The Transcendental Non-Dualism of Trika Śaivism

The basic principle of Kashmir Śaivism is that consciousness alone is real, and that which is not consciousness has no reality of its own, but is contingent on account of it being the expression of consciousness. It accepts *a priori* that consciousness alone is real, whereas what we cognize or perceive is nothing but what comes out of and from consciousness. The source of this thinking lies in the fact that it is in and through consciousness that we are empowered to engage in the process of reflective thinking, and due to it we become aware of what we are. This personal awareness gives rise to such reasoning which compels us to think that, a part from the body, there is existing within us a thinking principle, namely, the self. It is this inner self which is identified with the Absolute—and the Absolute is nothing but consciousness. Whatever we know or experience is because of consciousness. In the absence of consciousness, everything would be insentient, and there would prevail utter darkness of non-knowledge.

It is in the context of this thinking that Kashmir Śaivism has developed the philosophy of transcendental non-dualism that is theistically oriented, which maintains that the Absolute is none else than the core of myself. It is this self as the Absolute that expresses itself in and through the universe, which is to say that the phenomena are but the appearances of consciousness. Since everything is contained in consciousness, so nothing is different from consciousness. In this manner is established such a form of non-dualism that is both logical and experiential.

Moti Lal Pandit, trained as a theologian and linguist, has been engaged in Indological research for the last thirty years. He has published articles as well as books on a vast range of subjects. Initially, he began his research in Vedic religion and philosophy. Gradually, he shifted his attention towards Buddhism, and as a result of this shift, he has been successful in publishing a number of books on Buddhist philosophy and history. For the last several years, however, he has been fully engaged in the study of Trika Śaivism of Kashmir. Some of his publications are: *Vedic Hinduism; The Essentials of Buddhist Thought; Śaṅkara's Concept of Reality; Buddhism in Perspective; Being as Becoming; Towards Transcendence; Śūnyatā: The Essence of Mahāyāna Spirituality; Buddhism: A Religion of Salvation; Encounter with Buddhism; The Buddhist Theory of Knowledge and Reality; Transcendence and Negation; The Trika Śaivism of Kashmir; The Disclosure of Being; An Introduction to the Philosophy of Trika Śaivism; From Dualism to Non-Dualism;* and *The Philosophical and Practical Aspects of Kāśmīra Śaivism.*

The basic principle of Śaivism is that [illegible] consciousness [illegible] and that which is not [illegible] presupposes [illegible] the existence of consciousness [illegible] what is [illegible] consciousness [illegible] the process of [illegible] thinking [illegible] consciousness [illegible] the Absolute [illegible] the Absolute is [illegible]

The Transcendental Non-Dualism of Trika Śaivism

Moti Lal Pandit

Munshiram Manoharlal
Publishers Pvt. Ltd.

ISBN 978-81-215-1269-5
First published 2015

PRINTED IN INDIA
Published by Vikram Jain *for*
Munshiram Manoharlal Publishers Pvt. Ltd.
PO Box 5715, 54 Rani Jhansi Road, New Delhi 110 055, INDIA

www.mrmlbooks.com

Contents

Preface vii

1

The Philosophical Format of Trika Non-Dualism 1

2

The Essence of the Theory of Spanda 35

3

The Process of Manifestation of Categories 53

4

The Spiritual Hierarchy of Subjects 93

5

The Dyad of Bondage and Liberation 112

6

The Trika Absorptive Methods of Liberation 144

7

The Śākta–Śaiva Perspective 180

Preface

It is very difficult to say with certainty, in the absence of definite historical evidence, as to who were the ancient inhabitants of Kashmir and what type of religion they professed. The information that we have concerning the ancient Kashmir is mainly mythic in orientation, but within this mythos are contained such elements in which may be hidden some historical truths. And this mythic infomation is basically provided by the text of the *Nīlamata-purāṇa*, which mainly concerns itself with the history of ancient Kashmir. According to this text, the entire valley of Kashmir, while surrounded by the majestic mountains, was a huge lake. Prior to the draining off the waters of the lake by sage Kaśyapa, it is believed that the Nāga tribe mainly occupied the hinterlands of the valley, who most probably were polytheistic, but seem to have been favourably disposed towards Śaivism. Upon the draining off the waters from the lake, there emerged a landmass that became available for human occupation, which duly seems to have been occupied by such less civilized Aryan tribes as the Piśācas and the Dardas. As a result of the occupation of the valley by these tribes, there ensued strife between the Piśācas and the Dardas for supremacy. It seems that the Nāgas were so diplomatic in their dealings as to have brought peace between the warring tribes through mediation.

The Nāgas, though polytheistic in orientation, seem to

have given prominence to Śiva among the deities they worshipped. The Nāgas seem to have been successful in influencing the newly arrived tribes insofar as their religious practices were concerned. In this manner was facilitated the spread of the worship of Śiva and Śakti among the people of ancient Kashmir. Thus the spread of Śaivism in ancient Kashmir is in no way different from the popular forms of Śaivism that must have existed in other parts of India. However, it is impossible for any religious movement to remain, within the continuum of space and time, restricted to the popular conceptions of spirituality or of deity. As the laws of history demand change in terms of evolution, so also is the case with any kind of religiosity, and Śaivism being no exception to this general rule. The popular forms of Śaivism, with the passage of time, evolved both in terms of thought and practice, and the earliest such evolutionary trend found its expression in the establishment of the Pāśupata School, which spread throughout the country in the early centuries of our era. The Pāśupata School is pluralistic as well as realistic insofar as its philosophical thinking is concerned. It believes in the distinct existence of God, soul and matter. Insofar as its religious discipline is concerned, it is very austere and ascetic. A sub-sect of the Pāśupatas, namely, the Kāpālikas, go even so far as to make cremation grounds their residential abodes. The asceticism of the sect was such as would verge on the torturing of the body. It is because of this reason that Abhinavagupta speaks of the sect as being *dakṣiṇam raudrakarmāḍhyam* (*Tantrāloka*, 3.7–27).

The next Śaivite sect that seems to have emerged after the Pāśupatas is the school of Śaivasiddhānta of the South. Traditionally it is believed that the sect owed its existence to some ancient Āgama known as the *Nānmurai*. This so-called Āgamic text is no more available, as its loss is attributed to a devastating flood of a far distant time. The story seems to be more apocryphal than real on account of it being mythic in content. However, there may be some content of truth contained in the story insofar as the occurrence of the flood is concerned. There is, however, another line of tradition, which maintains that there existed a Śaiva sect in and around the temple of Mantra Kāleśvara on the banks of Godāvarī. The sect seems to have ensued from such teachers who seem to have belonged to the tradition of Amardaka. It is the teachers of this sect who, on the invitation of a Chola king Rājendra, are said to have preached the basic principles of Śaivasiddhānta in the South. Also there exits another tradition that asserts that the Śaivasiddhānta sect owes its existence to such Āgamic texts whose date of composition is as old as the beginning of Christian era. In whatever way the sect of Śaivasiddhānta might have come into existence, the fact remains that its very emergence points out one of the historical truths, which is the popularity of Śaivism among the general masses. At the philosophical level of thought, there is further development of realistic pluralism in terms of giving it a reasonable metaphysical foundation. Also the methods of yoga as well as of supernal knowledge are now incorporated into the over-all soteriological framework as necessary tools of liberation. Also devotional and ritual worship are given due emphasis, and it is because of this reason that Abhinavagupta has spoken of Śaivasiddhānta as consisting of *karmubahulām* (ibid., 37.27).

The other major Śaivite sect that emerged in the South is known by the name of Vīraśaivism. It is very popular among the masses of Karnataka. Although the present form of Vīraśaivism began to develop from the twelfth century onwards, yet its historical roots have been traced to such ancient Śaivite ascetics who must have left their mark upon the masses. Insofar as the theological principles of Vīraśaivism are concerned, they adumbrate such doctrines as would terminate in the philosophy of qualified non-dualism. It is because of its bent towards such non-dualism that is qualified that it adheres to the theory of homogeneity or equilibrium (*sāmarasyavāda*). Even though containing much more philosophical content than does Śaivasiddhānta, yet it cannot be denied that it is also overlaid with ritualism. In addition to the school of Vīraśaivism, there also emerged Vedāntic form of Śaivism of Śrīkaṇṭha, which has adumbrated the monistic theory of transformation (*abheda-pariṇāma-vāda*). The crux of the doctrine of this school is that the divine powers of God are so transformed as would result in the emergence of phenomena. Although calling itself as being monistic, yet, upon analysis, it resembles in many ways to the qualified non-dualism (*viśiṣṭādvaita*) of Rāmānuja.

The last major Śaivite School that emerged is the Trika Śaiva School of Kashmir. The traditional account concerning the spread of the Trika School of Śaivism in Kashmir is to be found at the end of the *Śivadṛṣṭi* of Somānanda. It is maintained that in ancient times the treasure of religious philosophy of Śaivism was mainly to be found among such sages who were highly evolved spiritually. However, with the commencement of the Dark Age (*kaliyuga*) these sages went to such far off places that no contact could be established with them. Once it so happened that Lord Śrīkaṇṭhanātha, who is one of the forms of Śiva, while roaming in and around Kailāsa, inspired sage Durvāsa concerning the revival of Śaivism. Durvāsa, being under the influence of divine inspiration, imparted the non-dualistic form of Śaivism to one of his disciples, namely, Tryambakāditya. It was the fifteenth descendent of the line of teachers of Tryambakāditya, namely, Saṅgamāditya, who is said to have settled in Kashmir by marrying a local Brāhmaṇa girl. Thus the line of teachers that followed from Saṅgamāditya were greatly responsible in spreading the Trika form of Śaivism in the valley of Kashmir—and Somānanda, the author of the *Śivadṛṣṭi*, was the twentieth descendent of the line of Tryambakāditya. It was Somānanda who really laid the foundation for non-dualistic philosophy of Trika Śaivism by composing his magnum opus, the *Śivadṛṣṭi*.

The Trika Śaivism as an ally of Tantrism is very catholic

and open-minded in its approach to such matters that have social or religious bearing. It is, thus, within the openminded conceptual framework that the Trika, although not completely antagonistic to Vedism, rejects all such Vedic injunctions and prohibitions that are restrictive and oppressive. It rejects such Vedic normative social and religious conduct that is based upon the differentiating marks of caste, creed, and sex. This restrictive approach of Vedism concerning the social and religious behaviour is totally rejected by the Trika Śaivism. It accepts all such persons into its ambit, without making any distinction of caste, creed, and sex, who have a genuine desire and thirst for supernal knowledge. Although not neglecting the theoretical aspects of knowledge, which means the study of scriptures, the Trika, however, lays more stress upon the practical aspects of religious discipline. Also it rejects the Vedic notion that liberation is possible only by following the path of wandering monks, viz., of renunciation. It believes that one can achieve the final soteriological goal of liberation as a householder provided the path of Śaiva-yoga is interiorized and practised diligently. It does not believe that spiritual sanctity of a person can be measured by putting certain marks upon the body, or by wearing white or ochre-coloured robes, and so on. The Trika rejects such ascetic discipline of the yoga of Patañjali that is aimed at suppressing the natural flow of the mind. Instead of suppressing the flow of the mind, it believes in so harnessing it as would result in its sublimation. It is within this perspective that the Trika system lays as much emphasis upon the worldly enjoyment (*bhaga*) as much it does on liberation (*mokṣa*). The spiritual trajectory that the Trika has envisaged is so synthetic as would include into its ambit both the paths, viz., the worldly path as well as the spiritual path. In this manner is reflected the pragmatic approach of the Trika with regard to activities that are worldly as well as with regard to norms that are spiritual. It sees no division between the two, because it is in and through the world that the goal of spirituality is realized.

The basic doctrinal principles of Trika Śaivism of Kashmir have their roots in the sacred Āgamic texts. It means that the Trika Śaivism owes its existence to the sacred scriptures called the Āgamas in the same manner as do the schools of Vedānta to the philosophical thinking that is adumbrated in the various Upaniṣadic texts. The relationship that eventuates between the Trika system and the Āgamas is the same that exists between the schools of Vedānta and the Upaniṣads. As to when, and in what circumstances, the Āgamic texts began to emerge is difficult to explain at this juncture of time. However, it can definitely be maintained that the Āgamas as a countervailing force against Vedism must have begun to emerge in the beginning of our era, which over a period of time ultimately found its concretization between the fourth and fifth centuries. It means that the composition of the Āgamas must have begun not earlier than the fourth century and not later than the fifth century.

Most of the Āgamas, due to the vicissitudes of history, have been completely lost, and we know the existence of some of them only through references. Some of them are known only for name's sake. Some of the main Āgamic texts that are available, fully or partly, at this time are the following: (1) *Mālinī-vijayottaratantra*, (2) *Svacchandatantra*, (3) *Rudrayāmala*, (4) *Netratantra*, (5) *Mṛgendratantra*, (6) *Vijñānabhairava*, (7) *Parātriśikā*, and (8) *Śivasūtra*. The range of thought and practice that is contained in these scriptural texts is vast and comprehensive. There are texts that are solely devoted to such philosophical theories that adhere to dualism (*bhedavāda*). There are also texts that subscribe to such philosophical thinking that is thoroughly non-dualistic (*abhedavāda*). Equally there are texts that follow a middle path between dualism and non-dualism, and the philosophical thought that is contained in such texts is of the nature of qualified non-dualism (*bhedābhedavāda*). It is within the frame of such division that the entire corpus of the Āgamas has been classified as being either dualistic, qualified non-dualistic, or non-dualistic.

Almost all the Āgamas are in a dialogue form between Śiva and Pārvatī, the consort of Śiva. The discussion is so characterized as would contain within its format the various philosophical and religious topics. The topics that are discussed are not in logical format, which is to say that there exists no logical sequence between one topic and the other. Thus the doctrinal principles or philosophical thinking is so scattered throughout the texts that an effort has to be made of collecting them in a format that is logical and sequential. The philosophical truths that are hidden in these scriptural texts have not only to be given a logical format, but also have to be so interpreted as would be contextual in the sense of meeting the philosophical requirements of the times. Most of the philosophical truths are so concealed in these texts that only a person of wisdom and of far-sight can probe into them. Such luminaries as Vasugupta, Kallaṭa, Somānanda, Utpaladeva, and Abhinavagupta accomplished the task of collecting, interpreting and explaining the diffused thinking of the Āgamas with great élan.

The revelatory content of the Āgamas remained for a long period of time scattered and in a state of diffusion. It was Vasugupta who made the first attempt at explaining logically and sequentially the diffused thought of the Āgamas through his composition of the *Śivasūtra*. The importance of this text in the Trika system is evidenced by the fact that it is accorded the status of revelation. Insofar as the actual authorship of the text is concerned, there is divergence of opinion among the scholars. Some of them think that Vasugupta was just a compiler of the *Śivasūtra*. These scholars believe that the actual author of the text was none else than Śiva himself. It is believed that Śiva revealed the entire text of the *Śivasūtra* in a dream to Vasugupta. There are also scholars who think that Śiva informed Vasugupta in a dream that the entire text is inscribed on a rock in the Mahādeva Mountain. There is also a third view that thinks that some Siddhas transmitted the text to Vasugupta. Whatever be the case with regard to the authorship of the text, the fact remains that Vasugupta, in one way or the other, is associated with its composition.

The text of the *Śivasūtra*, being the foundational text of the Trika, is greatly valued and esteemed, and because of this reason many original commentaries on it have been composed. The commentaries that have been written on it are (1) the *Vṛtti* of an unknown author; (2) the *Vārttika* of Bhāskarācārya; (3) the *Vimarśinī* of Kṣemarāja, and (4) the *Vārttikam* of Varadarāja.

Upon explaining and expounding the hidden doctrines of the Āgamas by Vasugupta in his foundational text, namely, the *Śivasūtra*, there arose simultaneously the need for such reflection as would delineate the Āgamic concept of the Absolute philosophically. It was, however, Kallaṭa who bridged the gap that existed between the philosophical reflection and the religious faith by composing the text of the *Spandakārikā*. The importance of the text may be gauged from the fact that it is responsible in giving rise to a school of thought after its name, namely, the Spanda School. The Absolute, who is of the nature of consciousness, is said to be constantly throbbing, which is to say that it is not at all static, but is so dynamic as to be pulsating continuously. This text is as important as is the *Śivasūtra*, and because of this reason the following commentaries have been written on it, and they are (1) the *Pradīpikā* of Utpala Vaiṣṇava, (2) the *Vivṛtti* of Rāmakaṇṭha, (3) the *Sandoha* of Kṣemarāja, and (4) the *Nirṇaya* of Kṣemarāja.

Finally, we have such literature as would be termed philosophical in formulation, orientation and content—and the nomenclature that is given to this literature is that of Pratyabhijñā, or the School (*vāda*) of Recognition (*pratyabhijñā*). It is such a philosophical school as would result, through the process of supernal logical reasoning (*sattarka*), in the *recognition* of one's essential nature (*sva-svarūpa*) as being non-distinct from the Absolute, viz., from Paramaśiva. It was Somānanda who, for the first time, formulated an outline of the Trika philosophy of Recognition through the composition of his magnum opus, namely, the *Śivadṛṣṭi*. It is on the basis of the philosophical content of the *Śivadṛṣṭi* that Utpaladeva, the foremost disciple of Somānanda, explored further the philosophical thought by composing the *Īśvarapratyabhijñā-kārikā.* This text of Utpaladeva, with the passage of time, gained such prominence among the Trika thinkers that the philosophical school itself was named as that of Pratyabhijñā. The significance of the text can be gauged from the fact that Abhinavagupta himself wrote two different commentaries on it, namely, (1) the *Pratyabhijñā-vimarśinī* and (2) the *Pratyabhijñā-vivṛtti-vimarśinī.* In addition to these two commentaries of Abhinavagupta, Utpaladeva himself composed the *Vivṛtti* on the text, which however is partially available.

While the various thinkers laid down the basic principles of both the Spanda and Pratyabhijñā branches of Trika Śaivism, it was however left to the genius of Abhinavagupta to complete the unfinished task of integrating and bringing together the diffused thought of the Trika. The genius of Abhinavagupta was such that he has overshadowed all the thinkers that have preceded or succeeded him. He was a prolific writer, and wrote numerous works on philosophy, theology and aesthetics. It will not be possible for us to deal here with the vast amount of literature he composed. We shall mainly concern ourselves with some of his important works that have a direct bearing upon the Trika.

The earliest literary phase of Abhinavagupta concerned itself with the *tāntrika* thought and practice, and accordingly composed such treatises that would unravel the esoteric aspects of Tantrism. One of the earliest compositions of this genre seems to have been the *Bodha-pañca-daśikā*, viz., *Fifteen Verses on Awareness.* Instead of fifteen, the text actually has sixteen verses. The first fifteen verses explain the Trika notion of Śiva and Śakti and their mutual relationship in the context of objective emanation/manifestation. The final verse, which is the sixteenth, attempts to explain as to what is the essential purpose of these verses. The purpose of composing this small tract seems to have been to enable his less intelligent disciples to have some kind of grasp about the essential aspects of the Trika. The important composition of his that concerns itself with the unravelling of *tāntrika* esotericism is his commentary on the *Mālinī-vijaya-tantra,* namely, the *Vārttika.* The most important commentaries that Abhinava composed on Tantrism are his *Vivaraṇa* and *Vivṛtti* on the *Parātriśikā* which forms a concluding part of the *Rudrayāmala.* Couched as it is in twilight language, so the text of the *Parātriśikā* is quite terse, difficult and complex, which means that it cannot easily be grasped unless accompanied by a good commentary. These two commentaries of Abhinava have unravelled the mysterious world of Tantrism in such a manner as would be possible to grasp conceptually the essence concerning the Word that is contained in the text of the *Parātriśikā.*

The most important work that Abhinavagupta composed on Tantrism is definitely his *Tantrāloka,* which is encyclopaedic in its range and depth. The text is a treasure-house of *tāntrika* thought and practice that is to be found in the sixty-four Bhairavāgamas. Both the ritualistic and philosophical aspects of Tantrism have been dealt with in this composition in equal measure. Although mainly concerned with the Kaula form of Tantrism, yet the text of the *Tantrāloka* does not neglect other forms of Tantrism, like those of Krama etc. The entire text consists of thirty-seven chapters, which, along with the commentary of Jayaratha, called *Viveka,* has been published in twelve volumes. Abhinavagupta also wrote a gist of this massive work in the form of the *Tantrasāra.* There is an another work of Abhinavagupta, namely, the *Tantravaṭadhānika,* which is a gist of the *Tantrasāra.*

In addition to the above massive works on Tantrism, Abhinavagupta wrote a small work, namely, the *Paramārthasāra*. In this text an attempt is made at explaining the essential aspects, in outline, of Trika thought and practice. The small tract is basically meant for the beginners. Abhinavagupta also composed a brief commentary on the *Bhagavadgītā*, which is known by the name of *Bhagavadgītārtha-saṁgraha*. The interpretation that has been offered by Abhinava is in accordance with the traditional Śaivite point of view.

Insofar as his important philosophical compositions are concerned, they are his two important commentaries on the *Īśvarapratyabhijñā-kārikā* of Utpaladeva. The commentary that Abhinava wrote on the *Vivṛtti* of Utpaladeva, which itself is a commentary on the *Īśvarapratyabhijñā-kārikā*, is known as *Lāghvivimarśinī*. It is also known as the *Vivṛtti-vimarśinī*. The aim of this commentary is to clear such cobwebs that have not been touched upon by Utpaladeva. The next commentary that Abhinava wrote on the *Īśvarapratyabhijñā-kārikā* is known as *Vimarśinī*. It is in these two commentaries in which Abhinava so develops the philosophy of Recognition as to make it universal.

Abhinava also wrote such seminal works on the philosophy of aesthetics as, for example, *Dhvanyāloka-locana* and *Abhinavabhāratī*. The former is a commentary on the *Dhvanyāloka* of Ānandavardhana, whereas the latter is the commentary on the *Nāṭyaśāstra* of Bharata. In addition to these works, Abhinava composed small tracts on Trika Śaivism as well as composed a number of devotional and philosophical hymns. Some of the hymnal compositions that have a philosophical tinge are, for example, (1) *Anuttarāṣṭikā*, (2) *Paramārthadvādaśikā*, (3) *Paramārthacarcā*, and (4) *Mahopadeśaviṁśatikā*. The devotional compositions consist of (1) *Kramastotra*, (2) *Bhairavastava*, (3) *Dehastha-devatā-cakra-stotra*, (4) *Anubhavanivedana*, and (5) *Rahasyapañcadaśikā*.

The post-Abhinava period also produced some such important authors who wrote extensively on the Trika religion as well as on philosophy. One such important author definitely is Kṣemarāja. As a disciple of Abhinavagupta, he faithfully followed the path shown by his teacher in matters of religion, philosophy and poetics. The important works he composed on Tantrism are his commentaries, called *Udyata*, on such Āgamas as, for example, the *Netra-tantra* and the *Svacchanda-tantra*. The other important *tāntrika* work that he composed is his *Vijñānabhairavodyata*, which is a commentary on the *Vijñānabhairava*. He also wrote a work on poetics, namely, the *Dhvanyāloka-locanodyata*.

Insofar as his work on the Trika Śaivism is concerned, he composed very important commentaries on such seminal texts as the *Śivasūtra* and the *Spandakārikā*. The commentary that he composed on the *Śivasūtra* is known as *Vimarśinī* whereas on the *Spandakārikā* he composed two commentaries, namely, the *Spandasandoha* and the *Spandanirṇaya*: the former being the commentary only on the first verse, whereas the latter is the commentary on the entire text. In addition to these works, Kṣemarāja also composed the *Pratyabhijñāhṛdaya*, *Vivṛtti* on the *Stavacintāmaṇi*, *Parāpraveśikā*, *Bhairavaṅkuraṇastotra*, and *Paramārthasaṁgrahavivṛtti*.

Next in importance to Kṣemarāja is definitely Jayaratha, who on the behest of king Rājarāja (AD 1200) studied the *Tantrāloka*. Subhaṭṭa Datta accordingly initiated him into the secrets of Trika Śaivism. He is said to have written both on Śaivism and poetics. Among his available works are the *Viveka*, which is a commentary on the *Tantrāloka*, and the *Alaṁkāravimarśinī*, which is a work on pure aesthetics.

The other important writer who wrote on the Trika Śaivism is Maheśvarānanda of Cola country. He is also known by the name of Gorakṣa. He was the disciple of Mahāprakāśa, who was greatly influenced by Abhinavagupta both in poetics and philosophy. Upon having been initiated into the secret aspects of Trika, Maheśvarānanda is said to have, due to the grace of his guru, achieved complete freedom from the debilitating impurities of bondage. Accordingly he was able to master all the aspects of Trika Śaivism, which means of having gained proficiency in the Krama, Kaula, and Pratyabhijñā systems. The most important work he composed is known by the name of *Mahārthamañjarī.* He also wrote a commentary on it called *Parimala.* Apart from it, he also is said to have authored the *Saṁvidullāsa, Pādukodaya, Mahārthodaya, Parāstotra,* and *Sūkta.* All these works are no more available, and are known to us only through references. The other great thinker that came after Maheśvarānanda is definitely Bhāskarācārya. He commented upon the *Īśvarapratyabhijñā-vimarśinī* of Abhinavagupta, and the commentary is known by the name of *Bhāskarī.*

The Trika as a religious denomination is flavoured with the fragrance of Tantrism, and accordingly has inserted into its ambit such *tāntrika* methods as it considers to be conducive for effecting the soteric release or freedom from the phenomenal bondage by submerging, through the process of introversion, into what may be called the universal subjectivity. As a school of philosophy, it establishes the principle of recognition (*pratyabhijñā*) in terms of which the particular (*viśeṣa*) is subsumed by the universal (*sāmānya*). It was Somānanda who, for the first time, laid down the basic principles of Pratyabhijñā in his magnum opus the *Śivadṛṣṭi.*

The purpose of the theory of Recognition is not simply to sharpen the intellectual faculty of an individual, but to deliver him from the limitations of phenomenality. The aim, therefore, is through and through soteriological. It is within the soteric context that the Trika doctrine of Recognition provides the necessary philosophical tools that enable the individual to arrive at the ultimate goal of freedom. The philosophical tools are so structured as would cause the destruction of the layers of ignorance, which is viewed as being the main cause for the experience of non-freedom, which within the Trika framework is called bondage. Even though the Trika philosophy of Recognition, like the Advaita Vedānta of Śaṁkara, has a non-dualistic orientation, yet it differs from the latter insofar as viewing the nature of the Absolute is concerned. The Trika, having a theistic bent, does not accept the assertion of the Advaita Vedānta with regard to the Absolute as being inactive, a mere spectator. For the Trika the Absolute is intrinsically throbbing in such a manner as would reflect the dynamic aspect of it. It means that the Absolute is not simply Being, but is also Becoming. Also the Trika does not accept the Vedāntic assertion that the world is a false appearance. It is in the context of this view that the Advaita Vedānta upholds that the entirety of phenomena disappears in the undifferentiated unity of the Absolute at the time when a yogi experiences the ultimacy of non-duality. For the Trika nothing disappears, because both unity and diversity are cognized within the perspective of Śiva being All, and All being Śiva. In recognizing the ontic status of an entity as being identical with Śiva means that there is not allowed to eventuate any kind of negation.

It is the principle of negation that is responsible in giving rise to the theory of illusion (*māyāvāda*) in the Advaita Vedānta. The essence of this theory consists in the assertion that phenomena exist, but they exist like an illusion, which is to say that they have the same ontic status that an illusory object enjoys. It is means that the world out there is nothing but a vast expanse of illusion. It is simply a mirage. However, the illusory object disappears when it is negated through the proper tools of knowledge. The world as an illusory entity disappears upon realizing that *brahman* alone is real, and everything apart from *brahman* is either a construction of the mind or a mere linguistic fabrication (*prapañca*). This Vedāntic view is not acceptable to the Trika. The Trika system, instead, upholds that the experience of unity terminates in the true understanding concerning the facts of experience, and so there is no involvement of any kind of negation in the knowledge that is supernal (*alaukika*).

This Trika philosophy is termed as Recognition on account of it enabling an individual to have such *recognition* as would result in the knowledge of non-difference, which is to say in the emergence of knowledge concerning one's essential nature as being non-different from the Absolute, who is Paramaśiva. In the language of Pratyabhijñā it means that everything is but I-consciousness. The philosophy of Recognition, thus, involves itself in integrating the various states of consciousness into a single whole. We experience fragmentation in terms of particularity because of ignorance, which is to say that ignorance is nothing but impurity itself. As a result we experience limitation of every kind. It is this experience of non-freedom, in the form of limitation, which is termed as bondage. In order to transcend the impact of impurities, and thereby of ignorance, there is need of such tools which would enable an individual to *recognize* as to who he essentially is. It is this tool that the philosophy of Recognition has provided. However, mere philosophical reasoning is not sufficient for arriving at the ultimate goal of knowledge of identity or non-duality. The philosophical vision has to be integrated within the spiritual praxis, which the Trika, as a religious system, has integrated within its initiatory structure in such a manner as would result in the empowerment of transcendent freedom. It is, thus, through initiation that impurities, and thereby ignorance, are overcome, and upon their removal the individual is graced with self-knowledge (*ātma-jñāna*).

MOTI LAL PANDIT

New Delhi
25 December 2014

1

The Philosophical Format of Trika Non-Dualism

WHATEVER FORMS OF DOCTRINE, whether philosophical or theological, the Trika Śaivism may have adumbrated or enunciated, they are not different from other Indian schools of thought insofar as the search for ultimate meaning of life in the world is concerned. It is basically the way we confront the situation of life-in-the-world that is seen to be responsible in determining not only our metaphysical notion of ultimate reality or meaning of truth, but also determines as to what would be the appropriate goal and in terms of which ultimate meaning of life could be realized and apprehended. The basic existential problem that all of us confront is in terms of such a fundamental question as to what is the reason for this entire manifest order, called the world, to be out there? If the world is there, then why is it always under the threat of finitude? Moreover, the existents that exist in the world find no reasonable reason that would answer the query of the purpose for their very existence. In such a despondent situation the only despairing cry that a man could utter is the following: "Man comes without reason, prolongs out of weakness, and dies by chance" (Sartre). It is in the context of such existential query that the Indian thinkers have tried to discover as to what really constitutes the ultimate goal of life by so analyzing life-in-the-world as would be satisfactory and reasonable. Thus the ultimate goal of life in terms of its meaning is so conceived as would terminate in the final solution of embodied existence in the world.

Most of the Indian thinkers have located the basic human existential problem in the question that perceives life-in-the-world as being not what it ought to be, which is to say that life has become so limited and bound as to be devoid of freedom. In the language of the Trika thinking the basic problem with man is that he has somehow lost the capacity of recognizing as to who he essentially is. It is due to this non-recognition of one's essential nature that terminates in such experiences as would be dyadic, and so all forms of empirical experiences are constituted by such pairs of knowledge as, for example, pain and pleasure, heat and cold, defeat and victory, etc. It is this dyadic nature of our empirical experience that is termed as being bondage. It is so because of the fact that man is tied to these experiences in such a manner as to be non-free. Whatever feedom he may enjoy, it is always limited and relative. This so-called limited freedom is hampered by our incapacity of knowing more than few things and doing more than few deeds. Thus the basic problem with man in the world, according to the Trika, is the loss of absolute freedom. Such a conclusion is arrived at by the Trika on the basis of such thinking that conceives ultimate reality as consisting of unlimited, unimpeded, unbounded autonomy (*svātantrya*). It is within the framework of this understanding of ultimate reality that the Trika has discovered the meaning of life in terms of the ultimate goal, and that is nothing but the realization of oneself as being wholly free from the fetters of limitations that are experienced within the continuum of causally driven space and time. It would mean, in the theological language of Trika, that the ultimate soteriological goal of life is to realize oneself as being non-different from ultimate reality, which is Paramaśiva—and Paramaśiva is absolutely independent (*svatantra*).

Thus it becomes clear that the Trika system of thought is not different from other Indian schools of thought insofar as search for meaning of life-in-the-world as well as its ultimate goal in terms of the realization of freedom is concerned. Since the search is for freedom, so the Trika is as much concerned with such existential problems as suffering, non-freedom and the conditioned aspects of embodied existence as would be any genuine religious or philosophical system of thought. In its search for such ways and means, both theoretical and practical, that would terminate in the discovery (*āviṣkaraṇa*) of ultimate meaning of life, the Trika has accordingly discovered such a philosophical tool in the form of the principle of "recognition" (*pratyabhijñā*)[1] whereby the possibility as to who we really are can become an actuality.

The Conceptual Basis

This idea of self-autonomy as being the basic form of the Absolute has its source in the *tāntrika* notion of Energy (*śakti*). The idea of Energy is so used by the Trika as to integrate it with its doctrine of throb (*spanda*). According to this doctrine, the Absolute is inherently of the nature of pulsation, which is to say that reality, being kinetic, is not so passive and inactive as is the *brahman* of Advaita Vedānta of Śaṁkara. It is this conception of the Absolute of the Trika that differentiates it from the absolutistic philosophy of Śaṁkara. It is on the basis of this conceptual thinking that the Trika has made use of such philosophical terms as would establish the dynamic character of the Absolute—and the terms that express this idea are *prakāśa* and *vimarśa*. The entire Pratyabhijñā philosophical thinking concerning the nature of the Absolute revolves round these two terms.

The Pratyabhijñā philosophy of the Trika is of the view that the Absolute is absolutely autonomous precisely because it is not dependent upon anything, and so is absolutely free and independent. Since the Absolute alone is independent, it means that it alone exists truly. Whatever seemingly exists other than the Absolute is but the expression of the interior joy (*ullāsatā*) of the bliss that wells up (*ucchalatā*) within it. In other words, it means that the objective world that exists out there is the wonderful display of the divine powers (*vaibhava, aiśvarya*) of the Absolute. This amazing display of the powers establishes the glory of unimpeded freedom of the Lord and in terms of which is actualized the "appearance" (*ābhāsa*) of objectivity. In terms of the language of phenomenology it would mean that the Absolute, being pure consciousness (*śuddha saṁvid*), appears as this universe.

It is on the basis of such conceptual thinking that the Absolute, which is the Self, is said to be of the nature of consciousness.[2] And it is as consciousness that the Absolute "appears" as the manifest universe, which is to say that it is the very nature of consciousness to appear as this or that.[3] It is because of this reason that the Absolute as consciousness is spoken of as being of the nature of "light." It would, thus, indicate that whatever there is, is but consciousness, and so there would evidently occur its manifestation. Even the light of the sun, according to the Trika, is dependent for its appearance on the light that is consciousness (*cetanā*). The reality of the light of the sun depends for its confirmation upon the experience of the subject who affirms it as being the light. Insofar as the subject itself is concerned, it is said to be of the nature of consciousness, and so is in no need of being proved as such.[4] There is nothing that exists apart from the light of consciousness. Thus consciousness, even in the state of deep sleep (*suṣupti*) or in that of dreaming state (*svapna*), is always glowing with its own light. It is because of this light of consciousness that the subject affirms in the waking state that he had an easeful and relaxing sleep. This very affirmation of the subject denotes the fact that there must have been someone who, as a witness, must have been awake in the state of deep sleep. It is this witnessing consciousness as "I," which, according to the Trika, always shines. It is on the strength or basis of this shining that it is proved that this shining is not external to the self, but is its very nature. Insofar as the manifestation of external objects is concerned, they become manifest not because of their own light, but because of the light of I-consciousness. There would be some who may say that the light the "I" has, is not of its own, but is received through such mediums as the sense organs (*indriya*-s) or the inner organs (*antaḥ-karaṇa*-s). Even if this assumption is accepted, then the question can be asked as to how does the self remain awake during the state of deep sleep when both the sense organs and the inner organs are non-functional? This very wakefulness in deep sleep proves that it is the Self that is awake, and so is not dependent in any manner upon any kind of external light, which is to say that the self as "I" is by nature self-shining. However, insofar as the Self is reduced to the status of empirical ego through its association with mind, body, life force, etc., it accordingly is stained by the deformity of impurity (*mala*). However, the "I" that is pure is always transcendent to such products of *māyā* as the body, mind and life force, and so is characterized by the pure luminosity of light. It is this transcendent Self that is said to be completely full (*pūrṇa*) on account of it being of universal nature. Thus the Trika is of the view that apart from the light of I-consciousness nothing exists. Even the world of objectivity is manifest precisely because it appears as a reflection of the light of I-consciousness in its own mirror.

This thinking of the Trika concerning the nature (*svarūpa*) of the ultimate reality as being consiousness (*cit*) is not different from the conception of *brahman* that the non-dualism of Śaṁkara has propounded. Where the Trika, however, differs from the vision of Śaṁkara is at the point of looking at *brahman* simply in terms of *cit* or consciousness. The *brahman* of Śaṁkara as consciousness may be light, but this light is in no manner different from the light of an inert object like that of diamond (*maṇi*). As the inert diamond is not aware of its own light, so is the *brahman* of Śaṁkara. It is so because the *brahman* of Śaṁkara is so indeterminate and impersonal as to be inactive (*niṣkrya*). Such a viewpoint of *brahman* is unacceptable to the Trika thinkers. There is inherent danger in this kind of thinking of falling into the pit of such nihilism as is propounded by Nāgārjuna. It is because of this reason that the Absolute of the Trika has such properties of power as are innate to a theistic God, which means that the non-dualism of Trika has a theistic orientation. It is this theistic orientation of the Trika that has led it to coin such new and appropriate terms that would expresses the nature of the Absolute as being not simply luminous consciousness (*cit*), but as being endowed with the power of absolute autonomy (*svātantrya*). The term that explains the absolute autonomy of the Absolute is *vimarśa,* which through proper formulation would mean self-cognitive awareness. Thus the Trika non-dualism, in contrast to that of Śaṁkara, is such as would explain the nature of the Absolute as being I-consciousness.

The Trika Non-dualism

As to why the Trika has taken a different route towards non-dualism than that of Śaṁkara is because it does not want its Absolute to be so impersonal, inactive and indeterminate as to be like an inert and lifeless object. There is all the danger of falling into the vacuum of nihility if the Absolute is simply conceived as being a passive spectator or witness. In order to avoid this pitfall, the Trika accordingly has conceived the Absolute as being of the nature of light of consciousness (*prakāśa*) as well as being characterized by self-cognitive awareness (*vimarśa*). What it amounts to saying is that the Absolute as consciousness does not simply shine (*prakāśyate*) with its own luminous light, but is also aware (*vimarśana*) of itself as being of the nature of light of consciousness. The Absolute as light illumines, like the light of the sun, everything, including the sun, that there is, which means that the very manifestation of anything is possible because of the Absolute being luminous (*prakāśa*).

While being of the nature of light of consciousness, the Absolute thereby establishes itself as being so transcendent as to be beyond the reach of the mind and the intellect, which would, from an epistemic point of view, denote its ineffable character. This ineffability would mean that the Absolute is so transcendent as to be inconceivable and unthinkable. As such it is impossible to formulate such positive formulations that would terminate in the emergence of knowledge that would make it possible to express conceptually the nature of the Absolute. It boils down to saying that the Absolute can be approached only through such negations as have been enunciated by the Upaniṣads, namely, *neti, neti*. Whatever prepositional formulations in terms of dogmatics may have been formulated, they are only approximations, and so must be treated as being mere approximations.[5] Since there is no possibility of knowing the Absolute in itself through conceptual formulations, so the only way of knowing the Absolute is, according to the Trika, self-realization.[6]

Insofar as the Absolute is viewed as being transcendent, ineffable, luminous light of consciousness, there is no divergence of opinion between the Trika and the Advaita Vedānta of Śaṁkara. While agreeing with Śaṁkara about the Absolute as being all-inclusive as well as the ground (*ādhāra*) of the manifest order, the Trika, however, goes much further in its metaphysical formulation. It asserts that the Absolute, apart from being luminous consciousness, is also self-cognitive awareness (*vimarśamaya*). This insertion by the Trika into the metaphysical thinking is necessitated by the looming danger, on the one hand, of nihilism and, on the other hand, by reducing the Absolute to the status of an inert object (*jaḍatva*). We know that a diamond shines, but the diamond is unaware of its luminosity on aocount of it being inert. It is not, however, the case with Paramaśiva/Maheśvara. Paramaśiva is aware of itself as being of the nature of light of consciousness. In the language of the Trika, it denotes the immediate, non-relational awareness of itself as being the supreme "I."[7] It is awareness of itself as "I" that is encapsulated by the term *vimarśa*. It is by conceiving the Absolute as being not merely consciousness (*cit*), but as I-consciousness (*ahaṁ-vimarśa*) that the Trika thereby safeguards the Absolute from being a mere inert object.[8]

Thus it is in the very nature of luminous consciousness, according to the Trika, to be of the nature of self-cognitive awareness (*vimarśātmaka*), which in practical terms means that the very occurrence of cognition (*ābhāsa*) results simultaneously in the experience of self-awareness in terms of I-ness (*ahaṁ-pratīti*). This self-awareness as I-ness among the existents also signifies the appearance of the "I" as being of this type or of that type. This cognition of I-ness as appearance in the mirror of consciousness is always characterized by awareness, whereas the reflection that eventuates in an inert mirror is destitute of such awareness. The inert mirror may receive innumerable reflections, but it is never aware of them because the appearance does not occur in terms of I-ness.[9] It is the conscious subject who has the experience of reflections in the mirror. This appearance is actualized on account of the light of consciousness—and the cognitive aspect of consciousness concretizes this appearance in terms of the awareness of I-ness. Thus consciousness always functions through the dyad of *prakāśa* and *vimarśa*, which is to say that they are never separate from each other. Thus both appearance and awareness of I-ness constitute the activity of knowing and doing, which is to say that the luminosity (*prakāśatā*) of the light of consciousness (*prakāśa*) constitutes its awareness (*vimarśa*).[10] Likewise the cognitive awareness embodies the luminous aspect of consciousness. Thus both these aspects of consciousness are, in fact, identical, which means that they cannot be separated from each other. This state of identity or unity of Being is spoken of as being pure, infinite, unbounded and perfectly full. In theological terms this state of identity of Supreme Being is expressed through such linguistic formulations as Parameśevara, Maheśvara, Paramaśiva, etc. As being beyond conceptual determinacy, it is accordingly said to be such reality as to be transcendent (*anuttara-tattva*). It is this very Being that appears or manifests itself in different forms and shapes. This self-manifestation of Being embodies its intrinsic nature in terms of complete self-autonomy.

The Absolute as the Unity of Prakāśa and Vimarśa

It must be clear by now that the Trika conception of the Absolute is such as would facilitate the emergence of such definition in which action (*kriyā*) would be given due place. In viewing the Absolute in terms of the light of consciousness (*prakāśa*) and self-cognitive awareness (*vimarśa*), the Trika thereby has found it much easier to assert that the Absolute is both transcendent (*viśvottīrṇa*) as well as immanent (*viśvamaya*).[11] As consciousness, the Absolute is transcendent, but in terms of its activity the Absolute is said to be immanent. This conception of the Absolute, in the language of theology, is respectively embodied by Śiva and Śakti, which is to say that Śiva as consciousness is transcendent, whereas Śakti as activity is immanent. The Absolute as Śiva in its absoluteness is one without a second, and so is transcendent to all that that falls within the manifest order. Śiva accordingly is referred to as being supreme (*parama*) and transcendent (*anuttara*). In contrast to its transcendence, the Absolute as I-consciousness is seen to be the creative source of whatever is manifest, which would mean that Śiva is the foundation (*ādhāra*) of all forms of categories of existence (*tattva*-s), of proof and disproof and of knowledge. It is this aspect of the Absolute that is equated with immanence.[12]

At the theological level of thought it is Śiva that is seen as embodying the principle of transcendence, whereas Śakti, as the Energy of Śiva, denotes the principle of immanence. In terms of the language of philosophy it means that the Absolute is viewed both in terms of Being and Becoming. The Absolute is Being when abiding in itself, but represents Becoming when engaged in the creative activity of emission (*visarga*) of the categories. In the philosophical language of Pratyabhijñā it is due to the luminous light of consciousness (*prakāśa*), which is Being, that categories become manifest, but the process of their emission is because of creative activity, which is but *vimarśa.* And so *vimarśa* represents the very process of Becoming.[13] In the language of phenomenology it would mean that Being as self-shining consciousness expresses itself as the manifest categories in terms of Becoming.

The Trika premise concerning the Absolute as being identical with the self-shining consciousness is proved by the fact that each individual being is conscious of himself as an "I." If the Absolute were destitute of self-cognitive and self-shining consciousness, then it would be reduced to the status of inert objectivity, which would mean that everything would result in such a chaos as would eventuate when enveloped by the sheer mass of darkness. The very fact that the entirety of objectivity is manifest, and thereby within the ambit of knowledge, proves that the Absolute as consciousness is of the nature of light. From this it is not difficult to conclude that whatever there is, is because of the light of consciousness.[14] Since the entirety of objectivity is manifest, and thereby knowable on account of the light of consciousness, so it would be appropriate to assert that existence per se shines because of consciousness.[15] It is because of the shining nature of the Absolute as consciousness that the Trika non-dualism is referred to, and rightly so, as being experiential (*pratyakṣādvaita-vāda*).[16]

The Absolute is not simply the light of consciousness, but also vibrates (*spanda*) with its own inherent Energy (*śakti*), which in the Pratyabhijñā philosophy is equated with the activity of self-cognitive awareness (*vimarśa*). This self-awareness of the Absolute, at the level of theology, is so personified as to be given the nomenclature of the Goddess. It is this notion of the Goddess that encapsulates within itself the Energy of the Absolute as Śiva. Thus the Absolute is seen as the unity of Śiva and Śakti, of *prakāśa* and *vimarśa,* of consciousness and self-cognition, and of Being and Becoming.

When it is said that Śiva is inseparable from its own Śakti, it means that Śakti embodies power of self-awareness (*vimarśa*), which denotes the power of will (*icchā-śakti*). Thus the Trika has such an Absolute as would be characterized by the luminosity of consciousness as well as by self-awareness.[17] Even Śaṁkara seems to be adumbrating this viewpoint of the Absolute when he says: *śivaḥ saktyāyukto yadi bhavati śaktaḥ prabhavitum/ na chedevam devo na khalu spanditum api.*

The power of self-awareness (*vimarśa-śakti, icchā-śakti*), according to the Trika, is innate to Śiva. It is through this power that the absolute autonomy (*svātantrya*)[18] of the Absolute is expressed, which accordingly is equated with the infinite bliss (*ānanda*) in terms of the five powers of emanation (*sṛṣṭi*), preservation (*sthiti*), dissolution (*saṁhāra*), concealment (*pidhāna*) and revelation (*anugrha*).[19] It is in terms of self-awareness that the Absolute is spoken of as being characterized by perfect and full self-consciousness (*pūrṇāhantā*), and so accordingly is identified with absolute Egoity or I-ness (*ahaṁ-vimarśa*). It is as Ego that the Absolute is aware of itself as "I am," which simultaneously denotes that Śiva's self-awareness is identical with freedom (*svātantrya*) and bliss (*ānanda*). Being identical with freedom, and thereby with bliss, the Absolute accordingly brims over with its own glory of powers (*aiśvarya*). As Śiva is identical with its own Śakti, so the self-shining nature of consciousness is said to be non-different from the self-awareness of consciousness, which explains the vibratory character of consciousness. Likewise the self-shining of consciousness as self-awareness as well as absolute freedom and bliss, which, though seen to be pertaining to Śakti, are identical because bliss is nothing but the awareness of the spontaneous inner activity of consciousness, which apart from self-awareness is impossible to experience.

The Trika conception of the Absolute as being both self-shining and cognitively self-aware is contrary to the view that the Advaita Vedānta has propounded. For the Advaita

Vedānta the Absolute is simply pure consciousness (*cit*), and so is devoid of activity. For it considers the subject-object duality as well as any kind of duality as being the result of *māyā/avidyā* which is so elusive a power as to be identical with illusion. Being elusive, it is impossible to say whether it exists or does not exist. The Trika rejects this view of *māyā/avidyā* of the Advaita. Ignorance or *avidyā* is not to be seen as the absence of knowledge; rather it is knowledge that is incomplete (*apūrṇa-khyāti*). Insofar as *māyā* is concerned, it is viewed as the power of the Absolute, and so it is through it that the impure order of creation (*aśuddha-sṛṣṭi*) is brought about. Such conception of *māyā* would mean that it is not so elusive as would make it impossible to affirm or negate its existence. Also the Trika rejects the view of the Advaita Vedānta with regard to *brahman* as being so peaceful (*śānta*) as to be inactive (*niṣkriya*). The Absolute of Śaṁkara, though self-shining, is so devoid of motion as to be unaware of itself as being of the nature of luminous consciousness. Moreover, Śaṁkara thinks that the objective world is completely false (*mithyā*) on account of it being the product of elusive *māyā.* For the Trika such a view is unacceptable, because it considers the universe as being real emission (*visarga*) of Paramaśiva, which means that whatever appears exists, prior to its manifestation, potentially within Paramaśiva.[20] Whatever exists potentially in the Absolute, exists in the form of an integral "I." While existing as pure "I," the objective universe, upon its manifestation, is referred to as "this." Thus the objective universe is but the appearance (*ābhāsa*) of the Absolute—and this appearance is equated with the reflection that is reflected in a mirror or in a clean pool of water.[21]

This Trika conception of the Absolute as being the unity of Being (*cit*) and Becoming (*kriyā*), of *prakāśa* and *vimarśa,* would mean such a type of non-dualism that is basically a synthesis of opposites, or what may be called the *coincidentia oppositorum.* Such a view of the Absolute would be reflecting the Hegelian dialectic of thesis and antithesis, which ultimately terminates in the unity of synthesis. It is in terms of synthesis of the opposites that the perfect unity of Being (*tadātmyatā*) is realized. There is, however, the problem of explaining logically as to how the opposites can achieve synthesis. It is like saying that heat and cold, shade and light cannot only co-exist, but also can achieve identity in such a manner as would lead to the negation of individual identities. The response of the Trika to this problem is in terms of the assertion that maintains that the so-called opposites appear in thought, but in terms of essence they are one. It would, thus, appear that we speak of the unity of opposites for the sake of linguistic convenience. In fact, there is only one reality, and that reality is Paramaśiva.

The Fulness of Being

It is an a priori assumption of the Trika that the Absolute, which is Paramaśiva, remains, no matter what the condition be, always as consciousness (*saṁvid-rūpa*), which means that there does not arise a situation when the Absolute is not of the nature of consciousness. Even when appearing in objects that are insentient, the Absolute does not deviate from its essential nature of being consciousness. The very existential status of an object is affirmed only when, within the consciousness of an individual being, there is reflected the reflection of the object, which means that an object exists only when the subject perceives it. However, the perception of the object would be impossible if the light of consciousness does not reveal it. This proves that nothing exists apart from consciousness. Rather everything is pervaded by it. Thus the object also becomes one with consciousness during the period of its cognition. It is so because it is this very consciousness that reflects itself as the object in terms of its appearance to consciousness. If it were not consciousness that reflected the object in its own mirror, then there would be no appearance of the so-called object. Such an assertion is made on the basis that it is the very nature of consciousness to appear, and not of that which is insentient.[22] It would mean that the so-called empirical objectivity, in fact, is nothing but the manifest form of consciousness.

Since everything is the manifest form of consciousness, so it is but natural to maintain that the ultimate reality, which is Paramaśiva, is of the nature of consciousness. This very nature of Paramaśiva as being consciousness explains its supreme purity. Thus such limitations as those of space, time and form are not applicable to Paramaśiva due to its transcendence. It is due to the pulsation (*spandana*) of this very consciousness that there occurs the experience of manifestation of such forms of objectivity as are determined by space and time within the subjectivity of the subject. It is this very consciousness that is seen as the basis (*ādhāra*) of the limitations (*saṁkoca*) that are brought about by space, time and form. Even though the ground of these limitations, yet consciousness is not in any manner affected by them because of it being infinite, unbounded and unimpeded, and so accordingly denotes the fulness (*pūrṇatva*) of Being. Whatever appears, whether it is in the form of subject (*pramatā*), of object (*prameya*) or means of knowledge (*pramāṇa*), all of them always exist in that absolutely pure consciousness that is Paramaśiva.[23] This objectivity does not exist in supreme consciousness in the manner things are contained in a container. Rather it exists in consciousness in the manner oil is found in the oil-seed, or butter is found in milk. Oil in the oil-seed or butter in milk does not exist separately, but exist either as seed or milk. Likewise does this entirety of phenomena, prior to its manifestation, exist in consciousness, which is to say that they exist in identity with consciousness. While containing this entire manifest order, prior to its manifestation, within as one with itself, the supreme consciousness thereby expresses its fulness.[24] Even when the emission of the manifest order eventuates, there occurs no change in the Absolute, and so it overflows with such fulness as to lack nothing. Whether there is emission of the universe or its dissolution, the Absolute in both the conditions remains ever full. Thus the Trika conception of the Absolute is such as would indicate its purity, fulness and unboundedness.

The Emission of the Manifest Order

The Absolute of the Trika, namely, Paramaśiva, is not only self-shining (*sva-prakāśa*) consciousness, but is also self-reflecting awareness (*vimarśamaya*) and in terms of which it is aware of itself as "I am." It is through its own self-awareness that the autonomy (*svātantrya*) of the Absolute as self-will (*sva-icchā*) is concretized when the objective universe is emitted. Were the Absolute devoid of self-awareness and of freedom in terms of autonomy of self-will, then it would no more be the ultimate reality, but would be like an object that is inert. Accordingly, writes Abhinavagupta: "If the Supreme Being were devoid of the power of manifesting itself multitudinously, but remained (as it were) cooped within its uniform solidity, it would (no more) be Supreme Power or consciousness, but would be something like a jar."[25] While viewing the Absolute as being both consciousness and will, the Trika thereby is in a position to say that Paramaśiva is both the knowing subject (*jñātā*) and the doer (*kartā*) of deeds. This knowing and doing of the Lord is so autonomous as to be identical with absolute freedom.

The Lord's activity, according to the Trika, basically stems from his being so blissful as to let it overflow in terms of emission of objectivity. This creative blissful nature of the Lord is referred to as *vimarśa* or *śakti.* It is this aspect of the Lord that is seen as containing within itself all that there is or shall be. In the *Parātriśikā*[26] we are informed that whatever is manifest exists, prior to its manifestation, potentially in the supreme consciousness, which is Paramaśiva. The objectivity exists potentially in Paramaśiva in the manner a huge *banyan* tree exists in a seed: "As the extensive *banyan* tree exists in the form of potency in the seed, so also does this universe, in its entirety, exist potentially in the heart of the Supreme."

While overflowing with bliss, the absolute Lord (Maheśvara) lets the emission of objectivity occur through his autonomous will. The ideation with regard to the emission of the universe that is in the mind of the Lord gets itself objectified in terms of the congealment of consciousness, which is to say that the Lord through his free will lets himself be reduced to limited objectivity. This Trika understanding of the Absolute would mean that Maheśvara is totally free to emit or not to emit the universe out of himself. Free will of the Lord, according to the Trika, would denote such an absolute power whereby are accomplished all the tasks without any impediment or restraint. This is how Abhinavagupta has described the content of the sovereign or free will of the Lord:

> There the Lord, Paramaśiva, whose own-being is consciousness of the nature of *prakāśa* and *vimarśa,* who is the undeniable, ever-present reality, appears as subject from *Rudra* down to immovable entities, as objects like blue, pleasure, etc., which appear as if separate, though in essence they are not separate, through the glorious might of *svātantrya,* which is inseparable from *saṁvid* and which does not conceal in any way the real nature of the Supreme. This is the exposition of *svātantrya vāda.*[27]

Although manifesting itself in the form of objective universe that is subject to change, yet the Absolute in itself does not suffer from any kind of change. It is so because the Absolute not only is transcendent, but also is immutable. The Absolute is referred to as being pure and self-reflecting consciousness on account of the fact that, on the transcendental plane of its own background (*sva-bhitti*), it manifests out of its own free will (*svecchā*) this objective universe.[28] The objective universe, as already pointed out, exists within the Absolute as a potentiality like the plant in a seed or like the colourful plumage of a peacock in the yolk of an egg. The universe in its potential state does not exist separate from the Absolute. It is rather identical with Paramaśiva. It would mean that the Absolute alone is the background (*bhitti*), the ground (*ādhāra*) and the material (*upādāna*) for the manifest objectivity, which is the universe.

This view of the Absolute as being identical with what seemingly is outside of it establishes its all-inclusive character, which means that nothing fundamentally exists apart from, or outside of it. As pure subject, the Absolute is endowed with powers of will, knowledge and action—and it is through these powers that the process of manifestation is eventuated.[29] These powers, as it were, constitute the blissful as well as playful aspects of the Absolute, which is nothing but the expression of absolute freedom. By terming the Absolute as being self-reflecting consciousness, the Trika thereby asserts that the Absolute is pure "I." If the Absolute were devoid of self-reflection, viz., of Ego, it would thereby be reduced to mere nothingness (*śūnyatā*). These powers of the Absolute, according to the Trika, are not a mere chimera of imagination, nor are they considered as a kind of superimposition by *māyā,* as is the case with the *brahman* of Śaṁkara. These powers are real, and it is through them that the Absolute as Paramaśiva manifests itself as the universe. From this premise it is concluded that everything is Śiva and Śiva is everything, and so Śiva is both the subject as well as the object.[30]

The error concerning the nature of the Absolute emerges when the object, which in our case is the universe, is considered to be outside or independent of the projecting consciousness. Since everything, according to the Trika, is subsumed in the ocean of undifferentiated consciousness, so whatever kind of difference is experienced objectively is to be treated as being false. This is so because every kind of manifestation exists potentially within the womb of consciousness, which is the self. The manifest universe must not be treated as a kind of transformation (*pariṇāma*) or as a modification without change (*avikṛta-pariṇāma*) or as a false appearance (*vivarta*) of the Absolute. The phenomena as manifestation (*ābhāsa*) are real in the sense of them existing identically with the Absolute. The term *ābhāsa* in the Trika philosophical thinking does not have the same connotation as *vivarta* as false appearance has in the Advaita Vedānta. In the Trika the appearance (*ābhāsa*) of the Absolute as the universe is real. Also the terms like *māyā* and *avidyā* are not treated in the Trika in the manner they are understood in the system of Advaita Vedānta. The Trika considers *māyā* as being a real power of Paramaśiva, and it is through this power that the One appears as the Many. Insofar as the term *avidyā* is concerned, it does not denote the absence of knowledge, but signifies knowledge that is erroneous or incomplete (*apūrṇa-khyāti*).[31] The total absence of knowledge would mean of having no possibility for the emergence of knowledge, which, however, is not the case.[32]

The Theory of Appearance as Reflection

The Trika assertion that the universe is nothing but the self-congealment of Paramaśiva has its antecedents in the Sāṁkhya causal doctrine of effect being nothing but the actualization of the cause, which is to say that the effect, prior to its actualization, exists in the cause potentially. This Sāṁkhya causal doctrine is known as that of *satkārya-vāda*. While accepting this Sāṁkhya causal doctrine, the Trika, however, rejects the interpretation that is offered of it in terms of transformation (*pariṇāma*) of the cause (*kāraṇa*) into an effect (*kārya*). The danger that lies in this interpretation is that the cause, upon terminating into an effect, gets totally destroyed either through the process of transformation or through the process of being subsumed by the effect. If applied to Paramaśiva, it would mean that he either transforms himself into the universe or is subsumed by it. In either case the immutability of the Absolute is totally destroyed. It is because of such danger that the analogies of the seed and the plant and the presence of the colourful plumage of peacock in the juice of an egg have been found to be unsatisfactory by the philosophers of Pratyabhijñā. It is to avoid this danger of the cause being totally destroyed upon the emergence of the effect that the Trika has resorted to the theory of appearance (*ābhāsa*) in terms of which is interpreted the universe to be nothing but the reflection of the idea that is in the mind of the Absolute. Also the Trika does not want itself to be identified with the Advaita Vedānta theory of the world as being a mere false appearance (*vivarta*).

Thus the aim of the Trika is quite different from that of the Sāṁkhya as well as from the Advaita Vedānta. The goal is simply, on the one hand, to establish that the manifest universe is non-different from Paramaśiva and, on the other hand, to assert that no harm occurs to the immutability of Paramaśiva while manifesting itself as the universe. This twin goal or aim is achieved through the theory of *ābhāsa.* It is a priori assumed that the universe, prior to its manifestation, exists as an undifferentiated mass, which is to say that it exists as non-different from the Absolute. The universe in its manifest form, according to the Trika, has to be treated as being an appearance of Paramaśiva in the manner of appearance of reflection in a mirror. This assertion of the Trika would mean that whatever appears, whether it is the subject, the object or the means of knowledge, has to be treated as being a manifestation of consciousness, which is the nature of Paramaśiva. This appearance of Paramaśiva as objectivity eventuates in a limited manner, which means that every kind of objective appearance is subject to some kind of limitation.

The process of the occurrence of this manifestation/ appearance is explained by resorting to the theory of reflection. This theory is made use of in order to avoid the logical deficiencies that are found in the Sāṁkhya causal theory of transformation as well as in the Vedāntic doctrine of illusion. As to what the theory of reflection in a mirror (*darpaṇa-pratibimba-bhāva*)[33] denotes, is explained by Abhinavagupta thus:

> As it (so happens that) in a transparent mirror appear (such) variegated images as (those) of a city, village, etc., as being different from each other as well as from the mirror, though being non-different from the mirror, even so the world, though non-distinct from the taintless consciousness of Paramaśiva, appears to be distinct both with regard to the variegated (world) of objects as well as (from the) Universal Consciousness.[34]

Thus the theory of appearance is so made use of as to establish that the appearances, though appearing distinct, are not distinct from Paramaśiva in the manner the reflection of a city or a village in a mirror is not different, though appearing to be different, from the mirror itself. However, there exists some kind of difference between the reflection in a physical mirror and of the reflection of the universe in the mirror of consciousness. In the case of the physical mirror, the image that is reflected is external to the mirror. It is the external light that enables the object to cast its reflection in the mirror. The mirror, upon receiving the reflection, is not at all aware of the reflection due to it being insentient. This, however, is not the case with consciousness. The universe that is reflected in the mirror of consciousness is not outside of consciousness, but exists in identity with it. Also consciousness is not in need of an external light for the reflection to be reflected in its own mirror. It is through its own light that the reflection is effected. Unlike the insentient object, consciousness is always aware of itself as being consciousness as well as of the reflection that it reflects itself in its own mirror. The *ābhāsa,* thus, has to be viewed as a kind of projection of the idea that is in consciousness. The very process of *ābhāsa* is beautifully explained in the *Iśvarapratyabhijñā-kārikā*[35] thus:

> None (whatsoever) apart from the Lord, who is pure consciousness, has (the power) to manifest externally the entire phenomenal world that exists (potentially) within him. (He accomplishes this task) through the power of his will, just as a yogi does, without

(resorting) to the use of any substantive material for this purpose.

The Trika theory of appearance in terms of the analogy of reflection in a mirror is, thus, used to delineate the idea that the Absolute through its own autonomous will projects the universe on its own background (*bhitti*). In this manner the Trika endeavours to explain as to how the universe in terms of the reflected image in a mirror exists within the mirror-like consciousness of the Absolute. The process of appearance of the universe eventuates in such a manner as if it is different from consciousness that projects it. It is on account of the power of differentiation (*apohana-śakti*), which is also termed as the power of obscuration (*māyā-śakti*), of the Absolute that the universe is experienced as if being distinct from Paramaśiva, which in actuality it is not. When we speak of appearance, it does not simply mean the appearance of the objective universe, but includes within its ambit the subject, the object, the means of knowledge, knowledge, perception, conception, imagination, and so on. It means that the manifest object as well as the manifesting consciousness is identical. Insofar as the experience of difference is concerned, it is apparent on account of it being the outcome of Lord's powers of differentiation (*apohana-śakti*) and of obscuration (*pidhāna*), which are seen as the source of impurity.[36] In the ultimate analysis, it denotes that the Lord is absolutely free to reveal himself as much as he is free to conceal himself.

The Divine Dyad: Śiva and Śakti

The Trika understanding of the divine couple, namely, of Śiva and Śakti is more philosophical than theological or anthropomorphic. This does not mean that it rejects the theological concerns or religious attitudes of people. The Trika gives as much importance to theology as much it gives to philosophy. Shorn of its theological veneer, the Trika makes use of the conceptuality of Śiva and Śakti in such a manner as would contrast its understanding of the Absolute from that of Advaita Vedānta. The votaries of Advaita Vedānta consider the Absolute as being of the nature of pure knowledge, which is to say that the Absolute, being devoid of activity, is simply pure consciousness. Such an understanding would entail that the Absolute is always as inactive or lifeless as is an insentient object. The Trika outright rejects this kind of viewing of the Absolute. According to the Trika, knowledge is not so passive as the Vedāntins imagine it to be. It is so because activity is the very nature of knowledge, which is to say that the very process of knowing involves some kind of activity. It is impossible to have cognition of anything apart from the self or outside the scale of time. Both these relations concerning the self and time are considered to be the nature (*dharma*) of action. Thus knowledge is such an activity whereby the process of knowing gains clarity.[37]

Whatever actions we do or do not do, their performance or non-performance is always dependent upon the state of knowledge an individual has. It means that no action is performed unless one has sufficient knowledge concerning it. It is for this reason that conscious beings alone, in the midst of inert objectivity, are considered as having the capacity of performing action, which is to say that it is the conscious being alone who is the doer or agent of action. It means that action is present where there is knowledge. Likewise knowledge is present where action exists. Insofar as action in immobile objects is found, it is, according to the Trika, not of their own. It is so because they have no control over the actions that pass through them. Thus the immobile objects are considered to be so contingent as to have no independence of any kind.

It is Paramaśiva alone who is absolutely autonomous. Insofar as limited beings are concerned, they are relatively free. However, they transcend the relative realm of freedom the moment they realize their essential nature as being identical with Paramaśiva. Perfectly autonomous Absolute is both of the nature of knowledge (*jñāna-rūpa*) and of action (*kriyātmaka*), which in terms of Pratyabhijñā philosophy would mean that the Absolute is both *prakāśa* and *vimarśa.* The Absolute as the light of consciousness (*prakāśa*) embodies the knowledge aspect, whereas *vimarśa* or self-awareness represents the aspect of action.[38] This perfect identity (*paripūrṇa sāmarasya*) of knowledge and action embodies the nature of the Absolute, because they are mutually so interpenetrating as to be inseparable from each other. The identity of these powers is of the same nature as exists between fire and heat. It is the unity of these powers that is referred to as being of the nature of pure consciousness.

The Absolute as pure, unlimited and perfect knowledge is at the same time the embodiment of action. It is the knowledge aspect that is seen as being represented by Śiva. Likewise it is Śakti that is considered as concretizing the principle of activity of the Absolute. It is in terms of the glory of luminosity of consciousness that the Absolute is said to be transcendent (*viśvottīrṇa*). The immanence (*viśvamayatā*) of the Absolute is eventuated in terms of the glory of self-cognitive awareness as action. Thus Śiva represents the principle of *prakāśa,* whereas Śakti represents the principle of *vimarśa.* Even when immanent in the world, the Absolute remains ever pure consciousness. There never occurs an occasion when the Absolute is not pure consciousness.[39] From the point of immanence, whatever there is in the world, it is but Paramaśiva. Whether it is pain or pleasure, blue or yellow, or whether it be subject (*pramatā*), object (*prameya*) or the means of knowledge (*pramāṇa*)—all this multitude, in fact, is but Paramaśiva.[40] This immanent aspect of the Absolute has such an orientation as to conclude in action, which is to say that the immanence of the Absolute is expressive of its active nature. The effulgent Śakti remains hidden in what may be called the Śiva aspect of the Absolute. Likewise this aspect of Śiva is concealed in what is called the Śakti of the Absolute. If the Absolute had been simply of the nature of knowledge and of transcendence, then he alone would have existed and there would have been no possibility for the subject, the object and the means of knowledge to exist. Even whether the Absolute would have existed or not would be impossible to affirm, because there would be none to attest or deny its existence. It would mean that there would have pervaded such nothingness as would be unimaginable. But such is not the situation precisely because the Absolute, which is of the nature of knowledge, is also of the nature of action (*kriyātmaka*). It is the immanence of the Absolute in which is contained the universal seed of emanation. It is because of such orientation that the Absolute is also spoken of as being Supreme Energy (*parā-śakti*). The lordship of the Absolute consists in its being active. It is because of this reason that the Absolute manifests itself in the form of diverse objects and creatures of the world. The very forms that the Absolute manifests exist potentially within it. Thus whatever there is, is but consciousness, which is Paramaśiva.

The Absolute as Freedom

The Trika concept of the Absolute can properly be grasped in the context of the determinate causality that has been adumbrated by the Sāṁkhya philosophy. It adumbrates such kind of causality in which the cause gets totally destroyed in the process of the emergence of the effect. Thus the seed gets destroyed in the process of giving rise to a plant. Likewise milk remains no more milk when it gets transformed into curd. Likewise when the categories of the intellect, mind and ego emerge from the root-stuff (*mūla-prakṛti*), there eventuates the disappearance of the root-stuff. Such a situation emerges because the root-stuff transforms itself into the inner organs of intellect, mind and ego. At the time of dissolution, the categories revert back to the primal condition, which is to say they get themselves dissolved into what is called the root-stuff. Thus such categories that are insentient, according to the Sāṁkhya, are the result of the transformation of the basic element, which is the cause. The cause, while transforming (*pariṇāma*) itself into an effect, completely disappears. This kind of causality is determined and fixed. As there is no element of freedom in it, so its course cannot at all be changed. It is because of this reason that imperfection and incompleteness (*apūrṇatva*) characterize insentience.

This kind of causal determinacy, however, is not applicable to Paramaśiva, because of him being perfectly free and autonomous. When the Lord appears in the form of the world and creatures therein, there does not occur the disappearance of the powers of the Lord. The Lord remains the Lord in both the situations of emanation and dissolution of objectivity. In all the conditions the lordliness of the Lord is manifest. There occurs the emanation of categories from Śiva down to earth and of such entities therein as the subject, the object, the means of knowledge as well as of infinite diversity in the form of bodies, realms and objects when, through its own autonomous will (*svecchā*), the powers of the Absolute are reflected in its own mirror. Likewise occurs, through the autonomy of will of the Absolute, the dissolution of this entire manifest order (*prapañca*). This process of emanation/dissolution cannot be equated with transformation. It is so because the lordship of the Lord does not disappear upon the coming into being of the manifest order. It is now quite clear that neither in transcendence nor in immanence is found any kind of possibility for the transformation of the Absolute to occur. It is because of the fear of the causal transformation that the followers of the Advaita Vedānta have spoken of the Absolute as being inactive without taking into consideration the fact that inactivity pertains to such entities that are inert and contingent. Since the Absolute is of the nature of consciousness, so insentience and dependence are inapplicable to it. There is always a kind of pulsation of the nature of self-awareness (*vimarśātmaka*) in beings that are conscious. This pulsation of self-awareness constitutes the innate nature of a conscious being. From this it may be concluded that the Absolute, which is a mass of consciousness (*caitanya-ghana*), cannot at all be termed as being inactive.

The activity of self-cognitive awareness characterizes the lordship of the Lord, which is its nature. It is due to this innate tendency that the Lord always remains intent (*unmukha*) towards both emanation and dissolution of objectivity. The complete unfolding of this intentness expresses itself in terms of the display (*līlā*) of the powers of the Lord. If this intentness towards emanation/dissolution did not exist in the Lord, then he would be like blank space. He would no more be God.[41] This orientation of the Absolute towards action is due to its being of the nature of Energy (*śakti-ātmaka*), and due to which is established the absolute autonomy of the Absolute. It is Paramaśiva himself through himself and within himself, who, on the basis of his own power and glory, manifests the infinite wonderful variety that is constitutive of the universe. To accomplish this task, Paramaśiva is not in need of any support either from *avidyā* that is without origin (*anādi*) and unthinkable (*anirvacanīya*), or from desire that has no beginning, or from non-originated action. None of the above items influence his intentness towards the manifestation of the universe. It is his autonomous self-will that is responsible in actualizing the manifest order. Paramaśiva is not dependent upon such external supports as the root-stuff (*mūla-prakṛti*) or atoms for the purpose of effecting the emanation of the world.[42] The powers of Paramaśiva, though non-different, manifest themselves as being different, through the process of reverse order in the form of such categories as primal stuff (*prakṛti*), atoms (*aṇu*) and the knowable objects (*prameya*).

Paramaśiva, while engaged in the activity of cognition (*vimarśana*) of self-autonomy, is so delighted by his absolute freedom as would result in the emergence of desire towards externalization of itself. It is in this state when Paramaśiva through his is autonomous and unconstrained (*aniruddha*) self-will manifests the reflections of his own powers, which take the form either of emanation or dissolution of the universe.[43] Thus the appearance of the entire universe occurs in the form of reflection on the background of the self which is Paramaśiva. While these reflections may appear in the ocean of supreme consciousness, yet they do not effect it in the manner the purity of crystal is effected by the reflection of various objects. The reflection of the universe into the mirror of consciousness does not bring about any kind of deformity in its purity. The "I" as the light of consciousness remains always and uninterruptedly pure. It is Paramaśiva himself who within himself is continuously engaged in reflecting the images of contingent creatures, of limited lordship, of *māyā/avidyā*, of desires (*vāsanā*-s), of non-discrimination (*aviveka*), of false knowledge, of desire for action, and so on. In short, this entire expansion of what we perceive and experience externally and internally is the play of the powers of the Absolute in the form of reflections. It is this activity of the Absolute that constitutes his absolute freedom. It is absolute freedom because it is unconstrained and unrestricted.[44]

The Principle of Pulsation

The Trika system of philosophy has so understood the Absolute or Paramaśiva as to be equated with an infinite ocean of consciousness, and the nature of this consciousness is but absolute autonomy (*svātantrya*). This autonomy terminates into what is called the blissful delight (*vilāsa*). It is because of overflowing of blissfulness that the Absolute is spoken of as the Great Lord (Mahādeva). The very term *deva* denotes playfulness or blissfulness, and as the Absolute is Mahādeva, so it is his very nature to be playful precisely because of him being blissful. This playfulness of the Lord is termed as bliss (*ānanda*). The nature of the Absolute is consciousness, whereas the nature of consciousness is characterized by bliss. The innate nature of bliss is non-distinct from consciousness, viz., from Paramaśiva, which is to say that both of them are identical. It means that consciousness and bliss are so interpenetrating as to be non-different. If one of them predominantly manifests itself, the other remains present within the manifesting aspect.

The Absolute is always throbbing on account of the fact that there exists such a stir of bliss within as would not allow it to be so still as is found in the vacuity of space. This does not mean that the Absolute is devoid of the tranquillity of peace. The Trika accepts the assertion that the Absolute is both peaceful as well as active. The Absolute is peaceful because it is devoid of afflictions, which means that the Absolute is transcendent to afflictions that come about due to ignorance, desire for action, or due to internal senses, body, or due to the pairs of opposites. Free from the causes of affliction, the Absolute remains always as peaceful as an ocean without waves. However, the Absolute is not so inertial as is an insentient object, because of it being of the nature of throbbing consciousness. There, thus, always occurs such stir within the Absolute as would be of the nature of knowledge and action. It is this stir within consciousness that is termed as the bliss of the Absolute, and which characterizes its emissional nature.

The experience of bliss is always characterized by some kind of movement. It is this stir or movement of bliss within the Absolute that is termed as the seed of the unrestrained delight of its autonomy (*svātantrya*). It is this blissful movement of consciousness that is given the nomenclature of pulsation (*spanda*). When the bliss of the Absolute as consciousness, on account of it being of the nature of pulsation, allows the movement of stir to eventuate, there occurs a kind of wave within the ocean of consciousness. The waves that emerge within the ocean of consciousness are directed either inward or outward—and such a stir is termed as being of the nature of desire/will (*icchā*). The emergence of this desire/will should not be considered as being directed towards the attainment of that that has not been attained, nor is it directed towards the fulfilment of some new goal. It is simply the welling up of the innate nature of the Absolute. This desire/will of the Lord is always free from impediments; it is absolutely autonomous. The Lord accordingly appears the manner he wishes to appear. It is so because his will does not face any kind of impediment. The Lord, thus, appears both in the form of the objective world as well as in the form of contingent beings. This is what, according to the Trika, constitutes the divine play (*līlā*) of the Lord. While manifesting himself as the universe as well as in the form of contingent beings therein, the Lord, as it were, forgets his fulness, self-autonomy as well as his intrinsic nature of being pure consciousness. The Lord does this wilfully and without any constraint. When, however, the Lord recognizes himself as being perfectly full, infinite and absolutely free, he thereby manifests the other aspect of his divine play. The divine play, therefore, has two aspects, namely, of forgetfulness of the essential nature and its recognition, which is to say that recognition would not be possible unless there is forgetfulness. To forget as well as to recognize constitute the divine glory of the divine display that the Lord engages in through the process of manifestation and dissolution of objectivity. This divine play always eventuates in Paramaśiva, or should we say that Paramaśiva is constantly engaged in this divine play of forgetfulness and recognition, of manifestation and withdrawal.

The Glorious Powers of the Lord

The divine display of powers of the Lord express themselves through the five processes or acts, which are known as the five powers—and they are those of emanation (*sṛṣṭi*), preservation (*sthiti*), dissolution (*saṁhāra*), obscuration (*pidhāna*), and revelation/grace (*anugraha*).[45] The Lord engages in the activity of emanation of objectivity the moment he so reflects within himself the objective universe as if it is separate from him. Such an act of the Lord may be considered as being of the nature of basic emanation of objectivity. This basic or primal emanation of objectivity appears in the form of "this" (*idaṃ*), which is to say that the appearance of objects does not yet take place in terms of separate entities. The continuance of the manifest world in terms of its preservation has to be seen in accordance with certain norms—and this activity of the Lord is known as the play of preservation. Upon preserving the world for some period of time, the Lord engages in such an activity whereby its dissolution is effected, and in terms of which it submerges within the Being of Paramaśiva. In the process of manifestation, preservation and dissolution the Lord himself appears in the form of a limited being (*paśu*). As a result of this, the Lord, in the form of a limited being, forgets his essential nature as being identical with Śiva. This process of forgetting and thereby concealing the transcendent form and nature is such an activity of the Lord that is termed as being that of concealment (*pidhāna*). Finally, the limited being, through the study of scripture as well as due to the grace of guru, is so inspired as would lead him on to the path of spirituality. It is through this spiritual journey that the limited being intimately gains the possibility of recognizing his essential nature. This act of the Lord is known as the divine play of revelation/grace (*anugraha*).

Paramaśiva manifests himself in each sphere through five forms, and these five forms are known as five causes. These causes, as representatives, carry out the five deeds of emanation, preservation, dissolution, etc., of the Lord. And these five causes have been identified with Brahmā, Viṣṇu, Rudra, Īśvara, and Sadāśiva. Even though each one of the causes may have the capacity of performing all the five deeds, yet each one of them is qualified to carry out the single task that is given to them. It is impossible to count the number of universes in terms of the creative play that is enacted by the Lord.[46]

The lordship of the power of the Lord with regard to knowledge and action is termed as autonomy (*svatantratā*). A person is said to be Lord (*īśvara*) of that field in which he has gained perfection with regard to knowledge and action, which is to say that he has the power of knowing and doing whatever he wants to know and do in that sphere.[47] In this manner a person can be master of his house, of his village, of the district, of province, etc. Higher than the worldly masters are such masters as Dikpāla, Mahendra, Brahmā, Viṣṇu, Rudra, Īśvara, and Sadāśiva. But all of them are limited both with regard to knowledge and action. However, all these Lords of various realms owe their existence to Parameśvara. It is Parameśvara who endows them with the glorious powers of lordship. While bestowing upon these Lords the glory of powers, there does not occur any kind of contraction in the infinite reservoir of powers in Parameśvara. It is Parameśvara alone who, as the great Actor, enacts the play of the infinity of universes as well as of their respective Lords.[48] It is such Parameśvara that is spoken of as being transcendent (*anuttara*). Thus it is within the Absolute within whom are played these various roles of emanation, dissolution, etc. Whatever these roles may be, they are not different from Parameśvara, as he himself constitutes these roles. All this display of powers discloses the fulness as well as complete autonomy of the Absolute. It is the natural disposition of the Absolute to play these various roles of emanation, preservation and dissolution. If the Absolute were not autonomous, then nothing would have happened, which is to say that there would have been neither the manifestation of the various universes nor would have there been the Lords of these realms. This wonderful display of diversity owes its existence to the absolute autonomy of the Absolute.

References

1. The term *pratyabhijñā*, according to Abhinavagupta, consists of *prati + abhi + jñānaṃ*. *Prati* is said to denote *pratīpam*, viz., that which is contrary, or that which, though known, is now forgotten due to the

delusory influence of ignorance. *Abhi* means to face or that which is close at hand, whereas *jñānam* means illumination. So the term *pratyabhijñā* is said to be such a form of "recognition" whereby one comes to know what one has forgotten. With regard to the individual being it means the recognition of the essential nature that has been forgotten because of ignorance.

2. Vasugupta, *Śivasūtra*, 1.1: *caitanyaṃ ātmā*. It is to this aspect of the Absolute as consciousness to which the *Kaṭha Upaniṣad* (2.2.15) has referred to in the following terms: *tameva bhāntaṃ anubhāti sarvaṃ, tasya bhāsa sarvaṃ anubhāti.*
3. Kṣemarāja, *Śivasūtra-vimarśinī*, 1.1.
4. Utpaladeva, *Īśvarapratyabhijñā-kārikā* (*ĪPK*), 1.1.
5. Abhinavagupta, *Īśvarapratyabhijñā-vimarśinī* (*ĪPV*), 1.1.2.
6. Ibid.
7. Kṣemarāja, *Parāpraveśikā*, p.2: *akṛtimāham iti visphuraṇam. . . .*
8. Ibid., p. 2: *yadi nirvimarśaḥ syāt anīśvaro jaḍaśca prasajyeta.*
9. Quoted by Jaideva Singh in his *Pratyabhijñāhṛdayaṃ: The Secret of Self Recognition*, repr. New Delhi: Motilal Banarsidass, 2006, p. 19: *antar-vibhāti sakalam jagad-ātmana iha, yadvad citra-racanā mukurāntarāle/ bodhaḥ paraṃ nija-vimarśa-rasa-anuvṛtya viśvaṃ pramṛṣṭi no mukuras-tathā tu//*
10. *ĪPK*, 1.5.11: *svabhāvam avabhāsasya vimamarśaṃ vidur anyathā/ prakāśa-'rthaporakto pi sphaṭikādi-jaḍopamaḥ//*
11. Abhinavagupta, *Parātriśikā-vivaraṇa* (*PTV*), v. 9.
12. Abhinavagupta, *Tantrāloka* (*TĀ*), 1.104: *śāsana-rodhana-pācana-yogātsa sarvaṃ-upakurute/ tena patiḥ śreyomaya eva śivo nāśivam kimāpi tatra//*
13. Ibid., 1.154.
14. Ibid., 1.59–60: *anapekṣasya vaśino deśa-kāla-kṛti-kramaḥ/ niyatā neti sa vibhurnityo viśvakṛtiḥ śivaḥ// vibhūtvāt-sarvago nitya-bhāvād ādyānta-varjitaḥ/ viśvākṛti-tattvaccidacittad-vaicitrya-avābhāsakaḥ//*
15. Ibid., 2.30; 2.
16. Abhinavagupta, *Mālinī-vijaya-vārttika* (*MVV*), v. 1.
17. *ĪPV*, 1.8.11.
18. Ibid., 1.2.4.
19. *TĀ*, 1.70: *na cāsau paramārthena na kiṁcidbhāsanātrte/nahiyasti kiṁcit-śakti tadvad bhedo'pi vāṣtavaḥ//*
20. *ĪPK*, 1.5.10: *svāminaś cātmā-saṁsthasya bhāva-jātasya bhāsaṇaṃ/asty eva na vinā tasmād icchāmṛṣaḥ pravartate//*
21. *TĀ*, 1.92: *evaṃ svātantrya-pūrṇatvād-atidurghaṭa-kāryayaṃ/kena nāma na rūpena bhāsate parameśvaraḥ//*
22. *ĪPK*, 1.5.2: *prāg-ivārtho 'prakāśaḥ syāt prakāśāt mātaya vinā. . . .*
23. Ibid., 1.6.7: *tad evaṃ vyavahāre 'pi prabhur dehādim aviśan/ bhāntaṃ evāntara-artha-aughaṃ icchayā bhāsayed bahiḥ//*

24. Ibid., 1.3.6,7: *evaṃ anyonya-bhinnānām aparaspara-vedinām/ jñānānām anusaṁdhāna janma nasyej jana-sthitiḥ// na ced antaḥ kṛtānanta-viśva-rūpo maheśvaraḥ/ syād ekaś cid-vapur jñāna-smṛtyapohana-śaktimān//*
25. *TĀ*, 3.119.
26. *Parātriśikā*, v. 24.
27. Quoted by Jaideva Singh, op. cit., p. 17.
28. Kṣemarāja, *Pratyabhijñāhṛdayam, sūtra* 2.
29. Bhāskarācārya, *Bhāskarī*, ed. amd trans. K.A.S. Iyer and K.C. Pandey, repr., 3 vols. Delhi: Motilal Banarsidass, 1986; 2.2.11: *śremat-sadaśivodāra-parārambhaṃ vasudhāntakaṃ.*
30. Abhinavagupta explains this all-inclusive character of the Absolute thus: "It is (none else but) Śiva himself who, being (of the nature) of unconstrained will and pure consciousness, is uninterruptedly shining in my heart. It is (none else but) his supreme Energy that continuously plays on the edge of my senses. This whole universe (that we experience) is filled with the ever wondrous delight of I-consciousness. In fact, I know not as to what the sound 'world' refers to." Quoted by Maheśvarānanda in his *Mahārtha-mañjarī* (Trivandrum Edition), p. 25.
31. *TĀ*, 1.25: *ajñānaṃ iti na jñāna-abhāvas ca ati-prasaṅgataḥ/sa hi loṣṭādike 'pyāsti na ca tasyāsti saṃsṛtiḥ//*
32. Ibid., 1.54.
33. See Śaṁkarācārya, *Hymn to Dakṣiṇāmūrti*, v.1.
34. Abhinavagupta, *Paramārthasāra (PS)*: *darpaṇa-bimbe-yadvan nagara grāmādi citram-avibhāgi/bhāti vibhāgenaiva ca parasparaṃ darpaṇādapi ca// vimalatama-parama-bhairava-bodhāt todvad vibhāga-śūnyamapi/ anyonyam ca tato 'pi ca vibhātamabhāti jagad etat//*
35. *ĪPK*, 1.5.7: *cidātmaiva hi devo 'ntaḥ-sthitam icchā-vaśād bahiḥ/yogīva nirupādānam artha-jātam prakāśayet//*
36. *TĀ*, 1.23: *malaṃ ajñānam icchanti saṃsārāṅkurakāraṇaṃ. . . .*
37. Somānanda, *Śivadṛṣṭi* (*ŚD*): 1.24–25: *ghaṭādi-graha-kāle 'pi ghaṭa jānāti sa kriyā/jānāti jñānam-atraiva niricchorveda na kṣatiḥ// aunmukhyābhāvatastasya nivṛttir-nivṛti vinā/ dveṣe pravartate naiv na ca vetti vinā citaṃ//*
38. *ĪPV*, 1.8.11: *sa eva hi ahaṃ-bhāva-ātmā vimarśo devasya krīḍādimayasya śuddhe paramārthikyau jñāna-kriye/prakāśarūpatā jñānaṃ tatraiva svātantryātmā vimarśaḥ kriyā//*
39. *ĪPK*, 1.6.1: *ahaṃ pratyavamarśo yaḥ prakāśa-ātma 'pi vāgvapuḥ/*
40. Utpaladeva, *Śivastotrāvalī*, 6.5: *bhavad āveśataḥ paśyan bhāvam bhāvam bhāvanamayam/vicāreyam nirākāṅkṣaḥ praharṣa-paripūritaḥ//*
41. *TĀ*, 3.100: *asthasyad-ekarūpenavapuṣā cen maheśvaraḥ/ maheśvaratvaṃ samittvam tadatyakṣayad ghaṭādivad//*
42. *ĪPK*, 1.5.7.
43. *TS*, chap. 1: *evam yathā aitāt pratibimbitam bhāti, tathaiva viśvam*

parameśvara prakāśe/nanu atra bimbam kiṁ syāt/mābhūt kiṁcit/nanu kiṁ kāraṇakaṁ syāt/ hanta tarhi hetu praśnaḥ/tat kiṃ bimba-vācayo-yuktya/hetuś ca parameśvara-śaktir eva svātantrya para-paryaya bhaviṣyati/viśva-pratibimba-dhāritvac ca viśvātmakatvam bhagavataḥ//

44. *ŚD,* 1.2: *ātmaiva sarva-bhāveṣu sphuran-nirvṛta-cid-vibhuḥ/ aniruddha icchā prasaraḥ prasarad-dṛk-kriyāḥ śivaḥ//*
45. *Pratyabhijñāhṛdayam,* p. 1: *namaḥ śivāya satatam pañcakṛtya-vidhāyine/ cid-ānanda-ghaṇa-svātma-paramārtha-avabhāsine/*
46. *TS,* (KSTS, edn.), p. 64: *na ca brahmāṇḍānām saṁkhyā vidiyate/*
47. Utpaladeva, *Īśvarasiddhi,* v. 56: *svātmaiva ayaṃ sphurati sakala-prāṇināma īśvararo 'ntaḥ/kartā jñātā 'pi ca yadi paraṃ pratyabhijñāsya sādhyā//*
48. *IPV,* 1.1.1: *sambhavanti hi māyā-garbha-adhikārino viṣṇu-viriñcyādyaḥ, tadottīrṇa 'pi mahāmāyā-adhikṛtaḥ śuddha-aśuddha mantra-tad-īśatanmaheśātmanaḥ śuddha 'pi śrīsadāśiva-prabṛtayaḥ/ te tu yadiya-aiśvarya vibṛud-bahir-īśvarī-bṛtaḥ sa bhagavān anavacchinna-prakāśa-ānanda-rūpa-svātantrya-paramārtho maheśvaraḥ//*

2

The Essence of the Theory of Spanda

The Development of the Idea of Spanda

THE PHILOSOPHICAL-CUM-THEOLOGICAL IDEA of vibration, throb, pulsation (*spanda*) is so conceived in the Trika system as to facilitate the emergence of the notion of ultimate reality as not to be so passive, inactive and impersonal as is the ease with an insentient (*jaḍa*) entity. Behind this thinking lies the Tantric background in which the ultimate reality is viewed as being the unity of Śiva and Śakti, which in the language of Pratyabhijñā philosophy is equated with *prakāśa* and *vimarśa*, respectively. The Trika philosophical school of Pratyabhijñā does not look at the ultimate reality as being merely luminous consciousness (*cit*), as does the Vedānta of Śaṁkara, but also thinks of it in terms of cognitive self-awareness (*vimarśa*). If looked at from phenomenological perspective, it means that consciousness not only reveals, but also is so intentional as would result in the gathering of knowledge. It is against the background of such thinking that the Trika is not desirous of reducing reality to the status of inert objectivity.

The philosophical or theological implication of such thinking is to adumbrate a viewpoint in terms of which the Absolute is seen not merely a passive consciousness, but such consciousness that is dynamic and thereby always vibrating (*spandanaṃ*). It is because of this pulsation that the Absolute so emits the phenomenal becoming as would be identical with it,[1] though appearing to be different. It is, thus, the notion of *spanda* that would allow the Trika thinkers to weave such an explanation of the Absolute as would differentiate it from the inert (*śānta*) *brahman* of Advaita Vedānta. The *brahman* of Śaṁkara is so passive and inactive as to be a mere witnessing consciousness. Such a *brahman* would be so transcendent as would be, in the words of Karl Barth, totally "other," and so would have no possibility of forming any kind of relationship with the manifest universe. Also such a *brahman* would never have the possibility of being the source of what is regarded the manifest order of the universe. It is because of the inactivity of *brahman* that Śaṁkara had to resort to the principle of *māyā* as being the source of a false universe.

The Trika philosophers avoided or, rather, bypassed this problem of inactive *brahman* by looking at the Absolute as being a synthesis of transcendence and immanence, of peace and dynamism, of Being and Becoming. Such a formulation the Trika system could envisage within the framework of a non-dualism that is also sufficiently oriented towards theism. The Absolute of the Trika is not so transcendent as would be impossible for it at the same time to be immanent. The basis of this theistic absolutism lies in the idea of the Absolute as being of the nature of pulsation, which is to say that the Absolute of the Trika is not so inactive, indeterminate and abstract as to be lifeless and devoid of self-awareness. It is this theistic orientation that allowed the Trika thinkers to speak of the Absolute as being kinetic, and so, at the philosophical level of thought, this meant that the Absolute consists of both the light of consciousness (*prakāśa*) and self-cognitive awareness (*vimarśa*). At the popular level of religiosity, the Absolute is seen as being polar, viz., Śiva and Śakti, the former representing the principle of light of consciousness in terms of transcendence, and the latter embodying dynamism, and thereby immanence.[2] Such a conception of the Absolute, thus, serves both philosophical and religious goals of man-in-the-world.

It is Durvāsa who, within the Trika sacred tradition, uses this idea of the Absolute as being dynamic for the first time in his hymn, namely, *Parāśambhumahimnastava.* The principle of *spanda* is so made use of in this hymn as would reflect the absolute autonomy of God, and in terms of which could logically be explained the divine operations in such a manner as would result in the maintenance of the respective courses of the mental and physical phenomena.[3] The absolute autonomy or freedom (*svatantratā*) is possible only if the Absolute is conceived of as being active and dynamic (*sakriya*). An entity that is lifeless or inert cannot be imputed with freedom. Since the Absolute is of the nature of active consciousness, so it is viewed as having absolute autonomy. The Absolute is absolutely free because its self-will (*svecchā*) is unimpeded and unrestricted, which is to say that the Absolute is dependent on nothing. It is through its own free self-will that the Absolute, as it were, carries out the five activities of emanation, preservation, dissolution, concealment, and revelation.

This idea of the Absolute as being of the nature of pulsating consciousness was, for first time, made use of conceptually by Vasugupta in his *Śivasūtra.*[4] In the text of the *Śivasūtra* the idea of *spanda* is hinted at in the very first *sūtra* in which is adumbrated the notion of the self as being nothing but consciousness.[5] And consciousness always embodies within itself the idea of a thinking consciousness, which reflects the nature of consciousness as being dynamic. It was, however, the disciple of Vasugupta, namely, Kallaṭabhaṭṭa, who elaborated this idea of the Absolute as being identical with *spanda* in his *Spanda-kārikā.*[6] He also wrote a brief but explanatory commentary on it. The importance of the concept of *spanda* can be visualized from the fact that a number of learned commentaries on the text were written respectively by Rāmakaṇṭha,[7] Utpalavaiṣṇava,[8] and Kṣemarāja.[9] Somānanda and Utpaladeva gave the theory of *spanda* the necessary philosophical veneer in their respective texts, namely, *Śivadṛṣṭi* and *Īśvarapratyabhijñā-kārikā.* To convey the idea of the Absolute as being of the nature of pulsation, a new genre of terms is being used, and such new terms, for example, are *sphurattā, prasāra, mahāsattā, sāra,* etc. It was, however, Abhinavagupta who explained at length, both philosophically and theologically, the significance of *spanda* in several of his works, such as, *Īśvarapratyabhijñā-vimarśinī,*[10] *Parātriśikā-vivaraṇa,*[11] *Tantrāloka,*[12] *Tantrasāra,*[13] and so on. As to what is the etymological derivation of the term *spanda* has been elaborately discussed respectively by Utpaladeva in his *Īśvarapratyabhijñā-kārikā* and by Abhinavagupta in his *Īśvarapratyabhijñā-vimarśinī.*

The Content of Spanda

The idea of pulsation or vibration, conveyed by the term *spanda,* should not mistakenly be identified or equated with such forms of movement that occur, through space, in the physical or material world that we inhabit and of which we are a part and parcel. The motion that eventuates in the phenomenal world is always outward-oriented—and this motion as pulsation continuously occurs in such shapes and forms as sound, heat, light, etc. In contrast to such limited notion of motion, the Trika understanding is inclusive, broader and comprehensive. It is so because the Trika thinks of vibratory motion to be of spiritual nature, which is to say that this pulsation is not restricted to the phenomena outside, but has also an inward orientation. It boils down to saying that the pulsating motion occurs simultaneously within as well as without. The very spiritual dimension of pulsation denotes that it is not extrinsic to consciousness, but, rather, constitutes the very essence of consciousness. Since the nature of the Absolute is consciousness, so this spiritual stir pertains inherently to it, or should we say that the spiritual stir is constitutive of the Absolute. Since this stir is innate to consciousness, so it cannot be considered such a kind of motion that occurs at some location in space. Were we to make consciousness for this stir dependent upon some location in space, then there would occur some kind of change in consciousness, which would cause destruction to its immutability. It would be so because motion in space always entails change, and change denotes the destruction of the preceding state upon the emergence of a new state. Since consciousness is constant and immutable, so change in any form cannot be attributed to it. It is because of this reason that this spiritual stir is said to be identical with what may be called subjectivity or I-ness (*ahantā*). When, however, consciousness externalizes itself in terms of reflection in its own mirror, the reflection, which is the universe, is not different, though it may appear to be so, from consciousness.[14] Even though the *spanda* may not be such motion as to be external, yet it is so pervasive as to be the controlling centre of the manifest order. In this way the spiritual stir of consciousness not only is the source of physical motion, but is also the source of all mental processes that occur within the individual being.

Even though the term *spanda* may denote a kind of pulsation or throb, the question, however, arises as to why *kiṁcit-calana* is added to the root *spadi*? In doing so, the meaning of the term would denote "just a little movement." If the term signifies some kind of movement, then it has to be just that and nothing else. If so, it would mean that the addition of *kiṁcit* does not serve any purpose, because movement is movement. It matters little as to whether it is of short duration or of long duration, whether it is intense or weak. Also the weak or intense nature of motion does not alter the fact that motion always involves the change of position. From this reasoning it may be concluded that the addition of "just a little" does not change the basic fact of motion as involving the change of position in space. If, however, throb is not considered as motion, then speaking of *spanda* as being either of high intensity or of low intensity is simply a meaningless jargon. So to speak of *spanda* in terms of *calana* is like speaking of a shell that is devoid of inner content.[15]

However, Abhinavagupta has cleared the doubt with regard to *spanda* as to whether it is characterized by movement or not by explaining the root *spadi* in a secondary sense (*lakṣaṇa*).[16] The doubt as to whether *spanda* is of the nature of movement or not arises when its root—*spadi*—is interpreted in a direct and literal sense (*abhidhā*). The resolution of the doubt is offered in terms of considering the Absolute, who is of the nature of consciousness, as being changeless, immutable, transcendent and eternal, and so completely free from the operations of space-time bound causality. In viewing the Absolute as being transcendent to the manifest categories signifies that it in no manner undergoes any kind of change or modification. An entity undergoes change or modification on account of it being subject to motion, which means that it is motion that brings about change in entities that are manifest. Since the Absolute is transcendent, so the phenomenal laws of motion, and thereby of causality, are inapplicable to it. So to ascribe or impute change to the Absolute would be going against the basic metaphysical norm that maintains the transcendent principle cannot be brought within the ambit of space-time causality, which with regard to the Absolute would mean that it is totally free from the becoming process of phenomena.

Spanda as Flashing Forth

Even though the Absolute as consciousness is spoken of as being changeless and immutable, yet the assumption of it having within itself constant spiritual stir or throb would amount to assertinlg that the Absolute is not so static as are objects in space-time or as is the *brahman* of Śaṁkara. This dyadic notion of the Absolute as being both immutable and dynamic seems to be self-contradictory. It is logically impossible to maintain that one and the same entity would simultaneously be both static and dynamic. This logical impasse is overcome in viewing consciousness both as light (*prakāśa*) and self-awareness (*vimarśa*).[17] At the religious level of worship this dyadic aspect of the Absolute is equated with Śiva and Śakti. It is the immutable, and thereby the transcendent, aspect of the Absolute that is identified with the utter stillness of quietude. However, the dynamic aspect of the Absolute is explained in terms of it being constantly throbbing within itself. It is this constant throb of consciousness that differentiates the Absolute of the Trika from that of Śaṁkara. It is this notion of spiritual stir that has allowed the Trika to speak of the Absolute as being absolutely autonomous. It is because of this throb that the Absolute is always aware of itself as being the Absolute, which is to say that it is as self-awareness (*vimarśa*) and light (*prakāśa*) that the Absolute is said to be brimming over with bliss (*ānanda*).[18] The Absolute is bliss precisely because it is constituted by the inner throb, and so accordingly displays its playful nature by externalizing itself as the manifest universe through the innate five powers of emanation, preservation, dissolution, concealment and revelation. This flashing forth of the Absolute as this universe is explained thus:

> Since the Self has been spoken of as consciousness, so it cannot be said to be unconscious. And so this (consciousness) is identical with the activity of awareness, (and) due to which we can differentiate it from an insentient entity.
> The (very) essence of consciousness is to be self-aware. It is the supreme speech emerging out of itself, and is (accordingly) the self-sufficiency of God as well as his divine essence.
> This consciousness (as awareness) is proclaimed as being shimmering, pulsation of supreme (and) unconditioned reality. As the heart of supreme Lord, it (accordingly) is the essence (of *brahman*).[19]

The very assumption of the Trika system concerning the Absolute as being endowed with an innate, inward and subtle throb would mean that, while directing itself towards external manifestation, must, in one way or the other, undergo some kind of change/transformation. Such a conclusion seems to be inevitable due to the fact that movement, even if it is of subtle kind, cannot so alienate itself from itself as not to be the source of change. If such a conclusion is accepted, it would mean that the Absolute in the process of external manifestation must suffer from some kind of change, which would naturally cause the destruction of its indivisibility. In such a scenario the Absolute would no more be supreme, changeless and eternal, but would be as finite, and so susceptible to change, as any phenomenal entity.

It is to avoid this kind of logical impasse that the Trika has resorted to the theory of reflection (*bimba-pratibimba-vāda*) in terms of which is equated the manifestation of I-consciousness as "this" (*idaṃ*) to the reflection in a mirror. The object, while being reflected in the mirror, in no manner undergoes any form of change or modification. It is this principle of reflection that is applied to the Absolute. The Absolute or Paramaśiva reflects the universe in its own mirror, which is to say that the Absolute, out of its own free will, manifests the universe on its own background.[20] The crux of this theory consists of the assertion that the externalization of consciousness as this manifest universe must be treated like a reflection in a mirror. It is so because the Absolute, upon externalizing itself as the universe, does not undergo any kind of change like the object whose reflection is reflected in a mirror. The reflection in a mirror, however, has the possibility of suffering from some kind of deformity due to some defects in the mirror, but the object that is reflected remains unchanged (*nirvikāra*). Thus the manifestation of the Absolute as this universe should be understood as a kind of divine transmutation, which would mean that the phenomenal diversity that is experienced in the universe is to be viewed as a kind of self-division of the Absolute. And it is in terms of self-division that the Absolute, as it were, conceals its essential nature by atomizing itself in the form of finite entities. In this display of self-manifestation as the universe

Paramaśiva appears as if undergoing constant change and modification. This appearing of the Absolute as if undergoing change is due to the so-called semblance of movement, which is qualified by "little movement" (*kiṁcit calana*). However, this inner throb may be compared to such moments of bliss that are experienced within the recesses of one's own being. During these blissful moments there emerges such a kind of dynamism that is subtle as well as inexplicable.

Spanda versus Śakti

It would be erroneous to think of *spanda* as being equivalent to, or identical with, *śakti*. At the theological level of thought, the concept of Śakti is explained in terms of the Divine Couple that is constitutive of what may, in philosophical terms, be called the Absolute. As the dyad of Śiva and Śakti, the nature of the Absolute thereby is said to be both *cit* and *ānanda*, which is equated with the philosophical concepts of *prakāśa* and *vimarśa*. The Absolute as *cit* or *prakāśa* is said to be transcendent, whereas as *ānanda* or *vimarśa* it is said to be immanent, which is to say that it is Śiva that reflects transcendence, whereas Śakti embodies immanence.[21] It would mean that the Absolute in itself is both Being and Becoming. It is, thus, the Śakti aspect of the Absolute that, as it were, is responsible in effecting the external manifestation, which is the objective universe. It is because of this fact that the term *śakti* has become so inclusive and elastic as to be identical with the entire manifest order. It is within this frame of understanding that the concept of *śakti* also conveys the idea of the manifest order as consisting of certain hierarchical steps. The term *spanda*, in contrast to that of *śakti*, denotes such blissful spiritual stir that continuously emerges and subsides within Śiva on account of him being identical with Śakti. In other words, it means that the rise and fall of this blissful stir within Śiva eventuates by virtue of him being Śakti, which means that Śiva is never devoid of *spanda* because of him being at the same time Śakti. Thus *spanda* may be seen as being the interior manifestation within Paramaśiva prior to the occurrence of outward manifestation.[22]

The Absolute, or what is called Paramaśiva, is said to have such five innate powers as would define his nature as well as autonomous activity—and the powers are those of consciousness (*cit*), bliss (*ānanda*), will (*icchā*), knowledge (*jñāna*), and action (*kriyā*). The first two items in the series do not really embody the powers of the Absolute. They, instead, define the essential nature (*svarūpa*) of the Absolute as being consciousness and bliss. The Absolute is consciousness precisely because of it being Śiva and Śakti, viz., both Being and Becoming. In the language of Pratyabhijñā philosophy it would mean that the Absolute is simultaneously of the nature of light (*prakāśa*) as well as of self-awareness (*vimarśa*). Since the Absolute is said to be consciousness, so its nature is said to be that of bliss, which is to say that consciousness is essentially *spanda*. In the language of theology we may say that *spanda* embodies the power of bliss (*ānanda-śakti*) of Paramaśiva. It is due to the blissful stir (*spanda*) that there emerge infinitely varied waves in the form of categories of existence from the ocean of transcendental consciousness, which is Paramaśiva.

The Phases of Spanda

The Trika system is of the view that the *spanda* is so characterized by the three phases as would correspond to the categories of Paramaśiva, Śiva and Śakti. The first phase of vibratory activity (*paraspanda*) of the Absolute, viz., of Paramaśiva, is such as would simultaneously be disposed towards both the inward as well as outward throbbing. The category of Śiva embodies the static aspect of the immutable Absolute, whereas Śakti is seen to be the dynamic aspect of the Absolute. It is due to the kinetic nature of Śakti that the outward throbbing within the Absolute ultimately terminate in the emergence of external manifestation. Thus the Absolute is simultaneously both Śiva and Śakti because of *spanda*, which would mean that *spanda* constitutes the intrinsic nature of the Absolute. Were the Absolute devoid of *spanda*, there would exist no objective manifestation, which would mean that there would be nothing. It would be the Absolute alone, in the absence of *spanda*, who would perhaps be existing. There could, however, be the possibility for the Absolute not to be existing at all, because there would be none that could confirm as to whether the Absolute is existing or not existing. But such is not the case, because the Absolute is of the nature of *spanda*—because of *spanda* there is actualized the variegated manifestation of objectivity.[23]

The second phase of *spanda*, representing the category of Śiva, is said to be static and indivisible. It is a phase that is equated with the universal vibration (*sāmānya-spanda*). It is at this level or phase of *spanda* in which the entire objectivity exists in the state of potentiality in Śiva. The objectivity exists in the state of potentiality in the way a plant exists in a seed[24] or the colourful plumage of a peacock exists in the yolk of an egg. Insofar as the third phase of *spanda* is concerned, it represents the Śakti aspect of the Absolute. Since Śakti is dynamic, so it, as it were, motivates the Absolute towards the externalization of what lies potentially within it. It is because of this tendency towards externalization that this vibratory phase is termed as that of particularized vibration (*viśeṣa-spanda*).

The externalization of the particularized throb passes through four stages prior to the actualization of the outward manifestation. The first stage is such as would result in the infusion of life to the process of manifestation itself, and so this level is constituted by the life force. The next phase is such as would result in the endowing of life to the senses and the limbs of the body with the intention of making them functional. The third level consists of in the operationalization of the various systems of the body. The final stage is so oriented as to be completely outward, in that it is at this level of *spanda* at which the insentient matter is put in motion.

The spilling over of the droplets of bliss from the ocean of supreme consciousness, which is Paramaśiva, results in the manifestation of the objective universe—and this spilling over of bliss is due to the inward and outward movement of the particularized throb (*viśeṣa-spanda*).[25] The Lord, while enacting the drama of emanation of the universe, conceals his essential nature by so atomizing himself as to be a limited being (*paśu*), which, as it were, signifies the abandonment of freedom. It is due to this abandonment of freedom that each sentient creature experiences himself as being bound or in the state of bondage. By assuming the role of a limited being, the Lord accordingly experiences all such limitations with regard to knowledge and action that are operative within the structure of space-time. In contrast to concealment, the Lord also engages in the drama of what may be called the display of the power of revelation, which occurs in the form of the divine descent of energy (*śaktipāta*) upon the bound being. The act of divine disclosure is actualized the moment the Lord bestows his loving grace upon those who seek him. As a result of the fall of grace the individual being becomes so disposed as to turn towards the path of spirituality and in terms of which is cultivated such virtuous life as would result in trudging the paths of knowledge (*jñāna-mārga*), of devotion (*bhakti-mārga*), of action (*karma-mārga*), and of yoga (*yoga-mārga*). This disposition towards spirituality simultaneously terminates in the abandonment of such activities that are seen as impediments in the way of self-realization. Thus there occurs the deepening of interiority and in terms of which consciousness, as it were, is saved from the diffusion that is the bane of empirical mode of life. Finally, the individual existent has the realization of being non-different from Paramaśiva, and as a result of it the notion of limitation with regard to knowledge and action is transcended. It is self-realization in terms of such recognition as would terminate in the knowledge of identity with the Absolute. In terms of self-discovery it means that each individual being, nay the entire manifest universe, is Divine. The discovery or recognition of divinity within is in terms of self-bliss and is the result of the inward movement of *spanda*, which ultimately leads to the attainment of the universal *spanda* (*sāmānya-spanda*). The bliss that is experienced is known as being the universal bliss (*jagadānanda*).[26]

Spanda as the Unity of Powers

It would not be a far-fetched assertion of speaking of *spanda* as being the embodiment of the unity of all divine powers. The bliss of *spanda* can be experienced by each one us within the framework of every day activities of life as, for example, pain and pleasure, loss and gain, etc.[27] Insofar as the experience of the bliss of *spanda* is concerned, Abhinavagupta[28] explains it thus:

> (The experience of *spanda* is such an) absorptive self-awareness of a yogi which, (while) shining in the heart, makes him (viz., the yogi) to feel (as if) the entirety of phenomenal existence is being absorbed by his being. It is such a principle that is known in the scriptural treatises (*śāstra*-s) as the universal vibration (*sāmānya-spanda*). And (it is such a spiritual) activity that spills out of the self. (Even though an activity), it is (to be considered as) the most subtle movement of the inert entity. (Since it is free from duality), so no (form of) duality shines in it. (As) the upsurge of the ocean of consciousness, it is always replete with it (viz., with *spanda*).

The principle of *spanda* is so conceived as to be the impelling force behind every divine activity of Paramaśiva, particularly in relation to the order of manifestation of categories. Thus in the *Spanda-kārikā*[29] the principle of *spanda*, in its universal (*sāmānya*) and particular (*viśeṣa*) forms, is linked to the opening (*unmeṣa*) and closing (*nimeṣa*) of the eyes of God, which in turn correspond respectively to emanation and dissolution of phenomena. Each one of us accordingly is told to discover that principle (*tattva*) within which is responsible in bringing sentiency to such objects as, for example, the senses and the bodily limbs, that are basically insentient.[30] It is, thus, assumed a priori that the principle of *spanda* not only shines in the infinite and eternal consciousness, but also in beings that pertain to temporality. The presence of *spanda*, for instance, is experienced as and when an individual is emotionally charged. The amazing wonder that emerges upon experiencing the bliss of *spanda* is explained thus: "How is (it possible) for (such) a person (to fall into the trap of) miserable transmigratory existence who, (while having) observed the mastery over this nature (viz., *spanda*), has been (experiencing) relaxation in the state of wonderful astonishment?"[31]

Insofar as the attainment of such a state whereby the principle of *spanda* could be realized is concerned, it is said that the aspirant (*sādhaka*), through the maintenance of vigilant self-awareness, would be so empowered as would lead him to the discovery of the effulgent *spanda* in-between the emergence and submergence of ideas in the mind.[32] It is so because the endless series of ideas that rise in the mind owe their existence to the very throb (*spanda*) of consciousness. It would, thus, mean that it is the outward movement or stir of consciousness that is responsible in allowing the ideas to emerge, and thereby follow each other in a series. Likewise the submergence or dissolution of ideas into consciousness occurs when consciousness, instead of going outward, turns inward. It is these two movements of *spanda*—outward and inward—that are constitutive of consciousness: the former representing the tendency towards manifestation, whereas the latter that of resorption. The principle of *spanda*, in the soteriologieal context, is said to be the source of both bondage and liberation. Insofar as man does not realize the *spanda-tattva*, to that extent he remains in the thralldom of bondage. However, *spanda* bestows divine powers and freedom the moment an individual aspirant recognizes its true and authentic essence. It is asserted that *spanda*, as it were, becomes the source of bondage the moment there occurs outward movement of consciousness. As a result of this outward movement emerge from the universal *spanda* the currents that are known as being particularized (*viśeṣa*). The particularized currents of *spanda* appear in the form of qualities (*guṇa*-s), and thereby are responsible in concealing the essential nature of *spanda*. Consequently people are made to undergo the misery and pain of the cycle of rebirths. However, the ones who know the real nature of *spanda* are spared from the misery of the wheel of becoming (*bhava-cakra*).[33]

The principle of *spanda* is so formulated and interpreted as would make it possible to define the transcendent Absolute in positive terms. It is in the context of such an understanding that the Absolute is said to be the source of the entirety of phenomenal existence. It is the principle of *spanda* that is seen as the source and the sustaining power of what exists externally. The externalization of *spanda* results not only in the manifestation of phenomena, but also becomes the source of bondage to those who are devoid of supernal gnosis, which is to say who are bereft of the knowledge of the essence (*sāra*) of *spanda*. It is this very *spanda*, however, that also becomes the source of liberation from bondage for those who have inwardly realized its essence. The principle of *spanda* becomes the true and authentic means of self-realization for such an aspirant who is desirous of liberation.

The Trika system of Śaivism, being non-dualistic in orientation, is of the view that nothing exists apart from Śiva, which in the language of Pratyabhijñā philosophy would mean that whatever exists is but consciousness. Such an assertion would denote that it is Śiva alone that really exists, and so, when looked at from the absolute standpoint, it would mean that the phenomenal or manifest order has to be viewed as the expression of Śiva. It would mean that the world is contingent precisely because it owes its existence to Śiva. In other words, it would mean that both the sentient and non-sentient entities, nay the universe itself, have to be treated as being nothing else than Śiva. Whether the movement is that of unfoldment (*unmeṣa, vikāsa, prasāra*) of the universe or of its dissolution (*laya, saṁkoca*)—both of them are but the play of the Lord. This is a perspective that maintains that both liberation from bondage and bondage itself is nothing but Śiva. Such an understanding of reality would, thus, maintain that non-dualism pertains as much to Śiva as does dualism. It all boils down to saying that nothing whatsoever exists apart from Śiva, and everything has to be non-different from Śiva. They who have realized perfect identity with Śiva know and experience every phenomenal entity as the expression of Śiva.[34] It is because of this reason that this type of spirituality has been given the nomenclature of transcendent non-dualism (*parādvaita*).[35] It is so spoken because it looks both at knowledge and ignorance, liberation and bondage, as the expressions of Śiva itself. It thus differs from the Advaita Vedānta of Śaṁkara, in that it does not treat the phenomenal world and the limited creatures therein as being the false products of a false *māyā/avidyā*.[36] Instead of treating the world as being unreal, the Trika is of the view that the entirety of the manifest order is of the nature of Śiva (*śivātmaka*).[37] The beauty of the Trika spirituality lies in the fact that it does not arrive at the realization of truth through the principle of negation, as is the case with Advaita Vedānta. It is through affirmative transcendence that the Trika establishes the truth concerning the non-dual nature of the Absolute.[38]

References

1. *Śivastotrāvalī*, 16.30: *parameśvaratā jayatyapūrvā tva viśveśa yadīśitavyaśūnyā/ aparāpi tathaiva te yayedaṃ jagadābhāti yathā tathā na bhāti//*
2. *ŚD, na śivaḥ saktirahito na śaktirvytirekinī/śivaḥ śaktastathā bhāvanā-ecchayā kartum-īdṛśan/*
3. Durvāsa, *Parāśambhumahimnastava*, 6.4–5.
4. Vasugupta, *Śivasūtra*, with four commentaries, ed. and commented by Krishnananda Sagar, Shivoham Granthamala, 1984.
5. Ibid., 1.1.

6. Kallaṭabhaṭṭa, *Spandakārikā,* with his own *vṛtti,* ed. J.C. Chatterjee, KSTS no. 5. Srinagar, 1916.
7. Rāmakaṇṭha, *Spandakārikāvivṛtti,* ed. J.C. Chatterjee, KSTS no. 6. Srinagar, 1916.
8. Utpalavaiṣṇava, *Spandapradīpikā,* ed. Gopinātha Kavirāja, Yogagranthamala no. 3, Varanasi, 1970.
9. Kṣemarāja, *Spandasandoha,* ed. M.R. Shastri, KSTS no. 16. Srinagar, 1917. In this text Kṣemarāja has commented upon the first verse of the *Spandakārikā. Spandanirṇaya,* ed. wih English trans. M.S. Kaul, KSTS no. 43. Srinagar, 1925.
10. Abhinavagupta, *Īśvarapratyabhijñā-vimarśinī,* ed. M.R. Shastri, vol. 1, KSTS no. 22. Srinagar, 1918; vol. 2, ed. M.S. Kaul, KSTS no. 33. Srinagar, 1921.
11. Abhinavagupta, *Parātriśikā-vivaraṇa,* ed. M.S. Kaul, KSTS no. 18, Srinagar, 1918.
12. *Tantrāloka* with *Viveka* of Jayaratha, vol. 1, ed. M.R. Shastri, and vols. 2–12, ed. M.S. Kaul, KSTS nos. 28, 30, 35, 36, 39, 41, 47, 59, 52, 57, 59. Srinagar, 1918–38.
13. *Tantrasāra,* ed. M.S. Kaul, KSTS no. 17. Srinagar, 1918.
14. *ŚD,* 1.15–17.
15. See Jaideva Singh, *Spanda-kārikās.* Delhi: Motilal Banarsidass, 1980, p. xvi: "Spandana means some sort of movement. If there is movement from the essential nature of the Divine towards another object, it is definite movement. Therefore, *spanda* is only a throb, a heaving of spiritual rapture in the essentil nature of the Divine which excludes all succession. This is the significance of the word Kiñcit in *kiñcit calanaṃ* which is to be interpreted as 'movement as it were'."
16. *ĪPV,* 1,5,14: *spandanaṃ ca kiṁcit calanaṃ/eśaiva ca kiṁcitrūpatā yad acalaṃ 'pi calaṃ ābhāsate iti, prakāśa-svarūpaṃ hi manāgapi nātiricyate atiricyate iva iti acalaṃ-eva ābhāsa-bheda-yuktam-eva ca bhāti iti.*
17. *ĪPK,* 1.8.11: *sa eva vimarśattvena niyatena maheśvaraḥ/vimarśa eva devasya śuddhe jñāna-kriye yataḥ//*
18. Abhinavagupta, *Mālinī-vijaya-vārttika,* ed. M.S. Kaul, KSTS no. 31. Srinagar, 1921, 1.245–46.
19. *ĪPK,* 1.5.12–14.
20. *Pratyabhijñāhṛdayam, sūtra* 2: *svecchayā sva-bhittau viśva-unmīlayati,*
21. *ĪPK,* 1.8.11.
22. *ŚD,* 1.1.15–17: *bodhasya sva-ātma-niṣṭhasya racanāṃ prati nirvṛtiḥ/tad-āsthā-pravikāso yas-tad-unmukhya pracakṣayate//kiṁcid ucchūnatā saiva mahadbhiḥ kaiścid uccayate/ tasyaicchā kāryatam yata yaya sa icchāḥ sa jāyate// aunumukhyasya yā ābhogaḥ sthūlaḥ sa icchā vyavasthitā/*
23. Ibid., 3.3.
24. *Parātriśikā,* v. 24.
25. *MVV,* 1.276–77

26. Ibid., 2.30.
27. *ŚD,* 1.8-11.
28. *TĀ,* 4.182–84.
29. *Spanda-kārikā* (*SPK*), 1.1: *yasyonmeṣanimeṣābhyām jagataḥ pralayodayau/ tam śakti-cakra-cakra-vibhava-prabhavaṃ śaṁkaram stumaḥ//*
30. Ibid., 1.6–7: *yataḥ karaṇa-vargo 'yam vimūḍho 'amūḍhavat svayam/ sahānterena cakrena pravṛtti-sthiti-saṃhṛtiḥ// labhate tatprayatnena parīkṣyam tattvam ādarāt/ yataḥ svatantratā tasya sarvatreyam akṛtrima//*
31. Ibid., 1.11: *tam adhiṣṭhatṛbhāvena svabhāvam avalokyan/ smayamāna ivāste yastasyeyaṃ kṣrutiḥ kutaḥ //*
32. Ibid., 1.4.
33. Ibid., 1.19–20: *guṇādispandaniṣyandāḥ sāmānyaspandasaṃśrayāt; labdhātma-lābhaḥ statam syur jñasyāparipanthinaḥ//*
34. *ŚD,* 5.105–9.
35. *MVV,* 1.108; 2.18.
36. Gauḍapāda, *Māṇḍūkya-kārikā,* vv. 1–18.
37. Abhinavagupta, *Bodhapañcadaśikā,* v. 14; *TĀ,* 2.19.
38. *MVV,* 1.621.

3

The Process of Manifestation of Categories

The Conceptual Framework

THE TRIKA ŚAIVISM OF KASHMIR has so explained the cosmogensis as would enable it to maintain logically the absolutism that is at the same time theistic in orientation. The Trika has conceived the Absolute as consisting of theistic properties on account of the fact that it wants to avoid the pitfalls of Advaita Vedānta. The Absolute of Advaita Vedānta, being indeterminate and inactive, is unable to cause the manifestation of the cosmos. Thus the metaphysical absolutism of the Trika in relation to the manifestation of the categories of existence (*tattva-s*) is explained in such terms as would be contrary to the doctrine of illusion (*māyā*) of Advaita Vedānta. The Trika does not accept the notion of the world as being a mere illusion projected by ignorance (*avidyā*) or by the Lord (*īśvara*) who himself is considered, due to *māyā/avidyā*, as a superimposition (*upādhi*) upon the impersonal and indeterminate *brahman*. It is in the very nature of Advaita Vedānta thinking to reduce the world to epistemological illusion as well as to ontological nullity due to the fact that the world itself is viewed as having been produced by an illusory Īśvara. It is such-like epistemological and ontological shortcomings that the Trika wants to avoid when it maintains that the Absolute not only is consciousness (*cit*), but also is bliss (*ānanda*), which means that the Absolute is both knowledge and action. It is in terms of bliss of the Absolute that the manifestation of the cosmos is accounted for, which is to say that the world is seen as being the outcome of the spilling over of the bliss of the Absolute. It signifies that it is the very nature of the Absolute to cause the manifestation/emanation of the cosmos and in terms of which is established the dyadic aspect of the Absolute as being both consciousness and bliss, or what technically is called *prakāśa* and *vimarśa*. If the Absolute did not cause the manifestation of the categories, then it would be no more of the nature of consciousness/bliss, but would be like any other object.[1]

Although idealistic in tenor and tone, the Trika Śaivism does not reduce the status of the world to the category of illusion insofar as it is accepted as having emanated from the Absolute itself, which is known as Paramaśiva or Maheśvara. The manifest world, therefore, is real to the extent it is accepted as being the self-expansion (*prasāra, vikāsa*) of the Lord himself.[2] The problem concerning the ontological status of the world crops up when the entirety of the emanated world is seen to be different from the Absolute. Since the manifest world, as it were, is considered as being the emanation (*visarga*) of the Lord, so the question of *creatio ex nihilo* does not arise at all. In some theistic religions it is assumed that God has created the world out of nothing. This assumption of the world as having come out of nothing is rejected on the ground that it is logically impossible to maintain that something can come out of nothing. That which is non-existent has no possibility of giving rise to that that has existence. If it is maintained that the nonexistent exists, then it cannot be equated with non-existence, because of it being existing. It is because of this fact that the so-called material cause (*upādāna-kāraṇa*) of the world outside God is completely rejected by the Trika thinkers. It is at this point that we must take into consideration the Trika notion of absolute autonomy (*svātantrya*) of the Absolute, which means that the Absolute is not dependent on anything for causing the emanation of the cosmos. It is the self-will (*sva-icchā*) of the Lord that alone is the cause of the emanation of the universe.[3] In such a scenario, therefore, the question of internal or external necessity as being the cause of the universe is rejected.[4]

If it were assumed that the Lord needs some material stuff for the world to be, then he would in no manner be different from a potter. As the potter is dependent on clay and other accessories for fashioning the pot, so would be the Lord, which would mean that the Lord is not at all absolutely free to do what he wants to do. Such a view completely destroys the absolute autonomy of the Absolute, which is not acceptable to the Trika. Instead of material cause, the Trika has accepted the Sāṁkhya doctrine that maintains that the effect exists in the cause (*sat-kārya-vāda*). However, it rejects the Sāṁkhya notion that the effect (*kārya*) is nothing but the transformation (*pariṇāma*) of the cause (*kāraṇa*). Were it to accept that the effect is but the transformation of the cause, it would thereby go contrary to its theistic line of thought, which maintains that the emanation of the world is actualized in and through the sovereign will of the Lord, which is to say that the world is there because the Lord (*īśa*) desires it to be. The doctrine of *sat-kārya* is used in such a manner as would logically explain that the entirety of cosmos exists potentially, prior to its manifestation, in the Lord. The potential existence of the universe in the Lord is explained in terms of the analogy of the seed and plant.[5] As the plant exists potentially in the seed, so does exist the universe potentially in the Lord.[6] It is also maintained that the universe exists potentially in the Lord in the manner the colourful plumage of a peacock exists in the juice of an egg. Both these analogies are so used by the Trika as would result in the avoidance of the consequences of the Sāṁkhya doctrine of transformation. In doing so the Trika thereby safeguards the immutable nature of the Absolute. If the Absolute as cause were to transform itself into the universe, it would thereby destroy its own immutable nature.

The world existing potentially within the Lord, who in

philosophical terms is equated with the supreme consciousness, is explained in terms of the metaphor of seed. As the tree exists potentially in the seed, so exists this entire universe, prior to its manifestation, in the womb of the Lord. It would mean that the universal tree, prior to its manifestation, exists in the form of seed (*bīja*) in the Absolute. However, this explanation of the seed and the plant as well as of the variegated plumage of peacock and the juice of an egg do not completely stand the logical test. The seed is totally destroyed once a plant comes out of it, and the same is the case with the peacock's egg. If this analogy were applied to the Absolute, it would denote complete destruction of the Absolute the moment the universe is made manifest. In order to avoid such a logical deviation, the Trika has resorted to the theory of reflection (*bimba-pratibimba-vāda*), which maintains that the variegated universe, prior to its manifestation, exists as an undifferentiated mass within the supreme consciousness. Such an assertion is made on the basis that the underlying principle of all forms of manifestation is consciousness (*cit, saṁvid*), which is to say that the ever-changing objects of the universe, including the universe itself, are but the appearances of the immutable and eternal consciousness. Thus whatever appears, whether it is the subject, thc object, the knowledge, or the means of knowledge, are simply appearances or manifestations (*bhāsa*-s) of supreme consciousness. Whatever, therefore, exists is but a configuration of *ābhāsa*-s.[7]

The world as appearance is explained in terms of the analogy of reflection in a mirror. The reflection in a mirror may appear to be different from the mirror, but, in fact, it is not so. The reflection is non-different from the mirror. It would mean that the reflection of a tree, of a city, or of any object in the mirror may appear to be different from the mirror, but, really speaking, they are all non-different from the mirror. Likewise the objective world, though appearing to be different from Paramaśiva, is in actuality identical with him. The objective world, thus, is reflected in the mirror of supreme consciousness in the same manner as are external objects reflected in a mirror. However, there exist some differences insofar as the physical mirror and consciousness as mirror are concerned. One of thc differences consists in the fact that the object that is reflected in the mirror is external to it, whereas in the case of supreme consciousness it is not so, because it is its own ideation that is reflected in it. The other difference consists in thc fact that the reflection in the mirror becomes possible on account of the external light. However, in the case of consciousness it is not so, because it is through its own light through which is reflected the universe. Also the mirror, being inert, is not conscious of the reflection that is reflected in it. In the case of consciousness such a situation does not arise, because it is aware of its own ideation that is reflected within it. Thus the *ābhāsa*-s are nothing but the appearance of ideas in the form of external objects.[8]

Granted that the categories, whether pure or impure, prior to their manifestation-emanation, exist potentially, in the form of a seed, in the Absolute, which is Paramaśiva. Now the question that needs to be addressed in this context is as to how does the Absolute, which is pure consciousness (*cidātmaka*), initiate the process of the manifestation? It is at this point of philosophical necessity that the Trika has so conceived the Absolute as to assume the role of a theistic God. The Absolute, though of the nature of consciousness, is not at all destitute of activity. In terms of Pratyabhijñā philosophy, the Absolute is both light of consciousness (*prakāśa*) and self-awareness (*vimarśa*), which entails that to be conscious means to be conscious not only of something, but equally also of oneself. Thus thc Absolute of the Trika is not so passive or inactive (*śānta*) as to be inert (*jaḍa*). Rather the Absolute as consciousness is aware (*vimarśamayī*) of itself. When this thinking is translated into the theological conceptual framework, it would denote that the Absolute is not simply Śiva, but is also Śakti. It is in this context that the Absolute of the Trika is always characterised by what is called the internal throb (*spanda*), which, when activated, expresses itself in terms of the power of will (*icchā-śakti*), and this power is equated with the absolute freedom (*svātantrya*). In the light of this thinking it is said that the Absolute consists of five main powers, which are consciousness (*cit*), bliss (*ānanda*), will (*icchā*), knowledge (*jñāna*), and action (*kriyā*). It is through these powers that the Absolute carries out its fivefold tasks of emanation (*sṛṣṭi*), maintenance (*sthiti*), withdrawal (*saṁhāra*), concealment (*pidhāna*), and revelation (*anugraha*). The process of action towards the universal manifestation begins when within the supreme consciousness occurs what is called the internal throb (*spanda*), and it is this throb that terminates in the actualization of absolute freedom in terms of the activation of five powers. As a result of this internal stir is initiated the intentness (*unmukhatā*) towards the externalization of the categories that exist within Paramaśiva in a latent state.[9] This intentness towards externalization ultimately results in the manifestation of both the pure and impure categories from Śiva down to earth.

The Emanation of Pure Categories

The intentness of the supreme consciousness of going outwards initially results in the manifestation/emanation of such categories that are termed as being pure (*śuddha*). They are so termed because the experients of these categories are not subject to the malignancy of difference to which the beings of impure categories are. It is because of this fact that, in particular, the beings of the first two categories (*tattva*-s) are said to be completely devoid of the sense of "thisness" (*idantā*). These pure categories are free from the sense of difference on account of the absence of *māyā*. It is *māyā* that is seen responsible in giving rise to various types of differentiation among those beings that abide in the categories that are impure. Or should we say that these categories are called impure (*aśuddha*) due to the dominance of *māyā* in them. The total number of categories that are emanated are said to be thirty-five. The category from which all other categories proceed is the thirty-sixth, which is identified with Paramaśiva. It is due to this internal stir that there occurs descent of supreme consciousness in terms of which the categories become manifest and it is through this process of manifestation that the power of will (*icchā-śakti*) of the Absolute becomes actual in the form of freedom. It means that there would be no manifestation unless the Lord is endowed with unimpeded freedom. It is because of this unimpeded freedom that the Lord in accordance with his own will (*sva-icchā*) brings about the manifestation of the universe. In terms of theological thought it would mean that the power of will (*icchā-śakti*) is the perfect embodiment of the Śakti aspect of Śiva. Such an explanation appropriately takes into account the fact that the Absolute is not simply an impersonal and inactive consciousness, but also is characterized by self-awareness in terms of which absolute freedom in the form of power of will is made operational. It is this kind of understanding of the Absolute that has enabled the Trika to have a non-dualism that is at the same time sufficiently theistic.

The Pure Categories: The total number of categories that are constitutive of Paramaśiva are said to be thirty-five in number. These categories are so bifurcated as would demarcate the point from where the process of differentiation becomes predominant. It is in this context that the entire gamut of manifestation of categories has been divided into what technically is called "the pure course" (*śuddhādhva*) and "the impure course" (*aśuddhādhva*). The first five categories, which are termed as being those of Śiva, Śakti, Sadāśiva, Īśvara and Śuddhavidyā, are said to pertain to the pure course on account of the absence of dualistic consciousness in them. The first creative pulsation (*prathama spanda*) of Paramaśiva results in the emanation of *Śiva-tattva.*[10] The second category that emerges is known as *Śakti-tattva,* which operates, in the context of the knowledge aspect, as the principle of negation (*niṣedha-vyāpāra-rūpa*). It means that Śakti is responsible in negating the consciousness of "this" in Śiva. As a result of this negation, there is accordingly experienced perfect identity between "I" (*ahaṃ*) and "this" (*idaṃ*). Accordingly these two categories—Śiva and Śakti—are so conceived as to be the embodiment of pure non-difference (*abheda*), and it is for this reason that these two categories are respectivcly said to be characterized by consciousness (*cit*) and bliss (*ānanda*).[11] At this level of manifestation it is pure "I" (*ahaṃ*) that is predominant, whereas the awareness of "this" (*idaṃ*) is completely absent. The negation of "this," through the operation of Śakti, eventuates in what is called the state of void. The withdrawal of "this" denotes simply thc presence of "I." It is because of this reason that Śakti is spoken of as being the creative aspect of Śiva. Thus she is Śiva's I-consciousness (*ahaṃ-vimarśa*), or should we say that she represents the intentness (*unmukhatā*) of Śiva to emanate. It means that Śiva and Śakti are not separate from each other, but remain ever united both in the state of emanation and dissolution. In fact, the *Śiva-tattva* and *Śakti-tattva* have not to be treated as being emanated categories. They, rather, constitute the seed of the entire process of emanation. It is at the level of *Sadāśiva-tattva* that there begins the tendency of moving away from pure unity, which means that the movement is towards what may be called unity-in-difference (*bhedābheda*). This tendency from "I" to "this" occurs when Śakti polarizes consciousness into the subject and the object. Thus this category is characterized by the tendency of the will to have the experience of the "this" aspect of supreme consciousness. However, the awareness of "this" (*idantā*) is such as to be incipient and unclear (*asphuṭa*). Even though there may be occurring hazy awareness concerning "this," yet it is the awareness of "I" (*ahaṃ*) that is predominant at this level. As the awareness of "this" is faint, so the shining of consciousness is in terms of "I am this" (*ahaṃ idaṃ*).[12] The experience of "this," at this level, may be compared to the picture that an artist intends to paint. The idea as to what kind of picture that he should draw is so hazy as to be unable to draw an outline of it on thc canvass. It is in view of this haziness that Kṣemarāja speaks of this state as being so dominated by I-ness *(ahantā-acchādita)* as to have a faint idea of "thiss" (*asphuṭa-idantā-mayam*).[13] Although the awareness of "this" may be faint, yet there is some kind of awareness on account of which the *Sadāśiva-tattva* is considered to be the first manifestation (*ābhāsa*), which means that there is some kind of awareness of both the subject and the object. In our case it is consciousness that is both the subject and thc object. Thus it is consciousness that is aware of itself as consciousness.

The next stage of descent of consciousness is characterized by such awareness as would indicate the lessening of the predominance of "I" by becoming more prone towards objectivity. As a result of this tendency towards objectivity, the stage of *Īśvara-tattva,* which comes after the category of *Sadāśiva-tattva,* is such as would allow objectivity (*idantā*) to shine more clearly (*sphuṭa*). It is because of this tendency towards clarity that the *Īśvara-tattva* is considered as the facilitating point for the opening up (*unmeṣa*) of the universe. It is a state in which the awareness of consciousness is so shaped as would result in the utterance "This I am" (*idaṃ ahaṃ*). It may, thus, be said that in the *Sadāśiva-tattva* consciousness shines mainly in the form of "I," and so the utterance "I am this" (*ahaṃ idaṃ*), whereas in the *Īśvara-tattva* the awareness is directed towards "this" (*idaṃ*), and so the utterance "This I am" *(idaṃ ahaṃ)*.[14] The awareness of objectivity at the level of *Sadāśiva-tattva* may be compared to the idea that may be germinating in the mind of an artist. The idea in the mind is so unclear as would not result in the actual composition of a poem or of a painting. The idea, as it were, is in the process of being born. However, the awareness of objectivity at the level of *Īśvara-tattva* is as clear as would eventuate upon coming in contact, through the senses, with an external object.[15] It is, therefore, quite appropriate to maintain that in the *Sadāśiva-tattva* it is the power of will (*icchā-śakti*) that expresses itself predominantly, whereas in the *Īśvara-tattva* it is the power of knowledge (*jñāna-śakti*) that finds its proper expression. The source or seed of these powers is to be found in the *Śiva-tattva* itself and it is the throb (*spanda*) that activates the seed, and thereby puts into motion the divine powers through which the order of manifestation is accomplished. Finally, the category that pertains to the pure order of manifestation is called the *Śuddhavidyā-tattva*. In this category the experience of "I" and of "This" is of equal measure, which means that the experience is so balanced as to be like the evenly held pans of a balance (*sama-dhṛtatulāpuṭanyāyena*). It is at this stage where the power of action (*kriyā-śakti*) gains predominance. It is a stage that represents the experience in terms of diversity-in-unity (*bhedābhedavimarśanātmaka*). Although the experience of objectivity, at the level of thought, may be pronounced, yet this objectivity is felt as being an integral part of the "I." This category is said to be consisting of pure knowledge (*śuddhavidyā*) because it is at this stage where the true relation of objects is experienced. The experiences that eventuate from *Śiva-tattva* to *Śuddhavidyā-tattva* are in terms of ideation. It is because of this reason that it is called the pure order of manifestation (*śuddhādhvan*).

The Experients: The Trika Śaivism is of the view that all the categories, whether pertaining to the pure path or impure path, consist of such beings that are appropriate to them. Thus the beings of the categories of pure path would be pure in every sense of the word than would be the beings of the categories of impure path. The purity of a being is dependent, in a descending order, upon the purity of the category, which would in practical terms mean as to whether a category is permeated by the sense of duality or non-duality. The first two categories of manifestation, which are those of Śiva and

Śakti, are totally devoid of the sense of difference; it is the awareness of "I" that shines predominantly in them, which means that there is complete absence of the sense of difference (*bheda*). The beings of these categories are termed as Akala. As these beings are said to be of the nature of pure consciousness (*śuddha saṁvid*), so they accordingly abide in the permanent state of non-difference (*abheda*) and in terms of which they experience themselves as being identical with the perfect and non-dual I-consciousness. As a result of this experience of identity, the Akala beings are totally unaware of what is called objectivity (*idantā*). What it amounts to saying is that the so-called external objectivity is so dissolved into their subjectivity (*pramātṛtā*) as would eventuate the disappearance of objects in deep sleep (*suṣupti*). It is Śiva and Śakti who are the governing authorities (*adhiṣṭhatā*) of these categories respectively.[16]

The first two categories, namely, those of Śiva and Śakti, are characterized by the awareness of non-duality, which means that the Akala beings of these two categories are completely devoid of the sense of difference on account of them having perpetual experience of the unity of Being. Insofar as the third category, namely, that of *Sadāśiva,* is concerned, it is not so given to objectivity as is the case with the category of *Īśvara.* In the category of *Sadāśiva,* as already pointed out, the tendency towards the objectification of consciousness begins in an incipient and hazy manner. Thus the beings of this category, known as Mantramaheśvara-s,[17] are permeated by the awareness of identity in such a manner as would not completely negate the tendency towards objectivity. Although this tendency towards "this" may be faintly felt, yet it is there. The governing deity of this category is Sadāśiva himself. As the tendency towards difference is put into abeyance, and not eliminated, so the beings of this category, having Sadāśiva as their goal, remain immersed in the experience of the non-dual bliss of Being, which would mean that the tendency towards externalization hardly exists in the category. It is in the category of *Īśvara* in which the tendency towards objectivity, and thereby towards difference (*bheda*), comes into prominence. This tendency towards difference, at this level, attains clarity or becomes operational on account of the working of the power of action (*kriyā-śakti*). It is because of this fact that the governing deity of this category is given the nomenclature of Īśvara.[18] It is from this category onwards that the lordship of the Lord (*īśvara*) finds its fullest expression. It is Īśvarabhaṭṭāraka who so externalizes the divine powers as would result in the emergence of such diversity that would be characterized by sheer difference. Although even in the Vedānta school of Śaṁkara, it is Īśvara who is said to be the agent of emanation, maintenance and dissolution of the phenomenal universe, yet there exists considerable difference concerning the role of Īśvara between the Trika Śaivism and Advaita Vedānta. The difference lies in the fact that the Īśvara of Vedānta is the projection or creation of *māyā,* which exists and does not exist. Since whatever is projected by *māyā* is of illusory nature, so it would mean that the Īśvara of Vedānta too is illusory. It is this Īśvara, the product of *māyā,* that is superimposed onto inactive *brahman,* and due to this superimposition *brahman* is made to appear as if he is the agent, and accordingly is held responsible in bringing into existence the manifest universe. The fact, however, is that *brahman* by nature (*svabhāva*) is impersonal and inactive, and so in no manner can activity be attributed to it. Upon the removal of *avidyā,* the so-called Īśvara disappears in the same manner as an illusory snake is negated upon the dawn of appropriate of cognition.[19]

The Trika Śaivism outright rejects this view of the Vedāntins concerning Īśvara as being the product of *māyā,* and thereby enjoying the same ontological status that is accorded to an illusory object. It would mean that Īśvara is in no manner different from the illusory snake that is mistakenly imposed upon the rope due to the erroneous cognition. Further it would mean that Īśvara, like any illusory object, could be negated upon the dawning of right knowledge. Instead of looking at Īśvara as a product of *māyā*, the Trika thinks that it is Paramaśiva himself who, out of his own absolute freedom (*svātantrya*), abandons the state of non-difference by descending to the level of difference in terms of taking up the lordship of the Lord. So Īśvara is none other than Paramaśiva himself. Moreover, Advaita Vedānta has so conceived Īśavara as would enable him to relate to what is called *prakṛti* or the primordial stuff. In the Trika Śaivism Īśvara cannot be touched by *prakṛti* or by *māyā*, because the former is nine steps below Īśvara and the latter two steps. It is, however, accepted by the Trika that Īśvara descends to lower states in order to run and govern the universe. It is at the lower states where Īśvara comes in contact with *prakṛti*. He appears as Anantanātha once he descends onto the state of what is called Mahāmāyā. Upon assuming the attributes (*guṇa*-s) of *prakṛti*, he appears in the form of Śrīkaṇṭhanātha and Umāpatinātha. However, Īśvara is to be seen as consisting of pure consciousness when in the state of difference-in-unity (*bhedābheda*).

While the categories of *Sadāśiva* and of *Īśvara*, as well as the beings of these categories, namely, Mantramaheśvara-s and Mantreśvara-s, abide in the state of *bhedābheda*, there occurs descent towards the category known as *Śuddhavidyā* or *Sadvidyā*. This category is the fifth and the last category of the pure path. The beings that belong to this category are termed as Mantra-s or Vidyeśvara-s. The deity that governs this category is the incarnation of Īśvarabhaṭṭāraka known as Anantanātha. The order of manifestation of categories from Śiva to Śuddhavidyā is known as that of pure path on account of the fact that these categories are not touched at all by *māyā*, which means that there is no cognition whatsoever of any kind of difference. Within the category of *Śuddhavidyā* exist many such viewpoints in terms of which is established the purity of the category. One of the experiential viewpoints concerning the beings of this category is characterized by the perception of being of the nature of pure consciousness, which means that the existent of this category is completely free fiom the taints of ignorance. Even though considering himself as being of the nature of pure consciousness, yet there exists the tendency of considering himself as being different from Paramaśiva as well as from other existents. Thus there exists within the category of *Śuddhavidyā* the taint of *māyā*, and it is because of this that the sense of difference is allowed to emerge among the beings called Mantra-s. However, *māyā* is not in such a position as would allow it to influence the existents of this category in a major way. There is a viewpoint that maintains the existence of a state that exists between *Śuddhavidyā* and *māyā,* and which is known as *Māhāmāyā.* The tendency of this state is that of concealment of one's essential nature. Anantanātha, who is considered to be the incarnation of Īśvara, governs this category or state. The beings of this state, while recognizing their essential nature as consisting of luminous consciousness, remain however unaware of the wonder that is wrought by the power of action (*kriyā-śakti*). What it amounts to saying is that the existent of this category has to have such knowledge as would satisfy him of being of the nature of light of consciousness. He remains totally destitute insofar as the functioning of the power of action is concerned .[20] These cxistents, known as Vijñānākala, do not often undergo the painful process of rebirth, but are uplifted from the state of Mahāmāyā as and when they receive grace from the beings of higher categories, such as, Mantreśvara-s or Mahāmantreśvara-s.

The state of Mahāmāyā, if we may call it so, is not to be treated as a separate category. It exists within the frame of *Śuddhavidyā* category. In fact, the analysis of categories is carried out, on the one hand, for the purpose of understanding the real situation in the context of the manifest universe and, on the other, it is made use of in terms of what is called the path of categories (*tattva-adhva*) as a means of accomplishing the esoteric practices of the Trika. The number of categories could even be enlarged if analysis is carried out further. The number could also equally be decreased. There is, however, some debate concerning the number of categories. There is a viewpoint that maintains the number to be either thirty-seven or thirty-eight. Whatever be the number, the fact is that by and large it is the number of thirty-six categories that has been accepted. The Trika has so envisaged the number of categories as would enable the aspirant to make use of them in his spiritual praxis in a manner as would terminate in the transcendent absorption of identity. The first five categories, viz., from *Śiva* to *Śuddhavidyā*, are spoken of as pertaining to the pure path on account of the fact that these categories in no manner are influenced by *māyā* nor are the existents therein. Moreover, the existents of these categories are so pure as to be free from the ever-recurring cycle of birth and death. This nomenclature of pure path is given to these five categories due to the Trika spiritual discipline called *ṣaḍadhva*.

The Impure Course of Manifestation

The categories that are below *Śuddhavidyā* fall within the framework of impure path (*aśuddha-adhva*). These categories are known as being impure on account of them being under the influence of *māyā*. The impure path of manifestation begins upon the emergence of the category of *Māyā*. Anantanātha, who is supposed to be having his abode in what is called Mahāmāyā, initiates the emergence of *Māyā-tattva*. It is *Māyā-tattva* that becomes, as it were, the material cause for what may be called the material manifestation (*jaḍa-sṛṣṭi*). Being the material ground for the material manifestation, *Māyā-tattva* thereby itself is considered to be inert (*jaḍa*). It is the creative power (*māyā-śakti*) of the Lord that causes the emergence of *Māyā-tattva*, which means that it is the will of the Supreme Lord (*Parameśvara*) that actualizes, through *māyā*, the phenomenal existence. Thus it is but natural to think of this category as being the embodiment of materiality, and due to which it allows itself to be used as the material cause for such categories as those of *puruṣa, prakṛti* and *kañcukas.*[21] The existents within the *Māyā-tattva* have no awareness with regard to their essential nature, which is that of pure consciousness (*śuddha-saṁvit*). They, instead, think of themselves as being so inert and contingent as to be nothing. They look at themselves as being different from what may be called objectivity, which, in other words, means that it is the diversity of difference that is constitutive of cognition that is driven by *māyā*. It is because of this fact that from *Māyā-tattva* onwards the order of entire phenomenal manifestation is considered as belonging to the impure path, which means that these categories have to be seen as falling within the ambit of impure path.

Anantanātha is not totally free in bringing to the fore the order of impure categories. He, on the one hand, has to operate under the divine will of Śiva and, on the other hand, has to keep in mind the latent impressions that exist in beings that may be existing in the state of dissolution (*pralaya*). It all boils down to the fact that the re-emergence of existents is dependent not so much on the will of Anantanātha as much it is on the *karma*-s of existents called Pralayākala-s. Thus the phenomenal emanation is not the outcome of free play of Anantanātha. It is this kind of phenomenal emanation which in Advaita Vedānta has been assigned to Īśvara. However, insofar as *māyā* is concerned, it is said to be neither the creation of *brahman* nor of Īśvara. As a kind of adjunct of *brahman,* it exists beginninglessly, which means that we cannot locate its origin. It is because of this adjunct, which is *māyā,* that *brahman* appears in the form of Īśvara. And Īśvara brings the manifest order into being in accordance with the *karma*-s of existents. The Trika, however, is of the view that Anantanātha objectifies the general tendency towards objectivity that comes to the fore at the level of *Māyā-tattva.* It is this objectfication of consciousness that terminates in the emergence, through the agency of Anantanātha, of impure categories. Thus *māyā* in no manner is seen as being his adjunct. Instead it is seen as being under his control. It is Anantanātha who initiates change (*vikāra*) in the *Māyā-tattva,* and thereby is facilitated the emergence of such veiling entities (*kañcuka*-s) as *kalā, vidyā, niyati,* etc. Upon the emergence of veiling entities, Anantanātha initiates the emergence or appearance of the limited subject (*puruṣa*) as well as of objectivity (*prakṛti*).

The Trika considers *māyā* to be such a power that causes the cognition of difference in the subject (*pramātā*). It is also seen as the veiling power (*tirodhana-śakti*) of Śiva, viz., it is a power by which one's essential nature (*svarūpa*) is concealed.[22] Upon descending onto the *Māyā-tattva,* Śiva thereby assumes, out of his own free will, the state of limitation (*saṅkucita-avasthā*), and in terms of which he perceives his subjectivity, viz., the "I" (*ahaṃ*), as being different from the sheer mass of diversity, which is embodied by the term "this" (*idaṃ*). At this state the undifferentiated awareness, as it were, is so concealed as to give rise to perceptions that are grounded in difference. As a result of this concealment of one's essential nature, the limited subject experiences everything as existing apart from the self. It is at this level of difference that there occurs the appearance of the subject in the form of *puruṣa* (self-monad) and that of objectivity in the form of *prakṛti* (primal stuff). Thus eventuates the sense of difference between one subject and the other and between one object and the other. Thus the *Māyā-tattva* accordingly is pervaded by what may be called the phenomenal diversity.

The Five Kañcuka-s: It is out of the *Māyā-tattva* from where emerge the five veiling entities (*kañcuka*-s). These veiling entities come into being when Anantanātha, as it were, creates some kind of disturbance or agitation (*kṣobha*) within the *Māyā-tattva.* Upon descending onto the stage of *māyā,* pure and unlimited subject looks at himself as consisting of consciousness that is bound. Due to the sense of limitation, the subjectivity of the subject is termed as being equivalent to the void (*śūnya*).[23] The Trika view of the void in relation to the individual existent should in no manner be identified with the Buddhist notion of emptiness (*śūnyatā*). The Buddhist look at the world, including the existents therein, as being void due to the fact that there is no abiding self or ground that could be considered permanent. Since everything in phenomena, nay phenomena itself, is in the state of flux, so no permanency can be ascribed to phenomenal entities, which is interpreted in terms of the destitution of one's intrinsic nature (*svabhāva*). Insofar as the ultimate reality is concerned, which is *nirvāṇa*, it is so indeterminate that no affirmation can made as to its nature. It, thus, becomes quite clear that the Buddhist view of emptiness/void is quite different from the one that the Trika has propounded. For the Trika it simply denotes the phenomenal condition of existence, which is characterized by limitation with regard to knowledge and action. Thus the idea of the void denotes or explains the contingent aspect of the individual being. Since *māyā* is inert, so its products, too, would evidently be inert, which is to say that the inert reveals such aspects of the phenomenal state that are embodied by contingency as well as by the void. Thus the void or the contingent embody the inert. It is because of this reason that the individual being identifies himself with his body, which, as the product of *māyā*, is inert. Even though the individual existent may experience limitations of every kind, yet he is not so destitute of divine consciousness as to be totally inert and void. He is endowed with the divine consciousness, and it is through this consciousness that he carries out, even though in a limited manner, the activities of life.[24]

The dependent aspect of the individual being expresses itself in terms of the inability of knowing and doing whatever one wants to know or do. This limitation concerning knowledge and action of the subject is respectively called *kalā* and *aśuddha-vidyā*.[25] These two veiling entities (*kañcuka*-s) function with regard to the subject in such a manner as to conceal his essential nature, and thereby reduce his capacity (*sāmarthya*) of action as well as of knowledge. Thus the individual being is unable to do or know more than few things. Accordingly the subjectivity of the subject is disposed towards knowing only few things or engaging in activities that are so confined as to restrict their range. There, thus, arises a kind of contraction (*saṁkoca*) within the subject with regard to knowledge and action. This sense of contraction is further concretized by the veiling entity called "attachment" (*rāga*). It is due to the sense of attachment that the individual always desires to possess permanently the body that he possesses. As a result of this attachment he never wants to part with it. This identification with the body is the result of attachment. Attachment, which is the opposite of envy, is seen to be one of the characteristics of the mental apparatus (*antaḥ-karaṇa*). As such the individual is unable to comprehend the mystery of attachment. Although attachment may be the opposite of envy, yet at times it itself becomes a means of envy. Such an eventuality arises when the individual feels that the thing to which he is attached may be lost or snatched away. Even when envying, it is in the form attachment.

The fourth veiling entity is given the nomenclature of *niyati* or the law of restriction. The law of restriction always functions in relation to causality that operates within the bounds of space and time. The law of restriction functions in such a manner that every existent is made to experience the condition of phenomenal existence in accordance with the deeds that have been performed in previous existence. Thus every one of us, in one way or the other, is so bound that the fruit of the deeds previously done cannot be avoided. In this manner the power of action and of knowledge of the individual is made to suffer from further contraction.[26] The individual being, at the level of inner organs and of body, is so restricted with regard to knowledge and action as to be under the constant watch of *niyati*. It is *niyati* that, as it were, informs every aspect of existence in the world.

The last veiling entity is known as that of "time" (*kāla*). It subjects the individual being to such limitations that are constitutive of temporality. Although the individual is essentially of the nature of infinite and pure consciousness, yet he, on account of the influence of *māyā*, experiences himself as being so limited and contracted as would explain his contingency. Consequently he thinks in such terms as, for example, "I was," "I am," "I will be," and so on. As pure consciousness, the individual evidently should be free from the experience of the succession of time. But the existential fact of life is such that whatever experiences he is having as an embodied being, they are all in terms of succession, which is to say that each experience is succeeded as well preceded by another. Thus the temporality of time is experienced in terms of succession and precedence. It is because of this fact that there occurs division in time in terms of past, present and future, and it is within the frame of this division that the individual experiences himself in terms of I was, I am, and I shall be.[27] This experience of limitation in terms of succession is due to the influence of the veiling entity called time (*kāla*). Whatever actions an individual existent executes or performs, they are done with reference to time. In other words, it is time that determines every kind of human activity. Likewise the diversity of form (*mūrti-vaicitrya*) is also so confined as to remain within the boundaries of space (*deśa*). It is because of form that objectivity is perceived as being of the nature of difference. It is, thus, form that becomes the cause of difference between one object and the other. Although perceived as being different, the individual has the experience of mutual relationship of objects the moment he threads them together through his cognitive faculty.[28] The relationship that is perceived between the objects exists within the frame of space and time. So dependent becomes the individual upon space and time that he is unable to engage in any activity apart from them. Whatever events occur within the phenomenal realm are always with reference to time.

Whether it is the change of seasons, of the rising or setting of the sun, coming of the dawn or of night—all these events occur within the frame of time. But time needs space for the events to occur. Thus the events that occur within space are perceived with reference to time. It means that the veiling entity of time is so powerful that nothing in the universe remains untouched by it. It is because of this fact that time is seen as the great devourer, and this aspect of time expresses itself in terms of the process of succession as temporality.

It is the temporality of time that expresses itself in terms of birth, persistence and death. It is this idea of time as a kind of flow of temporal succession that has been applied to all the phenomenal entities, which means that the phenomenal entities, upon their birth, may last for some time, but would ultimately meet dissolution in terms of which their existence would come to an end. It is in the context of non-permanence of objects that time is spoken of as a great devourer. The Buddhists used this idea of non-permanence of objectivity in such a manner as to reduce everything to momentary (*kṣaṇa*) existence. It is, thus, in terms of the measurement of time that the activities of life are conducted in the world by maintaining that this child is sleeping, or that Devadatta would have a life of hundred years, or that there was momentary lightning yesterday.[29] Thus the activities of life are carried out within the bounds of time in terms of succession. Succession always occurs in objects that suffer from contraction, which is to say that it is in terms of the scale of succession that time is measured in relation to objects as pertaining to past, present and future. The cause for this contraction with regards to the subject and object is but *māyā* which means that time is nothing but the expansion of *māyā*, and accordingly limits the subjectivity of the subject in such a manner as to pervade his knowledge and action. Consequently nothing exists outside the ambit of time for the subject. He, as it were, becomes the creature of time.

Puruṣa and *Prakṛti:* The process of curtailment of freedom (*svātantrya*) of the pure subject, which is of the nature of consciousness, begins upon the emergence of the six veiling entities (*kañcuka*-s). By veiling the subjectivity of the subject, the veiling entities thereby facilitate the passage for the arising of the limited subject, which, according to the Trika, is *puruṣa* (self-monad). Thus the self-monad is a limited subject whose essential nature is totally veiled by the entities called *kañcuka*-s. He accordingly is referred to as being limited (*aṇu*) with reference to the divine fulness and perfection of the Absolute (*pūrṇatva-abhāvena parimitatvāt-aṇutvam*). This bound state of the self-monad is also equated with that of the void (*śūnya*). This Trika concept of the self-monad is quite antithetical to the one propounded by the Sāṁkhya thinkers. The Sāṁkhya philosophy conceives reality as consisting of the dyad of *puruṣa* and *prakṛti*—the former representing the principle of sentiency, whereas the latter is seen as the embodiment of the insensible or inert, and thereby is seen to be representing the objective side of manifestation. It is, however, *prakṛti* (primal stuff) that is seen to be responsible in evolving itself into the phenomenal categories. As the embodiment of barest objectivity, the primal stuff, prior to its further bifurcation, is said to be existing in a state of peaceful equilibrium with regards to her constituents called *guṇa*-s. The process of evolution of *prakṛti,* however, begins when there is caused disturbance in the peaceful co-existenec between the three constituents (*guṇa*-s) of *sattva, rajas,* and *tamas.* Insofar as the self-monad is concerned, it is said to be inactive, and so has no role to play with regard to the manifestation of phenomena. As to how it gets involved with the primal stuff is not explained satisfactorily. The involvement of *puruṣa* with *prakṛti* results in the former obtaining an embodied existence and in terms of which it undergoes the cycle of births and deaths. It obtains freedom from the cycle of becoming only when the knowledge of discrimination (*viveka*) emerges in the individual with regard the nature of *puruṣa* and *prakṛti.*

The Trika thinks of *puruṣa* as being the product of *māyā,* and so it is accordingly called the subject of *māyā* (*māyā-pramātā*), which means that the *Puruṣa-tattva* represents the "I" in its extremely limited form. In this state of limitation the self-monad either identifies itself with the void, or with the life force, or with the gross body.[30] This confusion exists within the self-monad on account of the influence of *māyā*. Insofar as *prakṛti* is concerned, it appears to the limited individual merely as "this" (*idaṃ*). However, the appearance of the primal stuff is always dependent upon some form or shape (*ākāra*). It is through some form that the self-monad apprehends the primal stuff. The entirety of phenomena as "this" (*idaṃ*) exists in the I-consciousness (*ahaṃ*) in the same manner as colourful plumage of a peacock exists in the juice of an egg. But this very absolute I-consciousness, in its bound state, is unable to recognize its essential nature as consisting of unlimited freedom.

The Absolute in its transcendent state not only has unlimited powers of knowledge and action, but also contains within itself the power of emanation (*visarga-śakti*). It is because of this inherent power of emanation that Paramaśiva tends to emanate the diversity of phenomena which, prior to emanation, exists in identity with him. In other words, the objective universe in its unmanifest condition does not suffer from the kind of difference that eventuates upon its manifestation. All the three powers or capacities of knowledge, action and emanation are to be found even in a limited being. However, these powers in the individual existent are, on the one hand, limited due to the emergence of contraction (*saṁkoca*) and, on the other hand, are always enveloped by the perception of difference.

Since Śiva and Śakti are always in mutual identity, so it means that these powers or capacities have to be treated as being nothing else but the powers of Śiva. However, these very powers in the context of an individual existent are termed as not being the powers of a limited being, but are termed as being his attributes or qualities.[31] Śiva knows the world as being non-different from his own self. Such cognition of non-difference is not found in the individual being to the extent he remains under the influence of *māyā*. The knowledge the limited individual has of objects is of such nature as can be measured in terms of its range and content. It is the power of knowledge of Śiva which, upon its contraction, appears in the individual being in its finite form. This appearance of knowledge as limited is spoken of as being the peaceful (*sattva*) constituent of the empirical individual. Likewise when the power of action of Śiva appears in the individual, it is called the constituent of passion (*rajas*). When the deluding power of Śiva (*māyā-śakti*) appears in the individual being, it is called the constituent of inertia (*tamas*). What it means is this: The attribute of *sattva* functions in the individual in such a manner as to terminate in the emergence of limited knowledge. Similarly the capacity to do only few things is because of the attribute of *rajas*. Insofar as the attribute of *tamas* is concerned, it always deludes an individual being. All these three attributes of *sattva*, *rajas*, and *tamas* are respectively the source of such experiences as are characterized by pain, pleasure and delusion—and it is such-like experiences that are constitutive of human existence in the world. Thus the seed of these three attributes exists within the three powers of Śiva.

The subject that has the vision of non-difference is termed as being the Lord (*pati*), whereas the subject who only perceives difference is called the bound being (*paśu*). The subject who has realized the state of lordship is always and in every condition so absorbed in the bliss of the self as to have cognition of everything as being identical with his own being. It means that his perception of non-difference is such as to lead him to the experience of identity in terms of which is realized that nothing is different from the mass of bliss of the self. Thus his knowledge as well action are characterized by the experience of bliss of the self. This experience of unlimited bliss, however, does not accrue to the bound being (*paśu-pramātā*). Even though capable of experiencing the delight of the objects, yet this delight is experienced to the measure the sense of "I" or of "mine" is extended. However, this delight of the objects, which the bound being experiences in his waking state, is not available to him during the state of deep sleep. As and when the bound being has the experience of delight of the sense objects, it is in terms of *sattva-guṇa*. But when there is the experience of the absence of this delight, it embodies the state of inertia (*tamas*).[32] There are also occasions when the bound being experiences the delight of the self as well as its absence partially. Thus he simultaneously experiences both pleasure and pain. It is an experience that makes the mind agitated as well as unsteady. Thus this experience of presence-absence as a mixture of *sattva* and *tamas* conjointly gives rise to what is called *rajas*. In this manner does the bound being experience pleasure, pain, and delusion, which correspond respectively to *sattva, rajas* and *tamas*.

These three strands or constituents (*guṇa*-s) of tranquility, activity and inertia, at the level of *māyā*, constitute, as it were, the nature (*svabhāva*) of a bound being (*paśu*). The impact of these attributes is such upon the individual that he looks at the sense objects as consisting either of pleasure, or pain, or delusion. In this manner the world of objectivity, viz., of *prakṛti*, is experienced in terms of constituents that are of triadic nature (*tri-guṇa-ātmaka*). In this state the condition of the self-monad (*puruṣa*) is charactcrized by such consciousness that is contracted, whereas the primal stuff (*prakṛti*) contains within itself the three constituents in a state of balance, which is to say that there is no disturbance insofar as the co-existence of the attributes is concerned. Since the attributes are still in the state of balance, there has not yet occurred any transformation in the primal stuff. Once there occurs disturbance among the attributes, there, then, is initiated the program of bringing such transformational change (*pariṇāma*) in the primal stuff as would result in its further division. As a result of this change in the primal stuff are evolved the elements (*tattva*-s) of senses (*karaṇa*) as well as of objects (*prameya*). When the attributes are in the state of balance, the twenty-three categories remain latent in the primal stuff. According to the Sāṁkhya thinking, there takes place agitation within the primal stuff on account of *rajas*, which disturbs the co-existence of the attributes. As a result of this agitation, there is spontaneously ushered in the process of transformation of the primal stuff. The Trika, however, does not accept this standpoint of the Sāṁkhya concerning the agitation (*kṣobha*) within *prakṛti* on the ground that the inert has no possibility of causing disturbance within itself. There has to be some agent who has the possibility of initiating disturbance within *prakṛti*. According to it, it is Śrīkaṇṭhanātha himself who causes this agitation or disturbance within *prakṛti*, and as a result of which the process of transformation is initiated. The process of transformation of primal stuff is so initiated as to serve an appropriate basis for the bound beings that would be born in accordance with their deeds done in their previous lives. It is because of this fact that the Trika thinks the entire process of transformation is directed and governed by Śrīkaṇṭhanātha so as to avoid the pitfalls of blind chance and necessity. Since *prakṛti* is inert, it cannot by itself initiate its own evolution. Were it to do so, then the evolution would have neither any direction nor any purpose to serve, and there would be utter chaos. It is this pitfall that is avoided by the Tirka when it maintains that the process of transformation occurs under the direction of Śrīkaṇṭhanātha. Thus it is Śrīkaṇṭhanātha who, in the process of initiating the agitation within *prakṛti*, is responsible in giving rise to the remaining twenty-three categories.

Insofar as the doctrine of *guṇa*-s is concerned, it owes its existence to the Sāṁkhya philosophy. In this philosophy primal stuff viz., *prakṛti*, is accepted as being constituted by the threefold *guṇa*-s, whereas the self-monad (*puruṣa*) is said to be devoid of such constituents. The Sāṁkhya philosophy, being dualistic in orientation, has so adumbrated its philosophical thinking as to remain confined only up to the categories of *puruṣa* and *prakṛti*. The Trika philosophy has, however, gone beyond the categories of *puruṣa* and *prakṛti*. It has added eleven more categories to the already twenty-five categories of the Sāṁkhya. Insofar as the *guṇa*-s are concerned, they constitute, according to the Trika, the three powers of Śiva. Moreover, the Trika is of the view that the objective entities (*prameya*) have no ontological status apart from the knowing subject (*pramātā*). An objective entity comes into existence only when it is made manifest by the cognitive light of the subject. What it amounts to saying is that when an object is perceived by the perceiving subject, only then does it attain the status of an object. It becomes clear that the arising of knowledge, at the level of *māyā*, will not occur unless both the subject and the object are present. However, this situation does not prevail with regard to the subjects that abide above the category of *māyā*, which is to say that the Akala subjects are not in need of an external object for the arising of knowledge. The Akala subjects perceive objectivity in the form of their own being, which is to say that the so-called objectivity is so dissolved as to be one with subjectivity. Everything, thus, is perceived or cognized as being identical with one's self which is but I-consciousness. Insofar as the Sakala subjects are concerned, they perceive objectivity as consisting of three attributes precisely because they think of the self-monad as being of the nature of three strands. It is because of this reason that the entirety of objectivity is also perceived in terms of threefold attributes. Since both subjectivity and objectivity, at the level of *māyā*, are viewed as consisting of threefold strands, so the subject at this level has such knowledge as would express its character in terms of one of the attributes. In this manner is vitiated the entire process of empirical knowledge. Thus would arise the epistemological problem concerning the substance and its attributes. The question would be asked as to whether attributes inhere in the substance or are simply added to it. It is this question around which most of the philosophical thinking concerning knowledge has revolved.

The Inner Organs: When the period of dissolution (*laya*) of the emanated manifest order comes to an end, and consequently there is the beginning of a new day, Śrīkaṇṭhanātha in accordance with his function creates the state of disturbance in the primal stuff (*prakṛti*).[33] There occurs, as a result of this disturbance, the appearance of the three strands (*guṇa*-s). It is because of these strands that the primal stuff is transformed into what is called the internal organs (*antaḥkaraṇa*-s), which consists of intelligence (*buddhi*), mind (*manas*), and ego (*ahaṁkāra*). Initially it is the *mahat-tattva* that comes into being, and in this category it is the strand of *sattva* that is predominant. This category is also known as that of intelligence (*buddhi*). Although inert (*jaḍa*), it is considered to be free from the taints precisely because the reflection of the object is reflected in it. If the category of intelligence were tainted, there would fall no reflection in it, which would result in the non-emergence of knowledge. It is because of its own purity that the category of intelligence absorbs the reflection of the objects in its own mirror. The category of intelligence is similar to the sense organs insofar as its functioning is concerned. The sense organs are considered to be such means as would terminate in the acquisition of knowledge or in operationalizing action. Likewise the category of intelligence carries out its assigned task when it manifests the reflected object within itself to the self-monad (*puruṣa*). It is intelligence that becomes the cause for such reflection (*pratibimba*) as would endow the reflected object with name-and-form (*nāma-rūpa*). Thus the category of intelligence enables the self-monad to have knowledge of the object through the process of name-and-form. Accordingly intelligence becomes the means for knowledge by naming the object. Equally it becomes a means for the execution of action when it conceives a definite form of the object. The category of intelligence, without relating itself to the external object, has the power of conceiving objects within itself through the process of name-and-form. Thus the intelligence is considered to be the nearest organ to which the self-monad can approach. It means that the self-monad has no possibility of conducting any kind of activity apart from intelligence. Thus intelligence always functions within the gross body of the self-monad. It is accordingly spoken of as being the internal organ (*antaḥ-karaṇa*). However, it cannot reveal the external objects without relying on the support of such sense organs as, for example, eye, ear, nose, etc. Likewise is the mind (*manas*) and ego (*ahaṁkāra*) considered to be the internal organs.

Thus the entirety of the mental apparatus consists of intelligence, ego and mind. Insofar as ego is concerned, it is simply a mental construct and has no ontological validity. It is because of this reason that the ego, while thinking of itself as "I," is identified with emptiness (*śūnyatā*). The identification of "I" with the body, etc., is simply the result of mental imagination.[34] Since the experiences of ego are always in the form of thoughts, so it always moves owards things other than itself. Insofar as pure consciousness (*caitanya*) in itself is concerned, it is devoid of mental constructs. The indeterminate state of pure consciousness, on the one hand, denotes its nature to be luminous (*prakāśamānatā*) and, on the other hand, signifies it to be devoid of thoughts (*nirvikalpa*). This state of purity of consciousness informs us that neither the mind nor the intellect can be of any help to the subject. When, at the empirical level, there falls the reflection of objects on consciousness through the senses, there initially eventuates such an experience as would indicate the existence of an object. However, at this level of understanding nothing definite can be said about the object, which is to say that the intellect is in no position of imputing any kind of definite name-and-form on to the object. Such subtle cognition is considered to be indeterminate from the relative standpoint. Since the mind is unable to have the grasp concerning the exact nature of the object, so it thinks of numerous possibilities with regard to the imputation of name-and-form upon the object. The mental power of the individual that conjures imaginary names and forms is called the mind.

The indeterminate knowledge concerning the object attains determinacy when the various intimations are given up in favour of definite name-and-form of the object. This state of definiteness about the object occurs at the second stage when the cobwebs of obscurity are totally abandoned in terms of what is called the clarity of thought. Thus this definite or determinate knowledge could be of any object; it could be of a cow, of a man or a woman, of a tree, and so on.[35] It is the mental power of reflection of the mind of the individual existent that causes the general emergence (*sāmānya unmeṣa*) of the sequence of name-and-form. It is ultimately the intellect that bestows definiteness to name-and-form. It is, however, ego that connects the individual being to determinate or indeterminate intimations of the object. Whether the intimation is definite or indefinite, in both cases reflection of the object falls within the mirror of the intellect. It is to this reflection to which the individual being imputes definite name-and-form, and accordingly asserts, due to the influence of ego, that he knows the object. Similar is the case with regard to the activities of the intellect, of life force and of the body. Also the individual being thinks of himself as being identical with the inner organs and life force. This sense of identification of the individual existent with the limited (*parimita*) and imaginary (*kalpita*) individuality occurs on account of ego.

Since ego, among all the mental organs, is seen to be the most undesirable, so its removal is sought on a priority basis by such thinkers who adhere to the principle of negation (*niṣedha*). The Trika, however, does not consider ego as a stumbling block in the way of spirituality. For the Trika the most desirable entity is the Ego. This is so because it considers that the essential nature of Śiva is nothing else but the pure and infinite "I." What for the Trika is rejectable (*heya*) is such thinking that gives rise to the sense of difference from the absolute "I." Thus, accordingly, the thinking that is centred on I-ness (*ahantā*) is the most acceptable (*upadeya*), whereas the thinking that terminates in "this-ness" (*idantā*) is to be considered as non-acceptable. It is within the framework of this thinking that liberation (*mukti*) is seen to be characterized by the viewpoint that looks at the entirety of universe as being non-different from the absolute "I." Insofar as bondage is concerned, it is characterized by the vision that looks at the universe as being different from the absolute "I."[36]

The identification of the constructed or psychosomatic ego with the "I," which essentially is unlimited and pure consciousness, occurs due to the impact of *māyā* upon the individual existent. As a result of this impact, the limited individual neither understands nor knows the exact nature of "I." Instead of understanding the nature of "I" as being infinite and unlimited, the individual initially identifies it with the void or with the life force (*prāṇa*). The "I" that is identified with the inert is not the real "I" but is a constructed one. On account of it being constructed, it is, therefore, not spoken of in terms of "I," but is given the nomenclature of ego (*ahaṁkāra*). It is because of this constructed ego that the individual identifies his real self with such inert entities as the void, life force, inner organs, the gross body, etc. It is also because of *māyā* that the individual ascribes the activities of the senses, of the body, the intellect, etc., upon the self. Insofar as an individual remains in the grip of *māyā* he will experience, in one way or the other, difference. It is by transcending the operations of *māyā* that one comes to realize the essential nature of "I," and accordingly is recognized that nothing exists apart from the absolute I-consciousness.

The Sense Organs: There is a threefold transformation of the principle of ego in terms of which come into being the five senses of perception (*jñānendriya*-s), the five senses of action (*karmendriya*-s) as well as the five elements of perception (*tanmātra*-s). The organs of perception are so oriented as to give rise to such forms of knowledge that is impure (*aśuddha-vidyā*), viz., knowledge that is the source of bondage.[37] Likewise the organs of action function in such a manner as would be divisive in nature. These sense organs operate in such a manner as would express the various conditioned capacities of man with regard to knowledge and action, which at the same time are to be treated as a means of conducting the practical affairs of life in the world. One of the functions, for example, of the organ of hearing is to apprehend the reflection of the sound as well as the objects that are of the nature of sound. Upon apprehending the reflection of the sound, the sense organ accordingly transfers it to intelligence. The apprehending of sound expresses the capacity of man insofar as the hearing of sound is concerned. This capacity of hearing lies in the ear of man, which forms a part of the gross body of the individual being. Rest of the sense organs also function in a similar fashion. Even these organs operate at the level of subtle body. It is because of this reason that the individual being, at the level of subtle body, has the capacity of apprehending every kind of sensation. The power to have the experience or knowledge of heat and cold, of what is soft and what is hard, is due to the sense of touch (*sparśa-indriya*). Insofar as the knowing of form, shape, colour, etc., is concerned, it is due to the sense of sight (*cakṣurendriya*), which exists in the eye (*cakṣu*). The capacity of tasting things as sweet, sour, pungent, etc., is due to what is called the organ of tasting (*rasanendriya*), which exists in the tongue. The power to apprehend the various types of odour lies in the organ of smell (*ghraṇendriya*), which is found in the nose. Thus the power to hear, to feel, to see, to taste, and to smell is carried out respectively through such sense organs as ear, skin, eye, tongue, and nose, and so they constitute the sense organs of perception of an individual being.

Insofar as the five sense organs of action (*karmendriya*) are concerned, it is through them that the practical aspects or activities of life are accomplished. The power of speech (*vāk-śakti*), for example, denotes the capacity of communicating, through the medium of speech, of what one wants to say or utter. The sense organ that carries out this activity is called the organ of speech (*vāgendriya*). And the power of speech lies in the tongue, which is located in the mouth. The uttered speech, which is of the nature of sound (*nādātmaka*), is technically called *vaikharī*. The speech that occurs at the levels of *paśyanti*, *madhyamā*, and *pada* does not fall within the realm of *vaikharī* or uttered speech. The action that involves seizing of something is carried out through the organ called hand (*hastendriya*). However, the hands do not have complete sway insofar as seizing of objects is concerned. It is also found existing in the other limbs of the body.[38] The third form of activity is characterized by such actions as, for example, of coming and going, of jumping, of walking, etc. The organ that engages in such activity is called the locomotive organ (*pādendriya*), and it is the physical limb called feet that carries out such-like actions. Then we have the activity that emits from the body the undesirable elements, such as, urine, excreta, sweat, etc. The organ that carries out this activity is known as the excreting organ (*pāyu-indriya*), which is located either in the generative organ or in the rectum. Also through skin, mouth, nostrils are emitted undesirable elements found in the body. Finally, an individual engages in such activity that terminates in the experience of sensual delight, and it is carried out by the sense organ whose location is in the generative organ (*upastha*). It is through these five organs of action that an individual carries out the activities of life.

Finally, we have the fivefold *tanmātra*-s, which are a kind of energetic mass of objects that are related to the five organs of perception. The principle of ego gets transformed into the five organ of perception when it is dominated by *sattva-guṇa*. Likewise the organs of action emerge when the *rajo-*

guṇa is predominant. Insofar as the five *tamnātra*-s are concerned, they come into being through the dominance of *tamo-guṇa*. The five *tanmātra*-s are so subtle as to be in the state of non-form. They exist simply as a mass of energy. These five subtle objects, in the form of energy, are sound-as-such (*śabda*), touch-as-such (*sparśa*), form-as-such (*rūpa*), taste-as-such (*rasa*), and smell-as-such (*gandha*). When these subtle objects become gross, they are respectively transformed into space (*ākāśa*), air (*vāyu*), fire (*agni*), water (*apas*), and earth (*pṛthvī*). It is accordingly said that the activity of hearing is characterized by sound, of air by touch, of fire by form, of water by taste, and of earth by smell. It is within space that the sound waves travel. It is through air that the sense of touch is actualized. Likewise fire expresses form, water contains the quality of taste and the earth that of smell. Sequentially the extent of the object decreases to the measure it becomes gross. The more an object becomes gross, the less is its range and extent. Space, among all these objects, has less grossness, or should we say that it is the subtlest among all the objects. Because of it being subtle, it is widely spread out, which is to say that almost every object lies within its lap. In contrast to the subtlety of space, we have gross earth. The category of earth, being gross, is not as spread out as is space, which means that it is more limited than is space. All the categories from *māyā* to earth are said to belong to the impure path (*aśuddha-adhva*). Being impure, these categories are not seen as being the result of the independent will of Śiva. It is only the five categories, from Śiva to Śuddhavidyā, of the pure path (*śuddha-adhva*) that are considered as being the result of the independent will (*sva icchā*) of Śiva. Since the categories of impure path germinate due to the working of Śrīkaṇṭhanātha, who happens to be the incarnation of Īśvara, so they are said to be contingent.

The Realms: Upon the completion of the emanation of the category of earth, there emerge such permanent, and thereby non-transformative elements as, for example, atoms (*aṇu*) and space (*ākāśa*). Upon the emergence of such permanent elements, there then is given rise to such realms as those of earth, moon, sun, etc. It is Brahmā who accomplishes the task of bringing these realms into the manifest order by combining atoms skilfully. Accordingly he also fashions the bodies of the living beings that are going to inhabit these realms. The fashioning of the body of each living being is done in accordance with the deeds each living being has done in his previous existences. Also the bodies of the creatures are so fashioned as would be appropriate for each realm. Along with the fashioning of the bodies of creatures there are also made available the necessary objects that would be needed by the different types of living beings in different realms. Such highly evolved beings as Dakṣa, Kāśyapa, Manu, and others, also extend their helping hand to Brahmā in the accomplishment of this task, which is that of bringing into being the various realms that are constitutive of phenomena. It is on the basis of the idea of Brahmā being the originator of phenomena that Nyāya-Vaiśeṣika school of philosophy gave birth to their doctrine of origination (*ārambha-vāda*). Insofar as the doctrine of transformation (*pariṇāma-vāda*) of the Sāṁkhya is concerned, it has its roots in the view of the manifest order as consisting of strands or attributes, and such a manifest order is given rise to by Śrīkaṇṭhanātha. The doctrine of appearance (*vivarta-vāda*) of Advaita Vedānta, however, seems to have derived its inspiration from the impure manifestation brought about by Anantanātha. None of the above theories seem to have at all grasped the significance of pure manifestation brought about by Śiva.

From the category (*tattva*) from which these thirty-five categories arise and into which they ultimately are dissolved or absorbed is the thirty-sixth transcendent category (*anuttara-tattva*) called Paramaśiva. Some Trika thinkers have added two more categories, namely, the thirty-seventh and thirty-eighth.[39] However, there exists no difference between these two categories insofar as their essential nature is concerned.

Whether the categories are thirty-seven or thirty-eight has no significance in the context of general acceptance of categories as being thirty-six. All the thirty-six categories have been classified into three groups. The first group of categories extends from earth to Māyā, which is known as *ātma-tattva.* The second group consists of categories from Śuddhavidyā to Sadāśiva, and is known by the name of *vidyā-tattva.* The third group consists of Śakti and Śiva, and is given the nomenclature of *Śiva-tattva.*[40] This triadic classification is much more prevalent in Southern Śaivism than in Kashmir Śaivism. The Trika Śaivism, however, has made the triadic classification in terms of Nara, Śakti, and Śiva. The term *Nara* denotes the bound being as well as the entirety of inert phenomena. Insofar as Śiva is concerned, it denotes the transcendent aspect of reality. Between these two is Śakti, and as the Energy of Śiva is responsible in bringing into being the entirety of phenomena.[41]

The Trika system, apart from the above classification, has made the classification of the categories in terms of five *kalā*-s and four spheres (*aṇḍa-catuṣṭaya*). The term *kalā* denotes the subtle aspect of a category, whereas its gross form is represented by a *bhuvana* (realm). Each *kalā* contains within its ambit a number of categories. The *kalā* that pervades the element earth is called the *nivṛtti-kalā.* It is at the level of element earth where the divine play of the Lord concerning the process of emanation comes to standstill, which means that there is no further emanation of any category.[42] The *kalā* that pervades the categories from water (*jala*) to the primal stuff (*prakṛti*) is called the *pratiṣṭhā-kalā.* It is upon this *kalā* that the entirety of subtle and gross categories rest, which is to say that it is such a ground as would become the foundation for each impure category.[43] It is *vidyā-kalā* that pervades the categories from *puruṣa* to *māyā.* In these categories the subjectivity of the subject, as it were, remains hidden. It is the tendency towards objective knowledge that seems to be in ascendance in this *kālā.* The *kalā* that pervades the categories from Śuddhavidyā to Śakti is known as *śānta-kalā.* There is cessation of the effects of *māyā* and its products upon the subjects in this *kalā.*[44] The *kalā* that is above and beyond the above mentioned four *kalā*-s, is known as the *śāntātīta-kalā.* Its pervasion exists in the category of Śiva. They who pursue the *āṇava-upāya* take the help of the *kalā*-s, in their practice of meditation, for attaining the absorption known as the *āṇava-samāveśa.* All the *kalā*-s from *pratiṣṭhā* to *śānta* respectively correspond to what is known as the spheres (*aṇḍa*) of *pṛthivī-aṇḍa, prakṛti-aṇḍa,* and *śākta-aṇḍa.*[45] Insofar as the category of Śiva is concerned, it is transcendent to all the spheres, and so this category cannot be imagined or thought of in terms of spheres. Likewise the thirty-sixth category, namely, that of Paramaśiva, is transcendent to the *kalā*-s. It is because of this reason that Paramaśiva is referred to as being *kalātīta.* In this manner is completed the entire process of emanation of categories, which, under the direction of Śrīkaṇṭhanātha and Brahmā, are so fashioned as to allow the emergence of various realms, objects and creatures. In this manner, thus, is effected the manifestation of categories from Śiva to earth, which involves the manifestation of both the pure and impure paths.

References

1. *TĀ*, 30.100: *asthāsyad-ekarūpena vapuṣā cen-maheśvaraḥ/ maheśvaratvaṃ saṁvitvam tadatyakṣayad ghaṭ-ādivad//*
2. This idea of the manifest world as being but the emanation of the Lord finds its earliest expression in such-like early Upaniṣadic texts as the *Chāndogya* (6.2.1–3). Thus we read there: *sadeva saumya idaṃ-agra āsāt-ekaṃ-eva-advaitīyaṃ . . . tad aikṣat bahu syām prjāyeya iti/*
3. The Absolute in the Trika is spoken of as Maheśvara on account of it being absolutely autonomous (*svatantra*). This absolute autonomy of the Absolute should not be treated as being a kind of blind force. Rather this autonomy is the very nature (*svabhāva*) of the Absolute. And it is through will (*icchā*) that this freedom is actualized, which in the case of the Absolute means that will is so free as not to be dependent on any external prop or internal need. This is how the

Absolute is spoken of in the *ĪPK*, 1.5.13–14: *citiḥ pratyavamarśātmā sva-rasoditā/ svātantryaṃ etan mukhyaṃ tad aiśvaryaṃ paramātmanaḥ// sā sphurattā mahāsattā deśa-kāla-aviśeṣinī/ saiṣā sāratayā proktā hṛdayaṃ parameṣṭhinaḥ//*

4. Since the Lord is totally independent in causing the universal manifestation, so he is totally free in accomplishing the task of manifestation. It is this idea of the Lord's free will as the cause of the universal manifestation that is given vent by Kṣemarāja in his *Pratyabhijñāhṛdayaṃ, sūtra* 1: *citiḥ svatantra viśva-siddhi-hetuḥ/*
5. *Parātriśikā*, 24: *yathā nyagrodha-bīja-sthaḥ śakti-rūpo mahādrumaḥ/ tathā hṛdaya-bīja-sthaṃ viśvaṃ-etat-carācaram/*
6. *ĪPK*, 1.5.7: *cidātmaiva hi devo'antaḥ sithitaṃ-icchā-vaśād-bahiḥ/ yogīva nirupādānam artha jātaṃ prakāśayet//*
7. *Paramārthasāra* (*PS*), vv. 12–13: *darpaṇa-bimbe yadan nagara-grāmādi citramavibhāgi/bhāti vibhāgenaiva ca parasparam darpaṇādapi ca// vimalatama-parama-bhairava bodhāt-tadvad vibhāga-śūnyamapi/ anyonyaṃ ca tato 'pi ca vibhaktamābhāti jagadetat//*
8. Quoted by Yogarāja in his commentary on the *Paramārthasāra*. See Jaideva Singh, *Pratyabhijñāhṛdayam*, p. 19: *antar-vibhāti sakalam Jagadātmana-iha, yadvad vicitra-racanā makurāntrale/ bodhaḥ punar-nija-vimarśana-sāra-yuktyā viśvaṃ paramṛśati no makuras-tathā//*
9. Maheśvarānanda, *Mahārtha-mañjarī* (Trivandrum edn.), p. 40: *yadā sva-hṛdaya-vartimana-ukta-rūpaṃ artha-tattvam bahiḥ kartum-unmukho bhavati tadā śaktir-iti vyavahriyate//*
10. *Ṣaṭtriṁśaṭ-tattva-sandoha*, v. 1: *yad-ayaṃ-anuttara-mūrti nijecchayā-akhilam-idaṃ/ paspande sa spandaḥ prathamaḥ śivatattvam-uccayate tajjñaiḥ//*
11. *Śivadṛṣṭi* (*ŚD*), 1.2: *ātmaiva sarva-bhāveṣu sphuran-nirvṛti-cid-vibhuḥ/ aniruddha-icchā-prasaraḥ prasarad-vikriyaḥ-śivaḥ/*
12. Ibid., 1.29–30.
13. *Pratyabhijñāhṛdayam, sūtra* 3.
14. *ĪPV*, 3.1.3: *tatra yadā ahaṃ-ity-asya yadadhikaraṇam cinmātra-rūpaṃ tatraiva-idaṃ-aṁśa-ullāsayati, tadā tasya asphuṭvāt sadāśivata ahaṃ-idaṃ-itya.*
15. Ibid., 3.1.2.
16. Ibid., 3.12.
17. *MVV*, 2.3.: *śiva-ādi-sakala-ātma-antaḥ śaktimantaḥ prakīritaḥ.*
18. *TS*, chap. 8, *etat saṁskāra (vidyā-kalā-saṁskāra) sa ca iva prabuddha-māna śuddhavidyā mantrasya (śaktiḥ)/ tat saṁskāra-hīna saiva prabuddhā mantreśasya/saiva icchā-śakti-rūpataṃ svātantraya-svabhāvam jighrikṣanti mantramaheśvarasya (śaktiḥ)//*
19. *ĪPV*, 3.1.2: *yestu sadāśivabhaṭṭaraka īśvarabhaṭṭārakas ca dheyeyopāsya-ādi-rūpataya sa brahmā-viṣṇu-tulyaḥ pṛthaga eva mantavyo, na tu nāma sarūpayād-bhṛmitvayam/*

20. Śaṁkara on the *Brahmasūtra,* 2.1.14: *tadevaṃ-avidyā ātmaka-upādhi-pariccheda āpekṣyam-eva-aiśvarasya-īśvaratvam/*
21. *ĪPK,* 3.2.6–7: *śuddha-bodhātmakatve 'pi yeṣām nottamakartṛtā/nirmitaḥ svātmano bhinna bhartrā te kartṛtātyayat// bodhādi-lakṣaṇaikeya 'pi teṣām anyonya-bhinnatā/ tatheśvarecchā-bhedena te ca vijñāna-kevalaḥ//*
22. *TS,* chap. 7: *tasya ca sṛjataḥ parameśvarecchāmayaṃ, tat eva ca nityaṃ, sṛkṣaya-māna-vastu-gatasya rūpasya jaḍatyā-ābhāsayiṣyamānatvāt-jaḍam, sakala-kārya-vyāpana ādi-rūpatvāt ca vyāpakaṃ māyāmayam tattvam upādāna-kāraṇam/*
23. *ĪPK,* 3.1.7–8: . . . *tirodhāna-karī māyā abhidhā punaḥ/ bhedetvekarase bhāte ahaṃtayāna-ātman-īkṣite/śūnye buddhau śarīre vā māyā śarīre vā māyā-śaktir vijṛmbhate//*
24. *TĀ,* 6.9–10: *saṁvinmātram hi yat śuddham prakāśa paramārthakam/ tanmeyamātmanaḥ projaya viviktam bhāsate nabhaḥ// tadeva śūnyarūpatvam saṁvidaḥ parigīyate//*
25. *ĪPV,* 3.1.9: *evaṃ kalā-kāla-rāga-niyati-bhirotaproto māyāyāpahṛta-aiśvarya-sarvasvaḥ san punarāpi prativitīrṇa-tat sarva-sva-rāśi-madhya-gata-bhāga-mātra evaṃbhuto ayaṃ mitaḥ pramātā bhāti/*
26. Ibid., 3.1.9: *asya śūnyādera-jaḍasya vidyā kiñcit-jñatvā-unmīlana-rūpa buddhi-darpaṇa saṁkrāntam bhāva-rāśim nīla-sukha-ādi vivinakti/ kalā kiñcit kartṛtvopodvalanamayī kāryam-udbhāvayati/kiñcit-jānāmi kiñcit-karomi-ity/*
27. *TS,* chap. 7: *asmin na eva kartṛtvam-ity-atra-arthe niyate-vyāpāraḥ/ kārya-karaṇa-bhāve 'pi asya eva vyāpāraḥ/*
28. *ĪPV,* 3.1.9: *kālaḥ kramamasūtrayan pramātari vijṛmbha-mānas-tadanusārena premeye 'pi prasarati/yo'haṃ kṛśo-abhāvam sa sthūlo varte, bhaviṣyāmi sthūlataraḥ itya-evaṃ-ātmānam deha-rūpaṃ karma-vanta-iva parāmarśaṁs-tat-sahcārini premeye 'pi bhūta ādi-rūpam kramạ prakāśayati/*
29. *ĪPK,* 2.2.4: *svātma-niṣṭhā viviktābhā bhāvā eka-pramātari/ anyonya-anvaya-rūpa-aikya-yujaḥ saṁbandha-dhī-padam//*
30. *ĪPV,* 2.1.3: *ye iyattaya pariniṣṭhitā ābhāsaḥ siddhaḥ, tad yathā candra-sūrya-ādinam, sahakāramallika-kaṭuja-ādinam, śītoṣṇādeḥ, parabhṛta-mad-vilāsa-ādeḥ, sa eva kālaḥ/ yato apariniṣṭhita gamana-pathana-ādi taira-iyattaya pariniṣṭhīyate, parivartakaira-iva kanakaṃ/sa eva ca sūrya-ādinam svabhāva-viśeṣas-tattvataḥ paramārthataḥ kramo, na anyaḥ kaścit kramo nāma/krama eva ca kālo, na anyo asau kaścit/*

    See also *ĪPK,* 1.6.4-5: *cit-tattvam māyayā bhinna eva avabhāti yaḥ/dehe buddhāvatha prāṇe kalpite nabhaśiva vā// pramātṛtvena-ahaṃ-iti vimarśo 'nya-vyapohanāt/vikalpa eva sa para-pratiyogy-avabhāsa-jaḥ//*
31. *ĪPV,* 4.1.5: *bheda-sthiteḥ śakti-mataḥ śaktitam napādiśyate/ eṣām guṇānām karaṇa-kāryatva-pariṇāminām//*
32. Ibid., 4.1.5: *sattānandaḥ kriyā patiyus tad abhāvo 'pi sā paśoḥ/ dvaya-ātma tad rajo duḥkham śleṣi sattva-tamo-mayam//*
33. *TS,* chap. 7: *sa ca kṣobhaḥ tattveśa-adhiṣṭhanād-eva/ anyathā niyatam puruṣam pratati na siddhayet//*

34. *ĪPV,* 1.6.5: *cit-tattvasya-aiśvarasya māyā śaktyā bheda-āvabhāsini śarīre buddhau-antare sparśe tadottīrṇe va ākāśe va śūnya eva kalpite 'haṃ iti pramātṛ bhāvena vimarśa tad-tad-abhāsamāna-śarīra-ādi-prati- yogya-apohana karaṇād ghaṭo-ayaṭo-iti-vad-vikalpa eva/*
35. *ĪPV,* 1.6.1: *vividhā kalpanā, vividhatvena ca śaṁkitasya kalpo naya-vyavachedanam vikalpaḥ/*
36. *Śivastotrāvalī,* 12.12: *tvaya nirākṛtam sarvaṃ heyam-etat tadeva tu/ tvanmayam samupadeyam-iti-ayaṃ sārasaṃgraha//*
37. *Śivasūtra,* 1.2: *jñānaṃ bandhah.*
38. *ĪPV,* 3.1.11: *sarva-deha-vyāpakāni ca karmendriyāni ahaṁkāra-viśeṣa-ātmakāni/tena vicchinna-hasta bāhubhyāmāddanaḥ pāṇi-naiva-ādite/ evaṃ-anyat/*
39. *TS,* chap. 8: *sarva-avaccheda-śūnya śiva-tattvam ṣaḍtriṁṣam / tad-yat upadīśyate bhāvyate vā yat-tat-pratiṣṭhāspadam, tat saptatriṁśam/ tasminnāpi bhāvyamāne-aṣṭatriṁśam/ na ca anavasthā/ tasya bhāvya-manasya-anvachinna-svātantrya-yogino vedyikarane sapatriṁśa eva paryavasanāt/*
40. *Mālinī-vijaya-tantra,* 2.47: *vijñānākala-paryantaṃ-ātma-tattvamudāhṛtam/ īśvara-antam ca vidyāhvaṃ śeṣa śiva-padam vidhuḥ//*
41. *Parātriśikā-vivaraṇa* (*PTV*), p. 80: *nara-śakti-śiva-āveśa viśvam etat sadā sthitam/*
42. *TS,* chap. 10: *pṛthivyam nivṛttiḥ/ nivartate yataś-tattva-sargaḥ/*
43. Ibid., chap. 10: *jala-ādi-pradhāna-ante varge pratiṣṭha/*
44. Ibid., chap. 10: *śuddha-vidyā-ante-śānta/kañcuka-taraṅga-upaśamat/*
45. Ibid., chap. 10: *etad-eva-aṇḍa-catuṣṭayam-pārthiva-prākṛta-māyīya-śākta abhidhānam/*
See also *PS,* v. 4: *nijaśakti-vaibhava-bharād-aṇḍa-catuṣṭayam-idaṃ vibhāgena/śaktirmāyā prakṛtiḥ pṛthvī ceti prabhāvitam prabhuṇā//*

4

The Spiritual Hierarchy of Subjects

THE TRIKA has so conceived the spiritual hierarchy of the subjects as would correspond to the bifurcation of the manifest categories from Śiva to earth into what is called the pure and impure courses (*śuddha-aśuddha-adhva*). It is in this context that the cosmological theory of the Trika consists in the assertion that the entirety of the manifest order consists of thirty-six categories (*tattva*-s), which is bifurcated into the pure (*śuddha*) and impure (*aśuddha*) courses (*adhva*). The first five categories, viz., from Śiva to *Śuddhavidyā*, are termed as being pure on account of the fact that they are not tainted by *māyā* in any manner. The purity of these categories, from a philosophical point of view, denotes that the subjects (*pramātā*) of these categories are free from the sense of difference, which is to say that their spiritual vision is characterized by non-duality. In other words, the subjects of these categories experience perfect identity with the supreme consciousness (*para saṁvid*), which, in the language of theology, is called Paramaśiva. Insofar as the impure course is concerned, it extends from Māyā-tattva to the element earth. All these categories, being the products of *māyā*, are accordingly *māyayic*, which is to say that they suffer, in one way or the other, from some form of differentiating deficiency. And this deficiency is the result of some impurity, viz., the subjects of the impure path retain within themselves one of the impurities or all the three impurities together.[1] Thus the subjects of the impure path, called Sakala, suffer adventitiously from such ignorance as would deprive them of the knowledge concerning their essential nature (*svarūpa*). This ignorance is the direct result of impurities, and so ignorance accordingly is equated with impurity per se. The nature of this ignorance consists in perceiving everything in terms of difference (*bheda*), which results in the emergence of the subject (*pramātā*), the object (*prameya*) and the means of knowledge (*pramāṇa*), which, as it were, constitute the phenomenal diversity. It is in terms of this triad that seems to be constitutive of the manifest diversity.

These thirty-six categories, when looked at from the point of spiritual praxis, are said to contain within themselves one hundred and eighteen realms (*bhuvana*-s). These realms are inhabited by the multitude of subjects (*pramātṛ-gaṇa*). A subject is considered to be such a being who has the capacity (*sāmarthya*) of knowing and doing. Thus these subjects have different capacities of knowing and doing depending on their spiritual worth and stage. The spiritual worth of an existent is determined as to whether he belongs to a pure realm or to an impure realm. If an existent belongs to a pure realm, it would mean that the existent is pure and so, when compared to an impure being, has a high spiritual value in terms of knowledge and action. The capacity to know and to do of such a being would not only be pure and of a very high quality, but also would be free from such constraints and impediments that is the bane of the subjects of phenomenal realm. Even among impure beings exists a kind of hierarchy in terms of which is measured the spiritual worth of a particular being. There are beings whose impurity is thin, and equally there are beings whose impurity is very gross and thick. Thus the knowledge and action of a being whose impurity is thin would be of superior quality than of a being whose impurity is thick and gross. It is, thus, on the basis of impurity that the hierarchical analysis of the existents is made, which is to say that a being would be considered to be pure, and thereby of a superior quality, if he belongs to the pure path. The impure being, however, would evidently be considered, in comparison to a pure being, of an inferior quality. It is, therefore, necessary that we make an analysis as to what impurity denotes in the Trika system of thought, and how its classification has been made. It is in the context of such an analysis of impurity (*mala*) that we shall be able to proceed further with regard to the typology of existents.

The Nature of Impurity

The concept of impurity in the Trika is such as would have a direct bearing upon the epistemological status of knowledge, which is to say as to whether knowledge, in the presence of ignorance, is possible. The Trika system does not differentiate between impurity and ignorance. They are seen to be interchangeable terms for the simple reason that the function of both is to veil or conceal one's essential nature, which is said to be nothing but the ever-luminous consciousness. And when this luminosity of consciousness is veiled, it is said to be due to the presence of impurity or ignorance. Thus impurity or ignorance in relation to Being functions in such a manner as would impede or obstruct its disclosure. This obstruction operates in the manner clouds obstruct the rays of the sun by veiling the glowing light of the sun. It is for this reason that the Trika considers impurity as being of the nature of ignorance (*ajñāna*).[2]

However, ignorance has not to be understood in terms of the absence of knowledge (*jñāna-abhāva*). If the absence of knowledge would be considered to be innate to an existent (*puruṣa*), there would, then, be no possibility for its removal, which would mean that the arising of any form of knowledge would be impossible. It would be so because the innate nature of anything cannot at all be negated or eliminated. It is because of this logical impassability that ignorance (*avidyā*) is considered to be adventitious. Thus ignorance is so unnatural or constructed (*kṛtrim*) as is the imposition of an illusory snake upon the real rope. Were the snake on the rope real, then it could not be negated through any means of knowledge. Since the snake is unreal (*asat*), so its removal is actualized through the application of right means of knowledge. From this the Trika concludes that ignorance is not innate to man, even though the knowledge that results from ignorance may be erroneous or incomplete (*apūrṇa*). This conclusion is based on the premise that the essential nature of an existent is but consciousness, and consciousness, according to the Trika, consists in knowing and disclosing. It means that consciousness and knowledge are identical. And for this reason the Absolute is spoken of as being of the nature of *cit*, which accordingly has resulted in the following Upaniṣadic preposition: *stayaṃ jñānaṃ anantaṃ brahma.*

Instead of absence of knowledge or non-knowledge (*na-jñāna*), ignorance (*ajñāna*), according to the Trika, basically means such knowledge as is imperfect and erroneous (*apūrṇa-khyāti*). Thus the forms of knowledge that are equated with ignorance are always erroneous. The knowledge that ignorance gives rise to is considered to be imperfect knowledge because of it being characterized by such limitations as are availed within the crucible of space and time. Thus it is limited form of knowledge that is spoken of as being identical with impurity. Moreover, this limited knowledge is always characterized by difference, and so is considered, in the words of the *Śivasūtra*,[3] as the source of bondage. Such an understanding of limited knowledge as being differential would mean that all forms of empirical knowledge is erroneous, and so the cause of bondage. It is so because the emergence of empirical knowledge is not possible apart from concepts, and concepts always operate within the scheme of subject-object duality. It boils down to the fact that, according to the Trika, the knowledge that is dualistic, and thereby determinate, cannot be said to be authentic, because such knowledge, instead of liberating the bound being, binds him to the bond of bondage. It is because of this reason that the transcendence of such knowledge is sought in terms of knowledge that is indeterminate, non-conceptual and liberating.

The state in which the murmuring of intentness (*unmukhatā*) of consciousness towards self-congealment, in the form of contraction, begins and the state in which it is actually experienced is equated to the void (*śūnya avasthā*). This tendency from the subtle to the gross occurs when there is polarization of consciousness in terms of *ahaṃ* and *idaṃ*, viz., when there is movement from the subject to the object. This movement towards "this-ness" signifies, in the language of phenomenology, intentionality of consciousness, which is to say that consciousness, instead of abiding within itself, moves towards the object. However, this movement towards the object, according to the Trika, is to be understood in terms of the objectification of consciousness of itself. It is this state of objectification of consciousness that is termed as being impure precisely because of the occurrence of the fissure of subject-object polarity within consciousness. It also means that consciousness cannot know itself unless it objectifies itself by projecting itself both as the subject as well as the object. The knowledge that arises from a polarized consciousness is considered to be impure, and so the source of bondage.[4] There, thus, is a smooth transition from philosophy to theology when the determinate forms of knowledge are seen to be the source of bondage.

The Trika, however, is of the view that the self, viz., the subject, is really pure, unlimited and unbounded, which means that the self, being of the nature of consciousness, is always autonomous precisely because it is perfectly full (*paripūrṇa*). It is precisely because of its autonomy that the self is perfectly free to know and do what it wants to know and do. The self always shines with its own glory in its non-dual state. The self-shining of the self explains its freedom with regard to knowledge (*jñāna*). While appearing in this manner, the self at the same time cognizes itself in terms of its essential nature (*svarūpa*). This reflective cognition or self-awareness (*vimarśana*) of the self concerning its nature explains its autonomy with regard to action (*kriyā*). In actuality, the subject, which is the self, is essentially infinite, unlimited and perfect light of I-consciousness (*ahaṃ-prakāśa*). While being light, the self at the same time is constantly engaged in the activity of self-cognition. Thus the self as light explains its knowing (*jñātṛtva*) aspect. Likewise self-cognitive awareness of the self denotes its doing (*kartṛtva*) aspect.[5] It is the power of action (*kriyā-śakti*) that explains or expresses the innate glory of the powers (*Parameśvaratā)* of the Lord. It is because of the glorious nature of the powers that the self is spoken of as being the supreme Lord (*Parameśvara*). These powers of the Lord also tell us that nothing exists apart from him. Whatever activities are being carried out in the universe, all of them are seen as being the activities of the Lord. Such an understanding of the Supreme Being leads to the conclusion of viewing him as being the perfect doer. It is because of absolute autonomy that the Lord conceals his nature (*svarūpa*) by assuming the state of a bound being (*paśu-pramātṛ*). It is also because of this autonomy that he reveals himself as to what he is and in terms of which he tastes the bliss that he is. Thus the Lord, out of his own free will, assumes the role of the finite subject, and thereby wilfully forgets his nature as consisting of perfect light, perfect self-cognition and perfect doing. It is this forgetfulness that terminates in the contraction of knowledge of the Lord. It is this contracted or limited knowledge that is termed as being impure (*aśuddha*) because of it being contaminated by impurity (*mala*). This limited knowledge as impurity is equated with incomplete knowledge (*apūrṇa-jñāna*).[6] It is, thus, this incomplete knowledge that is identified with ignorance (*avidyā*).

The Classification of Impurities

The Trika is of the view that impurity as the cause of ignorance is identical with it, which is to say that both impurity and ignorance can be seen as interchangeable terms. This understanding of ignorance as being the effect (*kārya*) of impurity (*mala*) has its basis in the Sāṁkhya causal doctrine of *satkārya*. The effect, according to this theory, always exists potentially in the cause. This potential effect in the cause is actualized when necessary inputs are provided for the cause to operate. It means that ignorance, prior to its actualization, exists potentially in the cause, which is impurity. Thus, in accordance with this theory of *satkārya*, ignorance is nothing but another expression of impurity. It would not be wrong to maintain that the emergence of ignorance is dependent upon the existence of impurity.

As such impurity is said to be of three types, namely, *āṇava*,[7] *māyīya*,[8] and *kārma*.[9] The *āṇava-mala* explains the limitations of the individual with regard to knowledge and action. The *māyīya-mala* operates in such a manner as to be the cause of sense of difference, whereas the *kārma-mala* owes its existence to the actions that have been done in previous lives. The *āṇava-mala* begins to operate at that point of time when the Lord assumes the role of a limited being, and accordingly forgets his essential nature in terms of which he thinks of himself as being limited both with regard to knowledge and action. Instead of cognizing itself as being infinite I-consciousness, the self thinks of itself as being so limited as to be unable to know and do more than few things. Such a kind of limitation arises due to what technically is called the *āṇava-mala*. Thus the *āṇava-mala* is responsible in making the subject to forget as to what he essentially is, and as a result of this forgetfulness he identifies himself with such inert entities as the body, the intellect, etc. There are, however, some subjects who, though devoid of impurity, forget the autonomy with regard to action, and consequently, like the inactive space, consider themselves as being so passive as to be like the peaceful empty space. Such an understanding results in depriving themselves of the blissful joy that results from the glory of the circle of powers. Such a contracted vision is another kind of *āṇava-mala*.[10] Thus this impurity functions at two levels, which is to say that the operation of the *āṇava-mala* is such as to limit the individual's capacity of knowledge and action.

The limited individual not only experiences limitation with regard to knowledge and action, but he also, through the reduction of the self to mere ego, experiences difference (*bheda*) with regard to other creatures and objects. This limited vision of the contracted individual in terms of difference is in the Trika system called the impurity of *māyā* (*māyīya-mala*).[11] In the Trika the concept of *māyā* is so used as to denote the state or stage of difference. In other words, it is at the level of *māyā* that consciousness is so polarized as to give rise to the sense of difference in terms of subject and object. It is because of this reason that the viewpoint that is characterized by difference is termed as being the impurity of *māyā*. It is not only the sense of difference that owes its existence to *māyīya-mala*, but the other two impurities are also related to it. Moreover, there is Mahāmāyā that exists between the categories of *Śuddhavidyā* and that of *Māyā*, or should we say that Mahāmāyā is above *Māyā* but below *Śuddhavidyā*. The subjects that abide in Mahāmāyā, viz., Vijñānākala-s, are also effected by the impurity of difference, which is *māyīya-mala*.

The Trika, while adhering to strict non-dualism, accepts the fact that it is Śiva really who is the real agent of all forms of action. When, however, Śiva freely assumes the role of a limited individual, it is but natural that the actions, too, would be of limited content, which is to say that when there is, as it were, pervasion of contraction, there, then, is the appearance of the principle of ego in terms of which the limited individual thinks of himself as the doer of limited deeds. The doer of these limited deeds, when looked at from the absolute viewpoint, is but Śiva himself. It is so because the limited individual, in fact, does nothing that is not willed by the Lord. He simply does what the Lord wills him to do. This does not mean that the unrighteous deeds are also the result of the divine will of the Lord. In order to avoid such a pitfall, the

Lord has laid down specific forms of injunctions that an individual has to follow in his day-to-day activities. Thus it could well be said that it is not the individual existent that is the doer of actions; rather it is the Lord himself who wills them through the instrumentality of an individual.[12]

The individual existent is influenced by contraction to the measure there is expansion of supreme consciousness in terms of the manifestation of impure categories. While under the sway of contraction, the individual accordingly boasts with regard to himself as being the doer of action, which, in fact, he is not. Due to the sense of egoism, there develops special kind of desire for various types of action (*karma-vāsanā*). It is this desire (*vāsanā*) that makes him perform various kinds of deeds, and as a result of which he is made to reap the fruit of what he has done. Thus the individual accordingly is made to suffer from the ever-recurring cycle of rebirths. This sense of "I am the doer" as well as the desire for limited action is known as the impurity of action (*kārma-mala*). It is due to this impurity that an individual reaps the fruit, in the form of rebirths, of deeds that he has done in his previous existences. Insofar as the presence of impurities among the various types of existents is concerned, it is not necessary that all the three kinds of impurity would be existing simultaneously among all the existents.[13] There would be some individuals who would be under the influence only of one impurity. Equally there could be individuals who may be under the impact of two kinds of impurity. Also it could be a fact that some individuals may experience the presence of all the three types of impurity. There are also beings of higher type who are totally free from the impact of impurity. Likewise there are some beings in whom there is just a tendency towards impurity, which has not yet fructified. Also there are such beings that have allowed the emergence of impurity to take place. It is in this manner that the presence of impurity with regard to several kinds of subjects has been analyzed and understood.

The Classification of Subjects

The *Akala*-s: The highly evolved beings in the Trika are referred to as the Akala subjects. The subjects of this type abide at such a spiritual stage in which the sense of difference is completely absent. These beings uninterruptedly have the experience of their subjectivity, which is of the nature of pure consciousness in terms of it being unlimited, unimpeded and unfettered. It means that the Akala beings experience perfect unity of Being. The subject of this kind may be equated to the ocean of the universal bliss (*jagadānanda*) and it is from this ocean of Being from where arise innumerable waves of bliss which are turned either inward or outward. The highest type of Akala being abides either in the category of Śiva or in that of Śakti. The subjects that reside in the category of Śiva are known as Śāmbhava.[14] It is the wonder of luminosity of light (*prakāśa*), which is the nature of Being as consciousness, which is found to be prominent among these subjects. The subjects that reside in the category of Śakti are known as Śākta. In these subjects it is the wonder of self-cognitive awareness (*vimarśa*) that is predominant. Thus these subjects, whether belonging to *Śiva-tattva* or to *Śakti-tattva*, constantly experience the fulness of the self, which, according to the Trika, is the "I." Insofar as "this" (*idaṃ*) is concerned, it is so dissolved in the "I" as to be non-different from it. The "this" remains so dissolved in the "I" as is salt in water. At this plane there is not the slightest awareness of "this," which is to say that unity or identity between "I" and "this" is such as would eventuate between salt and water. These subjects are completely free from the influence of *Kalā-tattva*.[15] Being free from the influence of *kalā* these subjects accordingly are termed as being Akala. Thus the subjects of the categories of *Śiva-tattva* and of *Śakti-tattva* experience spontaneously the wonder of bliss, which denotes their spiritual state of unity in terms of I-consciousness (*ahaṃ-vimarśa*).

Mantramaheśvara and Mantreśvara: Below the Akala subject is the subject of *Sadāśiva-tattva*, namely, Mantramaheśvara.

Although effected slightly by the vision of difference, yet this vision is so absorbed by non-duality as to be non-existent. It is because of this reason that his understanding concerning objectivity is characterized by the utterance of "I am this" (*ahaṃ idaṃ*), which when translated into the language of non-dunlism denotes that "I am this object." It is this kind of experience that is predominant among the subjects of *Sadāśiva-tattva.*[16] As the tendency towards objectivity is unclear and incipient, so the subject of this category has the cognition of himself as being of the nature of glorious consciousness. Even though cognizing himself as being pure consciousness, yet this subject within itself accepts the reflection, though in a very weak form, of objectivity. This reflection of objectivity, however, gets lost within the multitude of rays of the light of subjectivity of the subject, which is to say of consciousness. Thus there does not occur the cognition of objectivity in the subject of *Sadāśiva-tattva.*

The subject that abides below the *Sadāśiva-tattva,* which is that of *Īśvara-tattva,* is known as Mantreśvara. The cognition the subject of this category has of objectivity is in the form difference-cum-non-difference (*bhedābheda*). However, the perception of objectivity is much more clear and pronounced, and consequently the subjectivity of the subject, as it were, becomes a mere adjective of objectivity. The subject accordingly has the perception in terms of: "This I am" (*idaṃ-ahaṃ*), viz., in terms of the preposition: "I am this object."[17] It is the object (*idaṃ*) that shines predominantly in the subject called Mantreśvara, which is to say that the shining of the "I" is more objective than subjective. It would mean that this state of the subject is predominantly characterized by the experience of difference. However, this state cannot be termed as being of the nature of difference, because it is the "I" that is experienced as "this", and "this" as "I." In this manner is experienced essential identity between subjectivity and objectivity. However, at the level of *Śuddhavidyā* the tendency towards subjectivity and objectivity becomes more pronounced, and is of equal measure, which is to say that the subject is as much inclined towards objectivity as much as he is towards subjectivity. The subjects of this category are said to be both pure and impure.[18] They are considered to be pure insofar as they are free from the taint of duality. They are seen to be impure on account of the perception of objectivity in terms of difference. However, this sense of difference is not so pronounced as to be under the influence of the threefold impurity of *āṇava, māyīya,* and *kārma.* Since the subjects are completely free from duality, so the question of *māyīya-mala* existing in them does not arise. Insofar as *kārma-mala* and *āṇava-mala* are concerned, they too are not found in these subjects. However, it is among the subjects of *Śuddhavidyā,* namely, Mantra-s, in whom the latent seeds of impurity begin to emerge. Even though the latent seeds may begin to emerge in them, yet these seeds do not so obstruct the subjects as to deprive them of the experience of absorption in Śiva (*śiva-samāveśa*). So it should be noted that these subjects remain in the state of non-dual absorption known as *śiva-samāveśa.* Since these beings are disembodied, so they do not operate in the manner of embodied beings. The form they have is of pure consciousness (*śuddha-saṁvid-rūpa*). Whatever activity is performed by them, it is accomplished by mere willing.

So far we have described the subjects of the categories of pure path. Prior to the coming into being of the impure path, there exists a category between *Śuddhavidyā* and *Māyā,* namely, the category of Mahāmāyā. The subjects of this category are termed as Vijñānākala-s. The subjects of this category, while considering themselves as being of the nature of pure light (*prakāśa*), are not aware of themselves as having the characteristic of self-cognition. No form of contraction occurs in their I-ness with regard to consciousness or self-cognition. Since no form of limitation eventuates among these subjects, so they are free from the operations of the impurity of limitation (*āṇava-mala*). Even though not experiencing limitation with regard to knowledge and activity, yet these subjects experience difference with regard to God, world and creatures. It boils down to saying that "this-ness" (*idaṃ*) somehow is predominant among these beings, which results in the experience of "I am I" (*ahaṃ-ahaṃ*) and "This is this" (*idaṃ-idaṃ*). Thus the thrust of this kind of experience is towards such a proposition that would contrast the difference between "I am" and "This is," which is to say that "I am" is experienced as being different from "This is." Since these subjects are subject to the experience of difference, so the presence of the impurity of difference (*māyīya-mala*) in them cannot be totally denied. Although the function of *māyā* is to conceal one's essential nature, yet it does not operate among these subjects in such a manner as would conceal their essential nature. In these subjects *māyā* remains in an undeveloped condition, and as a result of which this category is called Mahāmāyā.[19] Since the essential nature of the subjects of this category is not concealed by *māyā,* so they are accordingly said to be pure. But these subjects do suffer from the deformity of the presence of *māyā* in them, and as a result of which they are termed as being impure, which means that they contain within themselves the elements of both purity and impurity.

The abodes of all these subjects of the pure path, viz., from Akala to Mantra, are respectively the categories of *Śiva, Śakti, Sadāśva, Īśvara,* and *Śuddhavidyā/Mahāmāyā.* The governing deities over these abodes as well as over the subjects therein are Śiva, Śakti, Ṣadāśiva, Īśvara, and Anantanātha. It is, however, Paramaśiva who, through his unimpeded will, brings these governing deities into existence.[20] In the autonomous ocean of the absolute will of the Absolute there arise and subside, like the waves of the sea, every moment hundreds and thousands of multitude of both pure and impure subjects. This emergence and dissolution of the multitude of subjects and objects reflects the glory of the power of pulsation (*spanda*) of the Absolute. It also explains the absolute lordship of the Absolute in terms of which is actualized his unimpeded freedom (*svātantrya*). If the Absolute were to be devoid of this ever-recurring pulsation, then there would be neither emergence nor dissolution of anything, which would mean that the Lord alone would be existing. Even in this regard, however, nothing definite could be said as to whether he would be existing or not, because there would be none to affirm his existence or non-existence. Even if the Absolute existed, he would be existing like the inert empty space. Thus the Absolute would have no possibility of enjoying the glory of the powers of lordship (*parameśvaratā*) precisely because of him being reduced to the status of an inert object.

Since the existence of the Absolute is self-evident, so the display of the glory of the powers of the Lord manifests itself in the very emanation of the universe. It means that it is in the very nature of the Lord to celebrate the powers in terms of being the author of five powers of consciousness, bliss, will, knowledge and action. These very powers of the Lord express themselves through such five acts as emanation of the universe, its maintenance, and dissolution. Also the Lord, upon manifesting the universe, conceals his nature by reducing himself to the status of a bound being. Not only this, he reveals himself to those who seek his grace. Thus whatever there is, is because of the display of the powers of the Lord. It is because of these innate powers that the Lord within himself through his unimpeded and free will brings about the emanation as well as dissolution of the categories of existence, of the deities that govern these categories as well as of beings that reside in them. As there is a constant emergence and dissolution of the waves in the ocean, so there likewise occurs continuous arising and subsiding in the ocean of supreme consciousness, which is Paramaśiva, of the categories of existence.

It would not be out of place if further analysis is carried out with regard to subjects called Vijñānākala-s. The Vijñānākala is such a being who is neither wholly pure nor wholly impure. However, the condition of these beings is far inferior to the beings of the category of *Śuddhavidyā*, even though the beings of both the categories have much in common. The Vijñānākala beings are of such nature as to have no consciousness or awareness of objectivity. It is so because they do not experience "this-ness" (*idaṃ*) in any form. It would mean that the Vijñānākala beings are not so impacted by impurity as to be disposed towards objectivity, and thereby towards the diversity of difference. Even though cognizing themselves as being of the nature of pure consciousness, they, however, are deprived of self-cognitive awareness,[21] which means that they, while cognizing themselves as being pure consciousness, are completely incapable of engaging in any kind of activity. The disposition towards activity remains so latent in them as to have no knowledge of it. Consequently, they suffer from the presence of such contraction as could be identified with the impurity of limitation (*āṇava-mala*). Not only do these subjects experience the presence of the impurity of limitation, but they also have the experience of mutual difference.[22] Insofar as the presence of *kārma-mala* among the Vijñānākala-s is concerned, it remains in them in the state of potency. It is because of this fact that these beings do not often come into the grip of becoming, which is to say that they usually are not reborn at the beginning of new creation. So they supposedly remain for a long period of time in such a state where they enjoy the luminosity of consciousness, but are deprived of the delight of self-cognitive awareness. However, they arise from this ocean of "great void" (*mahā-śūnya*) when the grace of the Lord descends upon them through such highly evolved beings as, for example, Mantramaheśvara or Mantreśvara. These Vijñānākala beings do not often have the experience of the delight of the bliss of the self on account of the absence of the glory of divine powers. However, they do not have the experience of suffering precisely because they abide in the state of peace. The peace they experience may be equated to the peace that obtains in the void of space. However, the changing aspects of *Kalā-tattva* in terms of having a body, sense organs or the inner organs do not effect the Vijñānākala beings. It is so because he recognizes himself as being of the nature of consciousness. Thus he, as it were, remains for a long period of time as an Akala being. It is because of this reason that he is given the nomenclature of Vijñānākala.

Below the Vijñānākala are beings that are known as the Pralayākala-s, or the beings that pertain to the state of dissolution. The Pralayākala beings neither have the knowledge of themselves as being of the nature of consciousness nor have they the self-cognitive awareness. Instead of recognizing themselves as being of the nature of *prakāśa* and *vimarśa*, they identify themselves with such elements that are through and through inert. Their state of existence is so inert as to be identified with the state of deep sleep (*suṣupti*). As the state of deep sleep is such a state of void as to be characterized by non-awareness, so the state of Pralayākala-s has appropriately been termed as being that of sheer vacuity. Unaware of themselves as to who they essentially are, they thereby disclose the acute presence of the impurity of limitation.[23]

Insofar as deep sleep (*suṣupti*) is concerned, it is said to be of two kinds. In one kind of deep sleep the existent remains dissolved either in intelligence (*buddhi*) or in life-force (*prāṇa*). In this type of deep sleep the existent has the experience, at the subtlest level, of pain and pleasure. The existent, upon coming out of this state, remembers the kind of experience he had, and so would, without any hesitation, utter: "I had a very pleasant sleep," or that "all my limbs were quite relaxed in sleep." Such a kind of deep sleep is called the one in which awareness is not totally absent. The second type of deep sleep is such in which the existent remains dissolved in the absolute void. The existent, upon waking up from such deep sleep, says that he was so engrossed in sleep that he remembers nothing as to what took place during the period of sleep. Such deep sleep is known as the one in which awareness is completely absent. The beings of the state of such dormancy do not suffer openly from the impurity of difference (*māyīya-mala*). However, the impurity of difference is not completely absent from beings whose deep sleep is not such as to have no trace of memory when coming into the state of waking. Insofar as the impurity of action (*kārma-mala*) is concerned, it remains dormant for some time. Among both the types of Pralayākalas, the Trika is of the view that the Nyāya-Vaiśeṣika concept of liberation (*apavarga*), the state of isolation (*kaivalya*) of the Sāṁkhya-Yoga, and the Buddhist idea of *nirvāṇa* are nothing but the different forms of the state of deep sleep. The body, inner organs as well as the sense organs remain for some time in the state of dissolution of such seekers who attain such spiritual levels. While in the state dissolution, these seekers thereby gain freedom from the impact of the changing aspects of *Kalā-tattva*.[24] These beings remain for a long period of time in this peaceful and inert state, which may be linked to the inert peace of space.

It is Śrīkaṇṭhanātha who, at the time of dissolution, dissolves all the elements into what is called the root element (*mūla-prakṛti*). When the dissolution of elements occurs, there begins the night for the beings that are to be reborn at the time of new creation. It is night that embodies or represents the state of bound beings. While in the state of dissolution, the bound beings obtain freedom from *Kalā-tattva* to the extent they remain in this state. However, all these beings come out from the state of dissolution when there is ushered in, at the end of the night, a new day for Śrīkaṇṭhanātha.[25] They are, in accordance with their previous deeds (*karma*-s), brought under the influence of *Kalātattva*, which means that they come into the ambit of the circuit of becoming.

Lastly, we have limited beings called Sakala-s. These beings, in the hierarchy of beings, belong to the seventh stage. These beings are so engrossed in the cognition of objectivity as to be unaware of themselves as being primarily of the nature of pure consciousness. They view and perceive everything in terms of the subject-object difference. They are always in the tight grip of the constructed psyehosomatic ego, and so it is through the prism of this ego that the limited knowledge that they obtain is filtered into them. Also the limited actions that are performed by the Sakala beings is due to the prompting of this ego. It would, thus, mean that the Sakala beings are under the complete domination of all the three impurities.[26] The Sakala beings represent all the mobile and immobile entities as well as the beings that reside in heavenly abodes. These beings, according to the Trika, are basically subject to rebirth. Thus the Sakala beings are such beings that are bound on account of them being subject to rebirth.

References

1. The Trika has made a triadic classification of impurity in terms of the impurity of limitation (*āṇava-mala*), the impurity of difference (*māyīya-mala*), and the impurity of action (*kārma-mala*).
2. *MVT*, 1.23: *malam-ajñānam-icchanti saṁsāra-kāraṇam/*
3. *TĀ*, 1.25–26.
4. Ibid., 9.71: *malaścāvaraṇam. . . .*
5. *ĪPV*, 1.8.11: *prakāśarūptā jñānam tathaiva svātantrayātmā vimarśaḥ kriyā/* See also *TĀ*, 2.10: *saṁvid-tattvam svaprakāśanam ityasmin kiṁnu yuktibhiḥ/ tadbhāve bhāved viśvam jaḍatvād aprakāśam//*
6. *Tantrāloka-viveka* (*TĀV*), 1.25: *nanu ajñāna śabdasya apūrṇam jñānam arthaḥ/*
7. *TĀ*, 9.62, 65: *apūrṇam manyatā ceyam tathā-rūpa-avabhāsanam. . . .*
8. Ibid., 1.30.
9. *ĪPV*, 3.2.5: *dharma-adharma-rūpam kārmam malam. . . .*
10. *ĪPK*, 2.2.4: *svātantrya-hānir-bodhasya svātantryasya 'pi abodhatā, dividha-āṇavam malam-idaṃ svasvarūpa aphānitaḥ//*
11. Ibid., 2.2.5: *bhinna-vedya-prathā-atraiva māyā-ākhyam. . . .*
12. *ĪPV*, 2.4.21: *tasya ya ekam iti vicitra rūpecchā saiva kriyā iti sambandhaḥ/ tena maheśvara eva bhagavān viśvakartā/*
13. *ĪPK*, 3.2.5: *bhinna-vedya-prathā-atraiva māyā-ākhyam janma-bhogadam/ kartary abodhe kārmam tu māyā śaktyaiva tat-trayaṃ//*
14. *TS*, chap. 8: *atra tattveśvara-śiva śakti-sadāśiva īśvara-anantaḥ/ brahmaiva nivṛttau/eṣām sāmānaya rūpānāmānugati-viṣayaḥ pañca/ tad yathā-śāmbhavaḥ śāktaḥ. mantramaheśvaraḥ. mantreśvaraḥ, mantraḥ iti*

śuddhādhava/

15. *Kalā* denotes the limited capacity of an individual being insofar as action is concerned. It is because of *kalā-tattva* that all the *māyīya* products emerge. Thus the gross body, inner senses, sense organs are seen as the result of the transformation of *kalā*.
16. *ĪPV*, 3.1.2.
17. Ibid., 3.1.2.
18. Ibid., 1.1.1.
19. Ibdi., 3.1.6.
20. *TS*, chap. 8: *iti śuddhādhva/iyati sākṣāt śivaḥ kartā/*
21. *ĪPV*, 3.2.7: *vijñānam bodhātmakam rūpam svātantrya-virahitam-eṣām-iti/*
22. *ĪPK*, 3.2.7: *bodhādi-lakṣaṇaikya 'pi teṣām anyonya-bhinnatā/ tatheśvarecchā-bhedena te ca vijñāna-kevalaḥ//*
23. Ibid., 3.2.8: *śūnyādy-abodha-rūpaś tu kartāraḥ pralayākalaḥ/ teṣām kārmamalo 'py asti māyīyas tu vikalpitaḥ//*
24. *ĪPV*, 3.1.8: *pralayena kṛta akalaḥ, kāla-tattva-uplakṣitā-kāraṇa kārya-rahita-abodha-rūpaḥ kartārś ca/*
25. *TĀ*, 6.152.
26. *ĪPK*, 3.2.10: *devādinam ca sarveṣām bhavinām tri-vidham malam/tatrāpi kārmam evaikam mukhyam saṁsāra-kāraṇam//*

5

The Dyad of Bondage and Liberation

THE TRIKA NON-DUALISM is of such philosophical orientation as would assert that the manifest world, though consisting of diversity, is in fact non-different from the Absolute, which would mean that whatever exists manifestly or otherwise is essentially divine.[1] This assertion has its antecedents in the Sāṁkhya theory of *satkārya-vāda,* which maintains that the effect (*kārya*) is nothing but the transformation (*pariṇāma*) of the cause. The implicit existence of the effect in the cause is equated to the presence of oil of plant in the seed, viz., oil or plant, prior to their actualization, permeates (*vyāpta*) the seed. The Trika does not, however, go so far as to maintain that the external objectivity is the result of the transformation of the Absolute. Such an assertion would destroy the transcendence, and thereby the indivisibility, of the Absolute. It is because of this reason that the manifestation or appearance of objectivity is linked to the reflection that occurs in a mirror.[2] Further the Trika maintains that the non-existence is as much identical with Śiva as is existence. It would mean that both Being and Non-Being, presence and absence, have to be treated as the expressions of Śiva. From this is concluded that there is nothing within and without the universe that is false or unreal.[3] Whatever there is, is but fulness, which is the innate character of Paramaśiva. If everything is Śiva, then it would signify, particularly within the framework of soteriology, that bondage and liberation, knowledge and ignorance, dualism and non-dualism are non-different from Śiva. In other words, it means that it is Śiva who within himself concretizes both liberation and bondage.[4] The supremely awakened adepts experience the all-pervading presence of Śiva everywhere and in everything.[5] It is the unlimited and all-pervading experiential vision of the lordship of the Absolute that is termed by the thinkers of the Trika as being transcendental non-dualism (*parādvaita*). The transcendental non-dualism is such a vision in which are equally contained dualism, monism, bondage, liberation, sentience, insentience, etc., which is to say that it is a vision in which in equal measure are absorbed all forms of pair of opposites.[6]

This Trika assertion concerning the Absolute as being everything would mean that both bondage and liberation have significance only to the extent the actuality concerning one's essential nature is not known, which is to say to the measure the pervasion of the presence of the lordship of the Lord is not experienced. In other words, it means that bondage and liberation are real at the level of day-to-day activity (*vyavahāra*), but have no significance at the transcendent level. It also means that such thinking as is constituted by the pair of opposites would be considered to be real unless it is transcended. Both bondage and liberation, according to the Trika, would appear in the form of pair of opposites till the time of opening up (*unmeṣa*) of the vision of transcendental non-dualism. It is upon the emergence of the vision of transcendental non-dualism that one experiences as well as cognizes in equal measure the phenomena as being but Paramaśiva.[7]

Bondage and Liberation as Divine Play

The Trika assertion concerning the pair of opposites as being identical with Śiva is so contradictory as to be against the fundamentals of logic and laws of thought. It is not at all possible for the opposites to be identical in terms of their essence, because of them having opposite natures. To say that pain and pleasure, blue and yellow, high and low, heat and cold are identical to go against the nature of truth, which is free from contradictions. If it is accepted that the opposites are one and identical, then there would be no possibility for knowledge to arise, because knowledge arises only with reference to the dual structure of thought. We think of sin precisely because it has an opposite, which is virtue. In this manner the arising of knowledge concerning sin and virtue, good and evil, etc., becomes possible. It is this contradictory aspect of the Trika assertion concerning the Absolute as being both bondage and liberation which the critics have pointed out. It is against this possible or actual criticism that the Trika maintains that this seeming appearance of knowledge as consisting of the pair of opposites is nothing but the flashing forth of the power of absolute autonomy (*svātantrya*) of the Absolute. Thus all forms of appearance, at the practical level of life, have to be treated as being nothing more nor less than a mere display of the absolute freedom of the Absolute. This flashing forth or appearance of the Absolute consists of two aspects, namely, of thesis and antithesis.

This appearance of the pair of opposites seems to be telling us that the Absolute is not content with itself. There seems to be going on a kind of continuous friction or agitation within the Absolute. There is no such friction or agitation within the Absolute as would be contradictory to his essential nature. The Absolute is always so pulsating within with the bliss that it ultimately overflows in the form of the emanation of the universe, and the universe is nothing but the collection of objects. These objects, at the surface level, may appear to be opposites, but at the level of essential nature they are one and identical, because of them being nothing but the forms of consciousncss.[8] Thus the entirety of phenomena is seen to be identical with consciousness. Were they to be separate from consciousness, then they could not appear. It is in the context of this understanding that the following assertion is made:

> It would be impossible to establish the existence or non-existence, within the realm of the empirical, of the phenomena unless they are (seen to be) resting within consciousness. In point of fact, the phenomena (evidently) are revealing (*prakāśmāna*) (on account of them) resting within consciousness. And their very revealing (nature) in itself (proves) their oneness (*abheda*) with consciousness. (It is so) because consciousness is nothing but the fact of appearing (*prakāśa*). If it were asserted that they (viz., the phenomena) existed apart from the light (of consciousness) and that they (at the same time) reappeared, (it would be tantamount to saying that the colour) 'blue' (exists) apart from its (essential) nature. (Insofar as the colour 'blue' appears and is known as such), one (accordingly) says: 'This is blue.' Thus, in this sense (is proved that phenomena) rest in conscious-ness, (and so) they do not exist apart from consciousness.[9]

As a philosophical explanation concerning the manifest nature of objectivity, it may satisfy our mental curiosity, but the question that still remains unanswered is as to why should the Absolute appear as this phenomena? Is it because the Absolute is not content with itself, and so desires to give rise to such a kind of objectivity that consists of contraries and opposites. However, the Trika asserts that the Absolute appears in the form of the universe not because of dissatisfaction or lack, but it is the very nature of it to overflow with the bliss in the manner that would condense itself as the universe. Thus the fundamental cause of the existence of phenomena is the blissful nature of the Lord, which so overflows as would result in the emergence of such diversity that would be constituted seemingly by the opposites. Thus, it is upheld that the Absolute not only is the light of consciousness (*prakāśa*), but also is reflective self-awareness (*vimarśa*), which, at the theological level of thought, is translated as being Śiva and Śakti, viz., the Couple. In displaying this divine play, the Lord, as it were, discloses his nature as consisting of creativity, and it is this creativity that pours out in the form of entities that are constitutive of the emanated universe. Accordingly we are told:

> Bhairava and his power of emission constitute the Couple (*yāmala*). (While) one member (viz., Bhairava) rests in his eternal and unchanging nature, (which accordingly) is called 'repose' (*viśrāma*), the other (member) is his (viz., of Bhairava's) primal vibration (*prathama-spanda*), and is (accordingly) called emergence.[10]

The essential nature of the Lord consists of the boundless ocean of consciousness. The nature of consciousness expresses itself in terms of bliss (*ānanda*). This bliss of consciousness is always and constantly throbbing in such a manner as would explain the absolute freedom in terms of unimpeded will (*aniruddha icchā*) of the Lord. When this throbbing of consciousness turns inward, it is a movement that is equated with knowledge (*jañāna*), whereas its outward movement is identified with action (*kriyā*). It is this unimpeded will (*icchā*), which, being of vibratory nature, shines forth as absolute freedom (*svātantrya*). As and when the Lord, due to this shining of freedom, forgets his own essential nature, he thereby manifests himself, on the one hand, in the form of a limited individual and, on the other hand, as this universe. While existing in the state of a limited being, the Lord recognizes his already forgotten essential nature by following the path of spiritual methods and in terms of which is discovered the ultimate fulfilment. In the *Mahārtha Mañjarī*,[11] this entire drama of manifestation is so poetically expressed as would result in the experience of the plenitude of divine bliss:

> The supreme Lord's extraordinary state of emotivity (*asādhāraṇa-bhāva*) is the overflowing of pure Being (*mahāsattā*). It is manifest as the brilliance (*sphurattā*) of the universe which, upon deep reflection, (is realized to be consisting of) the single flavour (*ekarasa*) of the essence of Beauty, which is vibration of the bliss of one's nature.

It is one of the aspects of Paramaśiva to remain in the transcendent state of absolute lordship. The other aspect of

Paramaśiva is to immanentalize himself in such a manner as to become the universe. The recognition of both these aspects—of transcendence and immanence—is also innate to the divine nature of the Absolute. Paramaśiva is spoken of as being the Lord precisely because it is his nature to manifest himself in the form of the universe. The lordly powers of the Lord find their proper expression through the glorious process of manifestation, which is to say that the Lord is Lord precisely because of the power of manifestation (*visarga-śakti*). This immanence also explains and proves the transcendent aspect of the Lord. It is this intrinsic nature that shines forth in terms of the divine play of the Lord. Having a sporting nature, the Lord actualizes the manifestation, in accordance with the principle of reflection in a mirror, of multitudinous variety of subjects and objects within the miror of his own pure and luminous consciousness. The Lord accomplishes this task of manifestation of objectivity on the strength of his absolute autonomy and unimpeded will, as well as also because of him being of the nature of vibration. The Lord, while bringing about this objective universe in the form of reflection, forgets as a limited being that this appearance of the mass of objectivity is nothing but mere reflection. Instead of treating the extemal manifestation as reflection, the Lord in the form of a limited being considers it, at the levels of thought and practice, as being real due to the impact of three types of impurity (*mala*).[12] Surrounded by the impurities, the limited individual accordingly experiences himself as being so bound as to be devoid of freedom. It is in this conditioned situation that the limited being, due to the grace (*anugraha*) of the Lord, is so enabled as would result in the discovery of an appropriate spiritual teacher (*guru*). As a result of this grace, the limited individual is shown such spiritual path by the teacher as would lead him to the study of sacred scriptures as well as to the path of spiritual practice. Consequently, he gains such spiritual maturity as would terminate in the emergence of supernal knowledge and in terms of which is recognized one's essential nature as being undifferentiated mass of consciousness and bliss. It means that the adept recognizes his forgotten essential nature, and accordingly recalims that the appearance of the external world actually eventuates in the form of reflection. Such an adept is said to be an appropriate vessel for liberation (*mukti*). In fact, the dyadic process of forgetting one's essential nature as well of recognizing it again is the divine sport of the Lord, viz., of Paramaśiva.[13]

It is in the context of this dyadic process of manifestation and withdrawal, of forgatherness and recognition, that the Lord himself, as it were, encounters bondage and the possibility of release from bondage. The experience of dependence, of limitation and of difference expresses the state of bondage, whereas the recognition of the world as being the result of the shining of one's freedom (*svātantrya*) and so a reflection of one's consciousness is considered liberation (*mukti*).[14] It could, thus, be said that both bondage and liberation, at the epistemic level, is nothing but the result of thinking in a particular way. To think of oneself as being a limited individual would mean of experiencing the limitation of bondage. Likewise liberation is experienced when reflection is so directed towards Śiva as would result in the dissolution of particularity. Both of them—bondage and liberation—are but the display, at the macrocosmic and microcosmic levels, of the divine sport of the Lord. Being the result of divine sport, both of them are accordingly experienced as consisting of difference—and the presence of this difference between bondage and liberation will continue to be experienced till the time they are recognized as being a mere sport of the Lord. Upon the emergence of the vision of transcendent non-dualism, there is experienced the presence of the fulness of Paramaśiva, which is seen as underlying every phenomena that was, prior to this experience, thought to be different and dependent.[15] It would mean that every manifest category, being identical with Paramaśiva, participates in the intrinsic nature and fulness of Being. Thus is realized that the objective world

> is Śiva himself, of unimpeded will and pellucid cons-ciousness, who is even now sparkling in my heart. It is his highest Śakti herself who is ever playing on the edge of my senses. The entire world glows at one with that bliss (of I-consciousness). Indeed, I know not what the word *saṁsāra* refers to.[16]

Since Paramaśiva alone is real and actual, so his powers too would have to be considered as being real and actual on account of them being inseparable from him. As a result of this inseparability, the result of these powers, in the form of the manifest universe, has also to be viewed as being real and actual. Maintaining this line of thought, the Trika thereby rejects the view of the Advaita Vedānta that equates the world with illusion. For the Trika the world is not so unreal as to be equated with illusion, because of it being the result of the actual powers of Paramaśiva. It is by considering the world to be real that the carrying out of both pure and impure activities is made possible. How could activities like the study of scriptures, of listening to supernal discourses, of engaging in spiritual activities, be carried out in a world that is thought to be unreal? If the world were totally false, then no form of activity could be performed or would be possible. The world, instead, is neither absolutely unreal nor absolutely real. For the Trika the world is contingent, and so is real relatively (*saṃvṛti-satya*).[17] It is within this perspective that bondage, according to the Trika, is nothing else than the forgetting of one's essential nature, whereas liberation is but the recognition (*pratyabhijñā*) of this intrinsic nature.

Ignorance versus Bondage

The basic feature of bondage, according to the Trika, is characterized by ignorance (*ajñāna*), whereas that of liberation by knowledge (*jñāna*).[18] Ignorance, however, should not be equated with the absence (*abhāva*) of knowledge (*jñāna*); rather it is knowledge that is contracted, limited, and thereby erroneous (*apūrṇa-jñāna, apūrṇa-khyāti*).[19] If ignorance were to be equated with the absence of knowledge, then there would exist no possibility for the arising of knowledge. It would be so because the absence of knowledge would, as it were, be a kind of innate nature and that which is of the quality of intrinsic nature cannot be transcended or negated. Since there is the possibility for the emergence of knowledge, so ignorance accordingly cannot be identified with the complete absence of knowledge. Even ignorance is characterized by knowledge in the sense of it being, though imperfect knowledge. It would mean that ignorance is such knowledge that is deficient on account of it being erroneous.

The Trika is of the view that the self, which is of the nature of unrestricted and unlimited pure light of consciousness (*śuddha-prakāśa*), falls to the position of a limited being or individual due to the occurrence of contraction in knowledge. And accordingly the self under the influence of contracted knowledge, considers such insentient entities as the body as his own. In fact, the self intrinsically has unlimited (*aparimita*) powers of knowledge and action, but unfortunately, due to the influence of *māyā,* it considers itself as being a limited individual who has limited powers of knowledge and action. In this manner the self in the form of a limited individual, has such experience with regard to knowledge as to be extremely contracted. It is this contracted experience of knowledge that is considered by the Trika thinkers as being ignorance.

This ignorance, which is limited knowledge, is, according to the Trika, of two types, namely, *pauruṣa* and *bauddha.* The basis of the former kind of ignorance is the individual being (*puruṣa*) himself. It is because of this ignorance that the limited individual inherits, as it were, such forms of impurity as, for example, *āṇava-mala.*[20] Insofar as the latter kind of ignorance is concerned, it has its basis (*āśraya*) in the intellect (*buddhi*) of the individual being. The intellect of the individual being becomes, as it were, the abode of contracted knowledge when influenced by ignorance. In other words, it is the inherited ignorance (*pauruṣa-ajñāna*) that restricts the grasp of the intellect, and so accordingly is pursued such forms of knowledge that are identical with ignorance. The intellect's capacity for knowledge is, thus, so restricted by the inherited ignorance that it can do nothing else than be subservient to ignorance. It would mean that the type of knowledge the intellect gathers is always erroneous and limited. It is a knowledge that operates within the realm of ideas (*vikalpa*-s), and the knowledge that is rooted in thought-constructs is, according to the Trika, to be considered as being impure (*aśuddha*). The grasping of an entity as being of the nature of Śiva is the characteristic feature of pure knowledge (*śuddha-vikalpa*), whereas to grasp it simply in terms of an object (*prameya*) is the function of impure knowledge (*aśuddha-vikalpa*). Thus ignorance is nothing but to remain subservient to thought-constructs (*vikalpa*-s) that are through and through impure. In other words, it is the impurity of thought-constructs that is constitutive of ignorance. In the context of such formulation it would amount to saying that any form of intellectual understanding or knowledge is ignorance when viewed from the absolute standpoint. And the cause of this ignorance is such ignorance that is inherited, namely, *pauruṣa-ajñāna*. As a result of inherited ignorance, the imprint of individuality of the individual so lays its impressions upon the mind as would become firm and fixed. The feeling of individuality gains firm foothold to the measure the cultivation of the disposition or sentiment towards Śiva begins to recede. It is due to the influence of intellectual ignorance that an individual identifies himself with such insentient objects as, for example, the body, and accordingly conducts the affairs of life in the world. Depending upon the limited and contracted sense of I-ness (*ahaṃ-bhāva*) the individual carries out all forms of worldly activity. Instead of grasping the nature of objectivity as being non-different from Śiva,[21] he thinks of it as being insentient, and so possessable like a house, etc. In this manner the individual weaves ideas concerning his essential nature as well as concerning the objective world. It is this conceptualization that constitutes what, according to the Trika, is called intellectual ignorance.

Knowledge versus Liberation

It is the inherited ignorance (*pauruṣa-ajñāna*) as well as the intellectual ignorance (*bauddha-ajñāna*) that, according to the Trika, characterizes human bondage. In other words, it would mean that bondage is characterized by such ignorance as would be either innate (*pauruṣa*) or intellectual (*bauddha*). Insofar as this dyadic type of ignorance remains functional and operational, to that measure the individual will experience the bondage of limitation. It is upon the removal of both forms of ignorance that an individual has the possibility of actualizing release from the tight grip of bondage. The removal of intellectual ignorance is possible either by following the instructions of a spiritual master (*guru*) or by practising the spiritual methods or by studying the sacred scriptures. The individual who adheres to such a spiritual discipline is so empowered, at the level of the intellect, as would result in understanding himself as being of the nature of unlimited and pure consciousness, and so by nature non-different from the Omniscient and Omnipotent Supreme Lord (Parameśvara). But this intellectual knowledge (*bauddha-jñāna*) does not yield its appropriate fruit in the form of liberation from bondage till the time inherited ignorance (*pauruṣa-ajñāna*) continues to be.[22] The intellectual knowledge comes to the rescue of an individual in matters of conceptual understanding. It means that the destruction of inherited ignorance can come about only upon the emergence of knowledge that is innate to man (*pauruṣa-jñāna*).

If the removal of inherited ignorance is dependent upon

the emergence of innate knowledge, the question arises as to how would this knowledge emerge? The emergence of this knowledge, according to the Trika, is dependent upon the removal of three types of impurity, and the only way of washing off the stains of impurity is commensurate with the transmission of grace from a spiritual master (*guru*). It would mean that the very stain of impurity is washed off the moment the grace of the spiritual master falls upon or is transmitted to the disciple. The grip of the inherited impurity (*āṇava-mala)* begins to loosen in the disciple from that very moment he is initiated by the master in the secret spiritual path of Śaiva-yoga. And through the continuous practice of spiritual methods the impurity, step by step, is washed off. Upon the removal of inherited impurity the intellectual understanding becomes appropriately sharp and clear. If, however, doubts do not cease completely upon the destruction of inherited impurity, there remains the danger of its re-emergence.[23]

The cessation of both forms of ignorance, and thereby of impurity, is necessary in the development of spirituality. It is upon the removal of ignorance, and thereby of impurity, that spirituality blooms in its fulness. This blooming of spirituality results in the emergence of non-dual vision of the Absolute and in terms of which is experienced not only the pervasion of the self (*ātma-vyāpti*), but also what is called the pervasion of Śiva (*śiva-vyāpti*).[24] For the attainment of such a state of spirituality the cessation of intellectual ignorance is not only necessary but a pre-requisite, because there is no possibility, in the absence of intellectual knowledge, of having faith that is firm and convincing. A man of mere intellectual knowledge may have conceptual understanding with regard to the nature of the self, but he is totally destitute of having a direct vision of it. The destitution of direct perception (*sākṣātkāra*) of the Absolute results in the breeding of such doubts that completely derail the spiritual disposition of the adept. Thus both forms of knowledge—intellectual and innate—are necessary for the purpose of realizing release from the fetters of bondage. The interior of an individual adept has to be as much pure as his intellect is expected to be. It is upon attaining such a condition of purity that the knowledge of the adept would be free from defects, which would mean complete cessation of ignorance. The sharpness of the intellect as well as the practice of esoteric yogic methods is needed for the realization of liberation. All this boils down to the fact that the Trika is of the view that mere knowledge in itself is not sufficient; it has to be action-oriented. It is through action-oriented knowledge that an adept has the experiential vision concerning his ontic status as being non-different from Śiva. As a result of this experience the adept's faith in his Śivahood becomes firm and inflexible. Thus both forms of knowledge, viz., *bauddha-jñāna* and *pauruṣa-jñāna*, are transformed into *vijñāna* the moment the state of unity of Being within and without is experienced.[25]

The Content of Liberation

The adept who is firmly convinced with regard to his essential nature as being of the nature of pure consciousness and divinity being his natural nature attains such supernal state whereby he understands the entire world to be nothing but the display of the sporting self. It is this type of interior reflection with regard to objectivity that does not terminate in the emergence of the fetters of bondage. Such a person is never deluded by the external glittering show of phenomena. Whatever objectivity he experiences or perceives he looks at it as being nothing more than a play of the self. And accordingly he is always replete with the experience of bliss that is constitutive of the self. Thus the adept of supernal knowledge looks at the world as being the great play of the Lord. In viewing the world in this manner, he is never influenced or effected by pleasant or unpleasant experiences that the adept may have with regard to his day-to-day activity.[26] Of course, such an adept, at the empirical level of the body, has the experience of heat and cold, hunger and thirst, pain and pleasure, wonder, envy, anger, etc., but such experiences remain restricted to the level of sense organs (*indriya*-s), of internal organs (*antaḥ-karaṇa*-s), and of life-forces (*prāṇa*-s). The worldly events, whether good or bad, do not leave their imprint upon the heart of the adept. The worldly events occur, but for the adept they simply come and go, and so no importance of any degree is accorded to them. The liberated yogi so experiences these events as would their effect be momentary, and thereby would have no lasting impact upon the internal organs (*antaḥ-karaṇa*). The yogi, however, would have to undergo all types of experiences in, through and of the world to the extent his body lasts, and the content of these experiences would be determined by the deeds that have been inherited (*prārabdha-karma*-s) from previous lives.[27] While living a normal life in the world, the yogi of this type also simultaneously leads such adepts on the path of spiritual freedom that are appropriately qualified (*adhikārī*). Such spiritual condition explains the state of liberation of the yogi while alive. The yogi, upon departing from the body, attains complete and perfect unity or identity with Śiva.[28] Upon realizing the state of perfect identity with Śiva, there occurs accordingly within the cessation of the sense of difference (*bheda*). The occurrence of cessation of the sense of difference in this manner denotes liberation that is disembodied one (*videha-mukti*).

Forms of Liberation

Now-and-then it so happens that a yogi, upon leaving behind the mortal coils, is endowed with such a kind of body that not only possesses supernal qualities, but also is transcendentally divine. This type of divine body is purely of spiritual nature. While staying in this body, the yogi plays the divine sport, in accordance with the will of the Lord, of concealment and of revelation with regard to the world. When the yogi leaves this divine body, he merges fully in the absolute state of non-duality. This kind of liberation for the yogi of divine body is extremely replete with bliss. While the yogi of this condition has partly the experience of the divine powers of emanation, preservation, dissolution, etc., he simultaneously also continues to have the full experience of the wonder of the bliss of his actual essential nature. Such liberated yogis are given the nomenclature of liberated Śiva-s (*mukta-śiva*).

The liberated yogi of this type, according to the Trika, has been classified into three categories. This categorization of yogis is done in accordance with the classification of the viewpoint that is contained in the sacred scriptures, which is of the nature of dualism (*bheda*), mono-dualism (*bhedābheda*) and non-dualism (*abheda*). Each spiritual aspirant, depending upon his mental capacity and disposition, follows one of the ways in terms of spiritual praxis. Even upon achieving spiritual perfection, the yogi mostly adheres to the viewpoint he has been cultivating. The yogi who cultivates the dualistic viewpoint is called the one who has attained the perfection of Śiva (*sidhha-śiva*). Such a yogi is said to be of the same spiritual status as are the Siddhas of the class of Vidyeśvara. A yogi of the Siddha or Rudra type (*rudra-siddha*), while enjoying the spiritual status of Mantreśvara and Mantramaheśvara, follows the path that is characterized by a mono-dualistic viewpoint. The liberated yogi who cultivates the spiritual vision of non-duality is known as the Siddha of Bhairava type (*bhairava-siddha*). Such a liberated yogi is said to be of the spiritual status that is enjoyed by the beings of Akala plane. [29] A *muktaśiva* of dualistic and mono-dualistic types is always in need of the grace of Bairavas of Akala plane for attaining the perfect state of non-duality. It is due the grace of Bhairavas that their respective viewpoints are ultimately transformed into a viewpoint that is completely permeated by the vision of non-differencc, and accordingly they are enabled to enter into the plane of unity of Being and in terms of which are resolved the knots of doubt, ignorance and delusion.[30]

There are some such fortunate adepts who, while still existing in a body that is practically dead, have a partial experience of the glory of divine powers of emanation, preservation and dissolution concerning objectivity. Upon the activation of such an experience, there emerges such knowledge within the adept that makes his conviction firm with regard to the divine powers of the lord, and consequently he attains such a state of liberation that is equivalent to the state of liberated Śiva (*mukta-śiva*). This state of liberation for such perfected beings is full of bliss. While being in this state, these perfected beings have the opportunity of comparing their existing spiritual state with that that existed prior to it. As a result of this comparison, there is increase in their disposition towards Śiva. While endowed with the glory of divine powers, there are some such perfected beings who, upon the exhaustion of inherited *karma*-s (*prārabdha-karma*-s), attain to the state of disembodied liberation (*videha-mukti*). There are also some such perfected beings that are adorned with such divine bodies that have been described above. Also there are such liberated beings that are born as human beings, and accordingly have the opportunity of serving humanity. Durvāsa, the founder of the Trika non-dualism, was one such perfected being (*siddha-puruṣa*). These perfected beings, while being liberated, are so fortunate as to relish the plenitude of bliss of liberation.

Ultimately, the perfected beings as well as *mukta-śiva*-s, while abandoning their divine or non-divine bodies, enter the state of disembodied liberation whereby they are enabled to have the wonderful experience of all the five divine powers. The glory and wonder of this experience is always unrestricted and unlimited, and so is characterized by the fulness of Paramaśiva. It is such a state of bliss that is beyond any description. Paramaśiva alone has the experience of this transcendent bliss, and because of this fact it is called the universal bliss (*jagadānanda*). So the aim and purpose of our life should be the attainment of the wonder of this bliss that comes to be upon the attainment of disembodied liberation.

However, it is possible to attain the so-called the state of liberation through the exertion of what may be called the spiritual praxis (*abhyāsa*). The liberation that results from the cultivation of exertive practices is not, according to the Trika, actual liberation. Such a liberation is not lasting on account of not obtaining complete freedom from the actual and latent forms of impurity. Such an individual remains subservient to one of the forms of impurity, and so accordingly does not enjoy the fruit of perfect and complete liberation. Perfect liberation, according to the Trika, comes to be when there is the intense fall of grace. It is because of the transmission or fall of grace that the adept attains, through the study of the sacred scriptures and the cultivation of Śaiva yoga, supernal gnosis concerning the nature of the self. The adepts who, however, are disposed towards the non-Trika scriptures seek, on account of the influence of *māyā*, liberation (*mokṣa*) in non-liberation (*amokṣa*), and as such remain for some time in a spiritual state that is between liberation and non-liberation.[31] Such adepts either are born again in the world of mortals or, due to the grace of *mukta-śiva*-s, transcend the middling spiritual state by climbing higher spiritual stages till complete liberation in terms of merger in Paramaśiva is realized

There is, however, a state of liberation that is different from, and higher to, the one which *jīvan-mukti* embodies or represents. This state of liberation is known as that of total submergence (*samāveśa*) in the absolute I-consciousness. Such an experience of liberation is not the result of a graduated or progressive practice. The experience is said to be sudden and spontaneous. While being conscious of his individuality, the adept at the same time experiences the transmutation of his empirical consciousness into that of absolute I-consciousness.[32] The impact of this experience is so powerful as would lead to the immediate recognition (*pratyabhijñā*) of one's essential nature as being identical with

Paramaśiva. And at the end of the worldly journey, there are two courses open to such a yogi. He may either prefer to be drowned in the infinite ocean of consciousness, which is the nature of Paramaśiva, or he may, like a Bhairava, prefer to be born again with the intention of serving those who are desirous of liberation.

In addition to the above types of liberation, which are *jīvan-mukti*, *videha-mukti*, and *samāveśa-mukti*, there is an another type of liberation, which is known as that of *krama-mukti*, liberation by stages. It is a liberation that emerges on account of divine intervention, which is to say that this liberation is the result of grace. The volume of grace is dependent to what extent one is open to it. If grace were of low intensity, it would mean that the attainment of liberation would be in steps and would take quite a long period of time insofar as the attainment of liberation is concerned. If it were of medium intensity, then the span of time for gaining liberation would not be much longer. If grace is intense, then liberation could be sudden and spontaneous. Grace fundamentally is a free gift of God, and upon whom it falls, he is bound to enjoy the bliss of liberation.[33]

Different Approaches to Liberation

It would not be out of place if the Trika concept of liberation were to be evaluated against the concept of liberation that Nyāya-Vaiśeṣika, in particular, has adumbrated. The Nyāya-Vaiśeṣika concept of liberation (*apavarga*) is such in terms of which the liberated-one, while having inclination towards knowledge, pain, pleasure, desire, etc., is unable to translate such inclination into actuality on account of its non-occurrence. Remaining always in the zone of neutrality, the liberated-one continues to exist in a state that is as insentient as is the vacuity of space. Such a liberated-one, although free from worldly pain, has no capacity of performing any kind of deed.[34] It is illogical to maintain that there exists in the liberated-one a tendency towards such dispositions which, according to the Trika, pertain to the intellect (*buddhi*). Thus the liberated adepts of Nyāya-Vaiśeṣika type seem to have not gone beyond the realm of the intellect (*buddhi-tattva*). Such types of adapts do not at all have the real vision concerning their essential nature, which is of the nature of light of consciousness. It seems that the spiritual state they enjoy is even below the state of deep sleep (*suṣupti*).

In contrast to the Nyāya-Vaiśeṣika view concerning bondage-liberation, the Sāṁkhya–Yoga is of the view that the self-monad (*puruṣa*) somehow gets so entangled with materiality (*prakṛti*) as to be caught up in the vicious circle of rebirth. It is the association of the self-monad with matter that, as it were, is seen to constitute bondage. For the Sāṁkhya–Yoga release from bondage consists in attaining such a spiritual state whereby the self-monad completely dissociates itself from materiality, and this dissociation is characterized by "isolation" (*kaivalya*). For the Sāṁkhya the state of isolation is attained through the process of discrimination (*viveka*), whereas for the Yoga it is attained through enstasy. However, the self-monad in this state of isolation has hardly any cognition of itself in terms of I-ness. It is a state that is as inert as is the vacuity of space.[35] Thus this so-called release in terms of the attainment of the state of isolation is in no manner different from the one that eventuates in deep sleep.

Insofar as the Buddhist concept of release in terms of "blowing out" (*nirvāṇa*) is concerned, it does not seem to be different either from the Nyāya-Vaiśeṣika concept of *apavarga* or from the Sāṁkhya-Yoga concept of *kaivalya.* The *nirvāṇa* of the Buddhists could be termed as being a continuous state of deep sleep (*suṣupti*). Thus the individual existents of these three types of release, according to the Trika, are similar, nay identical, with the creatures of the "state of dissolution" (*pralayākala*). These beings as Pralayākala-s remain in this state of dissolution till the time the manifest objectivity with attributes (*guṇamaya-prakṛti*) does not get dissolved into what is called the primal or root materiality (*mūla-prakṛti*). Even when the manifest objectivity reverts to its primal condition, these creatures either abide in the category of self-monad (*puruṣa-tattva*) or in that of unmanifest matter (*prakṛti-tattva*). These creatures of the state of *apavarga*, of *kailvalya* and of *nirvāṇa* come out of this swoon-like condition when Śrīkaṇṭhanātha again creates such tension (*kṣobha*) within the unmanifest matter (*prakṛti-tattva*) as would result in its manifestation. Accordingly these creatures take birth in accordance with their previous deeds, and so are made to descend to the level of worldly beings (*sakala*-s). As Sakala beings, these creatures undergo the circuit of becoming till the time they attain perfect liberation in terms of submergence (*samāveśa*) in the Absolute, who is of the nature of consciousness-bliss.[36]

The state of *apavarga*, of *kaivalya* and of *nirvāṇa*, according to the Trika, cannot be identified with perfect liberation on account of them not being different from the state of deep sleep. Whether it be the state of *apavarga* or that of *kaivalya*, the individual existent, while dissociating itself from the becoming-process of *prakṛti*, remains stationed in the state of isolation, which is not different from the inert void of space. Whatever awareness such an existent has, it is only for namesake, because of it being non-functional (*niṣkriya*). Insofar as the state of *nirvāṇa* is concerned, it is of the same nature that emerges when a lamp is blown off, which would almost mean non-existence. According to the Vijñānavāda Buddhists, *nirvāṇa* is equated with the blowing off the flame of storehouse-consciousness (*ālaya-vijñāna*).[37] It is a state which, as it were, dissolves into the void, and which is equated by the Trika with the category of self-monad (*puruṣa-tattva*).[38] Thus these kinds of release are temporary, which means they do not last forever. The creatures that have attained this kind of release remain free from the impact of changing aspects of *kalā-tattva* till the time they abide in the state of dissolution. However, they do not obtain freedom from such forms of impurity as the *āṇava-mala*. This form of release cannot at all be called real liberation, because of it being temporary.

The concept of release in the Advaita Vedānta is far better than the views propounded by the Nyāya–Vaiśeṣika, Sāṁkhya–Yoga or by Vijñānavāda. The Advaita Vedānta upholds the view that the actual release is realized at that moment when perfect merger of the individual existent occurs in *brahman.* However, the view that the Advaita Vedānta has propounded concerning the nature of *brahman* is radically different from that of Trika Śaivism. For the Trika *brahman* not only is Being (*prakāśa, cit*), but is also of the nature of Becoming (*vimarśa*), which is to say that *brahman* as an active principle is the sole cause of objective manifestation. The Advaita Vedānta, on the contrary, thinks of *brahman* as being so passive and inactive (*niṣkriya*) as to be unable even to cause the manifestation of a single object. Thus *brahman,* according to the Advaita Vedānta, is of the nature of infinite light (*prakāśa-mātra*). The Absolute of Vedānta is so inert, passive and impersonal as to be completely devoid of any kind of pulsation (*spanda*), activity (*kriyā*) or powers (*aiśvarya*). Rather the passivity or inactivity of *brahman* is so conceived as to be identical with the quietude or peace of space, which is almost identical with the *nirvāṇa* of Buddhists.[39]

The Trika considers such a concept of *brahman* as being very close to the Buddhist notion of emptiness (*śūnyatā*). However, the idea of emptiness in the Trika system is so treated as not to be identical with sheer nihility. For the Trika emptiness simply denotes the light of consciousness that is contracted or limited, viz., when reduced to constructed individuality. However, the *brahman* of Vedānta is said to be of the nature of boundless light (*aparimita prakāśa*). Even though being of the nature of infinite light, yet this *brahman,* being devoid of self-awareness as well as of glorious powers, is much more close to such form of emptiness as are objects that are inert. This type of Absolute, no doubt, may be a mass of light, yet this light is in no manner different from the light of an inert diamond. The Absolute as light of consciousness shines exactly like the inert diamond. The Absolute of the Advaita Vedānta, like the diamond, is unaware of itself as being of the nature of luminous light. Thus the question arises as what purpose does such an Absolute serve in the context of it being devoid of the power of self-awareness (*vimarśa-śakti*), which within the Trika is equated with the power of action (*kriyā-śakti*)?

This inert-like Absolute, though possessing light, seems to represent the plane that eventuates when the yogic Fourth State (*turya*) begins to emerge. It is such a state in which the characteristics or features (*saṁskāra*-s) of the state of deep sleep (*suṣupti*) are inherited. Those who have attained this type of release are subject, due to the destitution of the glory of powers, to the influence of the impurity of limitation (*āṇava-mala*). However, these so-called liberated beings are not threatened openly by the impurity of difference (*māyīya-mala*). These beings cannot be considered as having attained perfect form of liberation on account of their equation with the existents known as Vijñānākala-s. The emergent state of the Fourth, however, is said to have its beginning in the condition of Vijñānākala. Having got rid of the impurity of action (*kārma-mala*), these beings accordingly are not subjected to the cycle of becoming, which is to say that they do not undergo any further the process of rebirths. Having partially experienced the Fourth State, these creatures, thus, do not very often descend downward. They remain stationed for a long period of time at a plane that is below Mahāmāyā, and the Mahāmāyā plane is below the category of *Śuddhavidyā* and above *Māyā* category. However, they can ascend to the plane of difference-cum-non-difference (*bhedābheda*) as and when some higher soul, in accordance with the will of Śiva, sends grace upon them.[40] Even though these beings may not experience the kind of bondage that is experienced by Sakala existents, yet they remain, due to the absence of the glory of powers, in the state that is inert and is open to the influence of the impurity of limitation (*āṇava-mala*). These existents, according to the Trika thinking, are not totally devoid of desire for perfect liberation. It is because of this desire for liberation that they trudge the spiritual path that would ultimately terminate in the realization of perfect unity of Being in terms of identity.

Insofar as the adepts of Bhāgavata and Pāśupata sects are concerned, they have the possibility of attaining to the plane of Vidyeśvara, which, due to the influence of *māyā*, is such a plane as would be characterized by the vision of duality. It would mean that the kind of release these adepts achieve or attain couldn't, in the real sense of the word, be termed as liberation from bondage. However, these existents fortunately abide at a higher level of Mahāmāyā,[41] and so do not descend to the lower levels of *māyā*. Instead they have the possibility of ascending to the higher plane of the category of *Śuddha-vidyā*. Such highly evolved souls as, for example, Mantreśvara-s and Mantramaheśvara-s, have their abode in the category of *Īśvara* and *Sadāśiva*, and are accordingly said to be relishing the absorptive bliss of liberation.[42] However, among these highly evolved souls there exists in a weak form the sense of duality. In comparison to such existents as Akala-s, there is hardly experienced any kind of plenitude of bliss that eventuates upon gaining liberation. Insofar as the Akala existents are concerned, their state of liberation is almost identical with the one that eventuates upon attaining the disembodied form of liberation (*videha-mukti*). It is at the plane of Akala that the Lord displays fully the play of emanation and dissolution.[43]

The adepts that follow the spiritual path of difference-cum-non-difference (*bhedābheda*) remain for a long period of time in the state of Mantreśvara-s and Mantramaheśvara-s, and as such taste the nectar of the bliss of submergence in Śiva (*śiva-samāveśa*). While relishing the taste of this absorprive bliss, these souls accordingly ascend to the plane of Akala-s. Such adepts, however, enter, without any impediment, into the Akala state who follow the path of non-dualism. It is, however, through the practice of *śāmbhava-yoga* that these adepts are so empowered as would result in the attainment of the Akala state. The liberation that accrues to these existents is of permanent nature, which means they are no more subject to the vicious cycle of rebirth. In this state of perfect liberation these creatures experience the purity of their subjectivity in terms of identity with Paramaśiva. As and when these existents, in accordance with the will of Paramaśiva, are submerged into the infinite ocean of consciousness, they accordingly are blessed with liberation that is of disembodied form. In the state of disembodied liberation these existents become, as it were, one with Paramaśiva, and so are practically non-different from Paramaśiva itself.[44] Thus the state of perfect liberation is characterized by such enlightenment (*prakāśa*) in terms of which, like the forgotten treasure, the lost treasure of freedom is recovered, and this lost treasure of inner freedom is but the state of one's unity with the All.[45] It would mean that the Trika notion of liberation basically denotes the recognition of one's essential nature,[46] which is equated with joy that is unlike the joy that is acquired or experienced, at the empirical level, through the senses.[47]

The Nature of Grace

The concept of grace in the Trika is so used as would indicate the dependence of the limited individual upon the divine intervention in matters that are beyond his capacity. The divine intervention is sought because the individual existent finds himself incomplete and ill-equipped for the task of reaching the ultimate goal of life, which is that of freedom from the limitations of temporality. It is in this context of existential despair that divine intervention, in the form of grace, is sought, and Trika Śaivism fully subscribes to this line of thought.

The Trika thinks of grace as a free gift of God, which is to say that grace is not dependent upon one's merits or demerits. As such grace is termed as being causeless and motiveless (*ahetukī*). If grace is a free gift of God, then the question arises as to why only few are showered with this gift and not others'? Does not this act of God of favouring some with grace and not others amount to divine arbitrariness? According to the Trika, God does not at all favour some at the cost of others. He sends his grace to those who deserve it, who seek it, and who are open to it. As a free gift, God showers grace upon those who surrender unto, and seek refuge in, him.[48] The measure of grace that one receives is dependent to what measure or extent impurities have been removed. There are individuals who are overwhelmed by impurities, whereas there are also some individuals who have successfully thinned the impact of impurities by cultivating spiritual practices, and one such practice would be complete surrender to God. Most of us, however, are in a state in which the impurities have not reached the point of ripening. The gradual process of ripening of impurities is called *malapāka*.

Since no cause is ascribed to grace, so, according to the Trika, it is God's playful nature that alone can be thought to be its cause. Whatever God does, he does it out of his own free will. And so grace is said to be a free act of God's divine will. This gracious activity has been accepted both in terms of worldly enjoyment (*bhukti*) and soteriological freedom (*mukti*).[49] Insofar as self-effort in the context of grace is concerned, it is not denied its role. Whatever kind of self-effort is made with regard to spiritual upliftment is itself seen to be the result of grace. Thus self-effort fulfils its goal when it is seen as being the result of grace itself. It is, therefore, grace which is the initial point of spiritual stir within an individual. Even the devotional attitude towards God is itself the result of grace. The moment divine grace (*śaktipāta*) falls upon the individual, that very moment he surrenders unto him. Thus divine grace and worship of God go together, one intensifying the other, and thereby enhancing each other. Such an understanding of grace would mean that the very emergence of the disposition towards spirituality within the individual would be considered as being the result of grace. As to when and in what manner an individual may reach the ultimate soteriological goal is also dependent upon the grace of the Lord. An adept takes on to the path of spirituality in proportion to the grace he receives.[50]

It is the fall of grace that is seen to be responsible in directing an individual to a preceptor (*guru*) who points out the way to liberation. The teacher itself is considered as being the form and embodiment of the Divine, and so for all practical purposes enjoys the status of divinity. Upon receiving necessary initiation (*dīkṣā*) from the preceptor, the adept thereby enters the path of spirituality. In addition to the impartation of theoretical knowledge concerning the nature of reality, the disciple is also taught the secret aspects of Śaiva-yoga. It is through the practice of Śaiva-yoga that the disciple is so empowered as would reach the goal of self-realization. It is through initiation that the process of purification is initiated in the disciple. It is through initiation that the disciple receives grace, and as a result of which he has a direct intuitive experience of the Absolute—and such supersensuous experience is called *pratibhā*.[51] The individual who is endowed with *pratibhā* is esoterically initiated by the benevolent powers of God called *aghora*.[52]

The Trika thinkers are of the view that the divine descent of grace is of three kinds: It can be of slow intensity (*manda*), of medium intensity (*madhya*), or of intense intensity (*tīvra*). Each of them is again classified into intense-intense, intense-medium, and intense-slow. Likewise is classified the medium and slow forms of grace. Each form of grace accordingly is sub-divided into nine types, which means that the total number of the forms of grace is twenty-seven. Even among the twenty-seven types of grace, there eventuates such diversity as would be infinite. It is this unfathomable wonder of grace that is constitutive of the play that the Lord enacts with regard to the diversity of the world. The Lord, however, is absolutely free in displaying this wonder of grace. Were the Lord to dispense grace within the ambit of restrictive laws, then he would no more be God. If seen from the absolute point of view, then nothing exists apart from the Lord, which would mean that the apparent diversity essentially is identical with the non-dual Absolute. This perspective of non-dualism tells us that whatever we perceive as being different is but Paramaśiva himself. There does not exist within the Absolute such a division as is indicated by the words "I" and "thou." It is a non-dualism in terms of which the descent of grace is interpreted as being free from such defects as, for example, favouritism. The descent of grace is not determined by our merits; rather it is a free gift of the Lord—and a gift that is totally free cannot be marred by the disposition of partiality.[53] Since grace is a free gift of God, so no external or internal cause can be ascribed to it. However, there is a viewpoint propounded in some scriptures that looks at grace as having a cause, which, however, is severely criticized by Abhinavagupta. If external cause were to be ascribed to grace, then it would no more be a free gift of the Lord, which would be unacceptable to the Trika. In order to maintain complete independence of the Lord, the Trika accordingly asserts that the grace that ensues from the Lord is a free gift.[54] It is in the context of this perspective that the Trika maintains that the Lord, in accordance with its own free will, manifests the wonder of infinite diversity through infinite forms. While manifesting the infinitely constituted objective diversity, the Lord accordingly enacts the play of bondage and release. It is what constitutes the Lord's divine powers, which is his intrinsic nature.

It is within the frame of this triadic classification that grace is said to have two aspects, namely, the initial grace that terminates in the attainment of the goal of liberation in terms of absorption in the Absolute and the grace that empowers one with supernatural powers (*siddhi*-s). The first form of grace is accordingly spoken of as being transcendental (*para*), whereas the second form of grace is termed as being relative (*apara*).[55] The transcendental form of grace is said to be quick (*tīvra*) and effective, whereas relative form of grace is either of medium (*madhya*) or of weak (*manda*) intensity. Thus those who seek supernatural powers are endowed with medium form of grace, whereas such seekers of liberation are endowed with grace that is of low intensity that are desirous of ascending the spiritual ladder in steps. Insofar as transcendental grace is concerned, it too has been classified into intense, medium and low. They who are qualified for intense grace attain liberation without any delay. They have a spontaneous knowledge of the Absolute. The individuals of medium type of grace do not have as quick intuition regarding the self as the individuals of intense grace. These individuals have such intuition as would not require any kind of initiation.[56] The grace that is of weak type creates, first of all, desire in the seeker for a right preceptor.[57] Upon approaching the teacher, the disciple undergoes such initiation as would result in the removal of impurities from him.[58] Upon the removal of impurities, the adept accordingly is freed from the impact of past deeds, which terminates in the recognitive experience of non-difference from Paramaśiva.

The spiritual goal of the Trika adept is the realization of the self, which is tantamount to saying of realizing one's ontic status as being non-different from Paramaśiva. It is a goal in which the perceptual and conceptual dualities are transcended by realizing the absolute unity of Being in terms of I-consciousness. This goal of unity of Being is reached both in terms of divine grace as well as by following and cultivating the yogic ways that the Trika has adumbrated.

References

1. *TĀ*, 4.185: *sārametatsamastasya yaccitsāram jaḍam jagat.*
2. Ibid., 3.4: "Just as earth, water, etc., are reflected in a clean mirror

without being mixed, so also the entirety of objects appear together in the one Lord Consciousness."

3. Utpaladeva, while commenting on Somānanda's *Śivadṛṣṭi* (2.78–79), maintains that the objective world issues forth from Śiva in accordance with his nature. As the universe is inseparable from the energies of the Lord, so it has to be treated as a form of Paramaśiva, which would mean that it is real and not an imaginary projection of the mind: *jagad 'pi tataḥ śivarūpāt śivarūpānurūpyeṇa tathā sarva śaktiyogāt yadā prasūtaṃ tadā śivarūpam eva, ata eva ca satyarūpam.*
4. The eight verses of *Anuttarāṣṭikā* are devoted to the analysis of bondage versus liberation. It is concluded that since Śiva is everything, so the question of bondage versus liberation should not arise. Both bondage and liberation are like the illusory shadow, and their removal occurs when one abides in one's essential nature. So bondage as well as liberation is like the illusion of "rope-snake or the shadow-ghost caused by false attachment," ibid., v. 2.
5. *ŚD*, 5.110: *evaṃ sarveṣu bhāveṣu sarva-sāmye vyavasthite/ tena sarva-gatam sarvaṃ śivarūpam nirūpitam//* See also *TA*, 15.265–66: *mahāprakāśa-rūpa he yeyaṃ saṃvid vijṛmbhate/sa śivaḥ śivataivasya vaiśivarūpyavabhāsita//*
6. *TĀ*, 2.16–19: *nīlam pītam sukham iti prakāśaḥ kevalaḥ śivaḥ/ pramuṣmin paramādvaite prakāśātmani ko 'paraḥ// upāyopeya-bhāvaḥ syāt prakāśaḥ kevalaṃ hi saḥ/idaṃ dvaitmayam bheda idam-advaitam-ityāpi// prakāśa-vapur-eva-ayaṃ bhāsate parameśvara/ asyām bhūmau sukhaṃ duḥkhambandho mokṣas cātir-jaḍaḥ// ghaṭa-kumbha-vad-ekārthaḥ śabdaste api ekam eva ca//*
7. *Śivastotrāvalī*, 6.5: *bhagvadāveśataḥ paśyan bhāvam bhāvam bhavan-mayam/ vicāreyam nirākāṅkṣaḥ prahṛṣa-paripūritaḥ//* The Trika non-dualism is not such as would consider the diversity of phenomena as being illusory. It is so because it looks, in the words of *Mahārthamañjarī* (p. 12), at the "various categories of existence (*padārtha*), though distinct from one another in their (external form), (yet they) must be (seen) in terms of their essential specific nature as a single collective reality." Abhinavagupta goes so far in his *PTV* (p. 188) as to say: *ata eva sarve pāśānatarutīryanmānuṣy-aevarudrakevali-mantra tadīśatan-maheśādika ekaiva parābhaṭṭarikabhūmiḥ sarvasarvātmanaiva parameśvararūpen-aste iti.*
8. *Śivastotrāvalī*, 2.8: *saṁsāraikanimitāya saṁsāraikavirodhine/ namaḥ saṁsārarūpaya niḥsaṁsāraya śāmbhave//*
9. *Īśvarapratyabhijñā-vivṛtti-vimarśinī*, 1.4.5.
10. *Paryantapañcaśikā*, v. 30.
11. *MM*, p. 40.
12. There are, according to the Trika system, three types of impurity

(*mala*), namely, the impurity of limitation (*āṇava-mala*), the impurity of difference (*māyīya-mala*), and the impurity of action (*kārma-mala*). The impurity of limitation, as it were, is inherited at the time of birth, and so serves as the base for other forms of impurity. Insofar as the impurity of difference is concerned, it functions in a manner as would give rise to the sense of difference between the subject and object. It is an impurity that clouds the purity of vision, and thereby conceals the undifferentiated nature of the Self. As far as the impurity of action is concerned, it determines our future in terms of our birth. It is because of this impurity that we are caught up in the vicious cycle of rebirth. See for further information. *ĪPK*, 2.3.5; *TĀ*, 9.65–66; *TĀV*, 9.62.

13. *Bodhapañcadaśikā*, v.6: *evam devo'nayā devyā nityam krīḍārasotsukaḥ/ vicitrān sṛṣṭi-saṁhārān vidhatte yugapada-vibhuḥ//*
14. Ibid., vv. 11–13: *yad-etasyaparijñānam tat svātantrayam hi varṇitam/ sa eva khalu saṁsāro jaḍānām yo vibhīṣikā//tat prasādavaśād eva guru-āgamata eva va/śāstrād va parameśasya yasmāt kasmāt-upāyataḥ// yat-tattvasya parijñānam sa mokṣaḥ parameśatā/ tat pūrṇatvam prabuddhānām jīvanmuktiś ca sa smṛtā//*
15. Ibid., v. 14: *etau bandha-vimokṣau ca parameśa-savarūptaḥ/ na biddete na bhedo hi tattvataḥ parameśvare//*
16. As quoted in *MM*, p. 24.
17. *ĪPV*, 2.2.3: *evaṃ saṃvṛtir-vikalpa-tad-vaśād ucyatā saṃvṛti-satyatvam, satyasyaiva tu prakārs-tat/ iti dvi-candra-vannāsatyatā/*
18. *TĀ*, 1.22: *iha tāvat samasteṣu śāstreṣu parigīyate/ ajñānam saṁsṛter-hetur jñānam mokṣaika-kāraṇam//*
19. Ibid., 1.25–26: *ajñānam iti na jñānābbhāvaś ca atiprasaṁgataḥ/sa hi loṣṭādike 'pi asti na ca tasyāsti saṃsṛtiḥ// ato jñeyasya tattvasya samastyenāprathātmakam/ jñānam eva tadajñānam śivaśāstreṣu bhāṣitam//*
20. Ibid., 1.36–38.
21. *ĪPV*, 2.4.1: *viśve hi bhāvāstyasyaiva śaktirūpena svarūpātmatvena sthitaḥ/*
22. *TĀV*, 1.44: *na ca aprāḍhvasta-pauruṣa-ajñānasyānena (bauddhena jñānena) kiṁcit-bhavati-itya-ukta-prāyam/ anyathā hi prekṣāvatām dīkṣāyām pravṛtir-eva na syāt/*
23. *TĀ*, 1.48–49: *dīkṣayā galite 'pi antarājñāne pauruṣātmani/ dhīgatasyā-nivṛtvādi-vikalpo 'pi hi smabhavet// dehasadbhāvaparyantaṃ ātmabhāvo yato dhiyi/ dehānte 'pi na mokṣaḥ syāt paruruṣājñāna-hānitaḥ//*
24. *PS*, v. 60: *mokṣasya naiva kiṁcid dhāmāsti na cāpi gamana-mantara/ ajñānagranthi-bhidā sva-śaktya abhivyaktatā mokṣaḥ//*
25. Abhinavagupta, *Gītārthasaṁgraha*, trans. with Intro. Boris Marjanovic. Varanasi: India Books, 2002, p. 43: *jñānam brahma vijñānam ca bhagavanmayīm kriyām/*
26. *ĪPV*, 2.3.17.

27. The concept of destined actions (*prārabdha-karma*) explains that the individual being has to reap the fruit of those past actions that have not so far fructified, and the liberated-one (*jīvanmukta*) is no exception to this rule, which is to say that he, too, is bound to the causal laws as any other embodied being.
28. Ibid., 3.2.12: *deha-pāte tu parameśvara ekaikarasa iti kaḥ kutra samāviśet /*
29. *MVV*, 1.391–92.
30. *PS*, v. 61: *bhinnājñāna-granthir gaṭasandehaḥ parākṛta-bhrāntiḥ/pṛkṣīna-puṇya-pāpo vigraha-yoge 'pyasau muktaḥ//*
31. *TĀV*, 1.54: *bhṛmayatya eva tan māyā hi amokṣe mokṣalipsaya/*
32. *TĀ*, 1.137: *tenājaḍasya bhāgasya pudgalānvādisaṁjñinaḥ/ anāvaraṇa-bhāgāṁśe vaicitryaṃ bahudhā sthitam//*
33. Ibid., 2.32.
34. Ibid.
35. Jayanta Bhaṭṭa, *Nyāya-mañjarī*, 1.1.17: *yadi nirvadher-duḥkhasyāntam cikirṣāsi sarvathā/ parihara mano-vāk-kāyānām pravṛttimanarglam.*
36. *TĀ*, 1.134.
37. *Sāṁkhya-kārikā*, vv. 66–68.
38. *TĀ*, 6.152: *sāṁkhya-veda-ādi-saṁsiddhān śrīkaṇṭhas-tadahar-mukhe/ sṛjatyeva punastena na samyak muktir-īdṛśī//*
39. See Aśvaghoṣa, *Saundarānanda*, vv. 16–29.
40. *SPK*, 1.14–15: *avasthā yugalam ca atra kārya-kartṛtva-śabditam/ kāryatā kṣayiṇī tatra kartṛtvam punarakṣayam// kāryonmukhaḥ prayatno yaḥ kevalam so 'tra lupyate/*
41. Gauḍapāda, *Māṇḍūkya-kārikā*, 3.38: *graho na tatra notsargas-cintā yatra na vidyate/ātma-saṁstham tadā jñānamājati samatām gatam/*
42. *ĪPV*, 3.2.10: *āṇava-māyā malau tu yad'pi na kāraṇam saṁsāre, tathāpi kārmena vinā tau dehādivicitrabhavabhir nirvartana-śakti-śūnyau vijñā-kalādiṣu/*
43. *TĀ*, 9.92–93: *vijñānakevali proktaḥ śuddha-cin-mātra-saṁsthitaḥ// sa punaḥ śāmbhavecchātaḥ śivabhedam parāmṛśan/ kraman mantreśatannetrarūpo yati śivātmatam//*
44. *ĪPK*, 3.2.9: *bodhānām api kartṛtva-juṣām kārma-kala-kṣatau/ bhinna-vedya-juṣām māyā malam videśvaras ca te//*
45. *Anuttarāṣṭikā*, v. 4: *sarvādvaita padasya vismṛtanidheḥ prāptiḥ prakā-śodayaḥ/*
46. *TĀ*, 1.156: *mokṣa hi nāma naiva anyaḥ svarūpaprathanam hi saḥ/*
47. *Anuttarāṣṭikā*, v. 4: *ānando na hi vittamadhyamadavan naivaṅganā-saṅgavat/*
48. *TĀ*, 13.117–18.
49. Ibid., 13.276.
50. *TS*, p. 123: *śaktipātāt sadguruviṣaya pipāsa bhavati/asad-guru-visyayam tu tirobhāva eva/ asadgurus-tastu sadguru-gamanam śaktipātad eva/*
51. *TĀ*, 13.142; see also *Yogasūtra*, 3.33.

52. Ibid.
53. Ibid., p. 119: *na ca vācyam kasmāt kasmins-cid-deva puṃsi śaktipāt iti/sa eva parameśvaras-tathā bhāti iti satattve ko'sau pumān nāma yad-udeśena viṣya-kṛta codaneyam/*
54. *MVV*, 1.688–92.
55. *TĀ*, 13.254–56.
56. Ibid., 12.132.
57. Ibid., 13.218.
58. Ibid., 13.220.

6

The Trika Absorptive Methods of Liberation

The Nature of Spiritual Absorption

THE ULTIMATE GOAL of Trika spiritual methods is not to gain such a spiritual experience in terms of which phenomenal existence is negated. It is, rather, to gain such spiritual absorption (*samāveśa*) in terms of which is affirmed that everything, including the empirical world, is nothing but the form of Śiva itself. It is such a state of inward absorption as would result in the attainment of the state of Śiva, which is equivalent to transcending the state of dependence or contingency (*paratantratā*) by having the experience of perfect identity with the Absolute, which is Paramaśiva. It is the experience of total identity with Paramaśiva which, on the one hand, is equated with transcendence and, on the other hand, is spoken of as being identical with absolute freedom.[1] It is so conceived because it is in and through this absorption that the last vestiges of non-freedom or limitation is overcome by letting the state of Śivahood emerge. It is the total absorption or submergence in Śiva that is given the highest priority in the overall spiritual scheme of Trika. Thus whatever be the spiritual method, it is always so oriented as would lead to some kind of inward absorptive experience of repose (*viśrānti*). The state of absorption can be realized either by making use of the technique of non-thought or through the use of such thoughts that ultimately terminate in the transcendence of thinking process itself. The success in the use of the methods of non-thought is dependent on the intensity and strength of one's will power (*icchā-śakti*). If the intensity of will is strong and durable, there will be spontaneous absorption, which is to say that absorption will be so spontaneous as is the flash of lightning.

The Trika has so devised the scheme of spiritual methods (*upāya*-s) of absorption as to meet the requirement of each individual type. There are such adepts who are highly evolved spiritually, and so are in no need to follow the rigorous discipline of the beginners. Likewise there are individuals who fall between the beginners and the highly evolved souls, and for such types of adepts the spiritual method has to be such as would lead to the highest point of absorption. It is in view of this typology of individuals that the Trika has adumbrated a spiritual scheme that consists of what may be called the four ways of liberation/absorption. The Trika thinkers have been of the view that one should straightway cultivate the superior ways of absorption. The inferior ways of liberation, according to the Trika, should be approached only if one does not obtain the required results by following the superior ways. Thus the four ways of absorption have been classified into what may be called the superior ways and the inferior ways. The superior ways of absorption consist of Non-Method (*an-upāya*) and the Method of Śiva (*śāmbhava-upāya*), whereas the inferior ways of absorption consist of the Method of Energy (*śākta-upāya*) and the Individual Method (*āṇava-upāya*). Since the Trika is of the view that one should straightway follow the superior ways of absorption, so we shall begin our account by explaining first the superior methods, and afterward we shall direct our attention towards the so-called inferior methods.

The Non-Method of Absorption

There are such highly evolved souls who, without resorting to the power of will, attain perfect absorption in terms of identity with Paramaśiva. Such individuals are not at all dependent on any kind of physical exertion or on mental contemplation for the deepening of introversion or for gaining access to the absorption of identity. Such individuals need merely an indication or hint concerning the nature of reality from their spiritual preceptor (*guru*). So it would be sufficient for them to be informed by the preceptor that you are essentially nothing else than pure consciousness (*śuddha-saṁvid*), which is the nature of the Absolute, viz., of Paramaśiva. As pure consciousness, you shine with the lustrous light of I-consciousuess. Such an indicative assertion would mean that for a highly evolved soul there is no need to resort to such absorptive methods that are dependent either on physical or mental exertion. It is so because that no physical or mental method can illumine the already illumined nature of the individual being. It means that an individual being is basically full of divine illumination on account of him being but pure consciousness.[2]

Whatever be the method, it cannot illumine one's essential nature precisely because the methods, being human devises, suffer from imperfections or defects. Instead of resorting to human devises or methods of absorption, the adept is asked to so delve deep into the interior of his being as would result in the recognition of his essential nature as being nothing else but pure and self-shining consciousness. While listening to such a kind of indicative discourse of the preceptor, the adept is accordingly so blessed by the divine grace of his guru as would lead him to the spontaneous realization of perfect absorption in Śiva (*śiva-samāveśa*). The preceptor imparts grace to the disciple either by looking into his eyes, or by touching some part of his body, or by offering a portion of his leftover food.[3] As a result of the impartation of grace, the disciple is so blessed as to have the experience of his own beingness as being non-different from Paramaśiva. While repeating this transcendental experience of identity uninterruptedly, the adept accordingly gains the supreme conviction with regard to his essential nature as being non-different from the Absolute, who is but Paramaśiva. While in this transcendental state of ecstasy, the adept does not give up his worldly activities. While remaining engaged in the day-to-day activities of life in the world, the adept at the same time experiences the wonder (*camatkāra*) of his subjectivity as being replete with the plenitude of bliss. It is this spontaneous and automatic transcendental absorption in terms of perfect identity that is spoken of as the absorption of Non-Method (*an-upāya*). The absorption is so spoken on account of it being not the result of any method.[4]

The experience of non-difference of Non-Method so empowers the adept as would free him completely from the fetters of bondage. The adept of such experience is referred to as the one who is liberated while still living (*jīvanmukta*). According to the Trika, this method or way of Non-Method is the most excellent precisely because it not only leads one to the experience of one's subjectivity as being divine (*ātma-vyāpti*), but also terminates in the experience of unity of Being in terms of identity with the Absolute (*śiva-vyāpti*). Thus this experience accordingly is identified with the plenitude of transcendental bliss (*ānanda*).[5] Since the characteristic feature of transcendental experience is in terms of bliss, so the Non-Method has appropriately been termed as the Method of Bliss (*ānanda-upāya*). It is also spoken of as the Method of Recognition (*pratyabhijñopāya*).[6] It is so spoken because recognition constitutes as a means of self-realization, which is not at all dependent upon external or internal props, such as, initiation.[7] Insofar as the recognition of the self itself is concerned, it consists in apprehending correctly the fact that the power of the self is characterized by its freedom (*svātantrya*), which is to say that the Absolute as the self is identical with absolute freedom. The individual self, being covered by the veils of impurity, is unable to recognize the essential nature of the self which is that of absolute free will. It is through the process of recognition that these veils of impurity are cut asunder, thereby resulting in the realization of the identification of the individual self with the cosmic self.[8]

The Trika has so conceived the Absolute as to be absolutely free, nay freedom itself. It is such a thinking that constitutes the core of the philosophical reflection of the Trika. It is such a philosophical viewpoint in terms of which, on the one hand, the absoluteness in terms of transcendence of the Absolute is established and, on the other hand, is affirmed that the manifest objectivity is the result of the divine free will of the Lord. It means that the Lord is under no compulsion, external or internal, while allowing the emanation of the objective universe to occur. "Freedom," thus, is seen as the embodiment of the supreme Energy of the supreme Lord and includes all the powers that can be attributed to him.[9] Kṣemarāja expresses this very idea thus: "By His own will, on Himself as the background, He unfolds the universe."[10]

The method of Non-Method (*an-upāya*) is considered to be the most excellent one on account of it being so synthetic as to include all other methods into its ambit.[11] As already pointed out, there is no effort of any kind involved in this method. In this Non-Method the individual adept receives grace of such intensity as would result in the immediate self-revelation.[12] Being independent of any human effort, the Non-Method seems to be the only cause of self-realization in terms of self-recognition.[13] The non-dependent nature of grace means that the Non-Method is unconditioned and indeterminate, which is to say that it is such an uncaused cause as would terminate in the deliverance of the individual self from the fetters of bondage. What initially seems to be the condition of grace is, in fact, the result of it.[14] It would be quite contrary to the very nature of grace to attribute to it some kind of qualification, because such an attribution would undermine the free will of the Lord, which is perceived as being engaged in the play of bondage and liberation. In this context it would mean that the very opening up of the heart towards the Divine is the result of grace. It would also mean that the individual adept obtains immediate release from bondage in terms of realization of identity with Paramaśiva the moment grace descends (*śāktipāta*) upon him. Even though still embedded to the body, the individual attains such a spiritual plane as would be ineffable (*bhairava-avasthā*), which is characterized by the pervasion of bliss that is of cosmic dimension (*jagadānanda*). And the true liberation is realized at that moment when the self assimilates the entirety of objectivity within itself and in this lies the authentic freedom. Abhinavagupta has expressed this urgency thus:

> The Master of the universe, even though continuously shining within as our Self, remains, nevertheless, unrecognized (insofar as) his essential nature (is concerned), (which is to say in terms of his) transcendence and sovereignty. (It is a condition in which) the heart is not full of the plenitude of his light. But (as soon as) the self is made aware of the true freedom of the Self and of its liberation from this (bound) life, perfection will be attained.[15]

It is well to remember at this point that it is only the adept of the Non-Method who is so blessed and elevated spiritually as to enjoy the bliss of perfect identity with Paramaśiva. While enjoying the bliss of perfect identity with Paramaśiva, he also simultaneously is endowed with his Energy, which in the language of Pratyabhijñā philosophy denotes self-awareness (*ahaṃ-vimarśa*). It means that such an aspirant is replete with self-consciousness as well as with the power of freedom. In terms of mystical language it means that the aspirant is endowed with the cosmic plenitude and in terms of which is expressed his beingness that flows forth from this spiritual state, which is the result of the union of the Divine Couple—Śiva and Śakti—and it is this state that is called the ineffable.[16] Accordingly such a person

> who has uninterruptedly practiced (what may be called) submergence in Śiva (*śiva-samāveśa*) and has perfectly recognized his powers of knowledge and action as being the pure freedom of

the Lord can then know and do all he desires even though he is still associated with the body. He is not only liberated-in-life (*jīvanmukta*), in the ordinary sense of the word, but he is basically free because he uses at will the divine powers belonging to the supreme Lord and lives in eternal freedom.[17]

The Method of Śiva

The aspirants who are unable to steady themselves in the path of Non-Method (*an-upāya*), or what is called the yoga of bliss (*ānanda-yoga*), are asked to follow the Method of Śiva (*śāmbhava-upāya*), which is one step below to the Non-Method. The Method of Śiva is also known as the method of will (*icchopāya*) as well as the method of non-difference (*abheda-upāya*).[18] The Method of Śiva is such a spiritual means in terms of which the body, the mind, or the intellect are used as tools for effecting the inward absorption. Instead of making any kind of mental or physical effort, the aspirant is asked so to tranquillize the inward mental operations as would facilitate the attaining of steadiness and stability of the mind. The steadiness and stability should not be in terms of suppression of the operations of the mind. Rather it should be easeful and spontaneous. Although the light of the self, viz., of consciousness, is constantly shining within, yet it remains concealed or non-disclosed due to the debris of ideas that continuously emerge and submerge in the reservoir called the mind. It is the appearance (*ābhāsa*) of the reflection of ideas in the mind that conceal the self-shining light of I-consciousness, which is the self. Just as the purity of the crystal is marred due to the reflection of various colours in it, likewise the stream of ideas conceal the self-shining light of consciousness. Just as the purity of the crystal is regained upon the removal of the reflection of various colours, so is recognized the self-shining nature of consciousness upon the tranquillization of the stream of ideas (*vikalpa*-s) in the mind. Consequently, the self shines in such a manner as to be the object of cognition to itself. In other words, it means that it is the self that has the direct and mediate (*aparokṣa*) cognition of itself as being of the nature of light(*prakāśamayī*). In this process of self-cognition is recognized the fact that it is the self that is the doer, the deed as well as the instrument of accomplishing the deed. Thus the aspirant, while remaining in the self-abiding state of the self, does not make use of his body, life-force or mind, nor does he renounce their use. The Method of Śiva is, thus, such a method as would not be dependent on any external or internal prop. It is a method that stabilizes the mental operations in such a manner as would lead to the cessation of the emergence of ideas, and thereby would bring to a point of standstill the appearance of reflection of ideas. The self through its own power of will accomplishes this task, which is to say that the goal of this method is to gain the self-abiding state (*sva-sithiti*).[19] The Method of Śiva terminates into Non-Method the moment the deficiency of instability of the mind is overcome, which means that this method attains the status of Non-Method upon the attainment of such perfection that results in the stability of mind in terms of the cessation of thoughts.

There is, however, such an aspect of the Method of Śiva in terms of which the power of will (*icchā-śakti*) is propped up by the power of knowledge (*jñāna-śakti*). Even in this kind of situation it is the power of will that remains predominant in the overall spiritual scheme. It is a method in terms of which the aspirant initially is asked to reflect over such statements as, for example, this objective universe, which is out there, exists within the mirror of my own consciousness as reflection. The reflector and the reflected are, thus, non-different from me, which means that the world as reflection does not exist as a separate entity from the reflector. Also the reflector of the reflection is not an entity that exists apart from reflection. It is the infinite number of divine powers within me that appear, while being reflected in the mirror of consciousness, in the form of thirty-six categories (*tattva*-s). The aspirant has to conduct his metaphysical reflection in such a manner as would enable him to have the cognition of the various powers within himself. The form of the powers in this practice, on the one hand, comes in the shape of letters from *a* to *ha*, which constiute the entirety of Sanskrit alphabet, and, on the other hand, appear as categories from Śiva to the element earth.[20] The first sixteen vowels, viz., from *a* to *ha*, are perceived to be reflecting the various wonderful cognitive experiences of what may be called the mood of Śiva (*śiva-bhāva*). And the wonderful process of manifestation of categories is further carried out, through the power of emanation (*visarga-śakti*), by giving rise to consonant letters from *ka* to *ha*, which through reverse order explains the order of manifestation from the element earth to Śakti. What it means is this: the process of manifestation appears in reverse order, which is from bottom to top. It is like looking in a mirror where the right side appears to be the left and the left as the right. It is exactly the same thing that happens when the image of the elements is reflected in the miror of consciousness. It is because of this reason that the reflection of the powers of Śiva begins to appear not from the category of Śakti, but from the element earth. In relation to appearance of letters of Sanskrit alphabet it would mean that the letter *l* appears as the element earth, whereas the letter *ha* appears as Śakti. The letters between *ka* and *ha*, through reverse sequence, constitute the order of manifestation from the element water up to the category of *Sadāśiva*.[21] The experiential cognition of oneself of one's divine powers, of the garland of letter (*varṇa-mālā*), of all the categories occur simultaneously in terms of identity or non-difference. The garland of letters, in its reverse order, is known as *mātṛkā*, viz., divine mothers. These letters are directly blended by the adept of this method in terms of perfect identity between Śiva and Śakti. The experience of identity is not the result of one's cognitive reflection, but occurs by itself, which is to say that in this path it is will that plays the predominant role insofar as the experience of the Divine is concerned. This does not mean that knowledge has no role to play. In this context it is well to remember that the five powers of the Lord, viz., of bliss, consciousness, will, knowledge, and action, are so mixed up that they can never be separated from each other. In fact, what happens is that a particular state is always dominated by one of the powers, which means that the four powers remain in a subordinate condition. Thus a state is known by the name of the power that is predominant in it. In fact, all the five powers together perform whatever action has to be accomplished.[22] According to this reasoning, it is the power of bliss (*ānanda-śakti*) that is predominant in *anupāya,* and this method is accordingly termed as being the method of bliss (*ānanda-upāya*). Likewise in the Method of Śiva it is the power of will (*icchā-śakti)* that is predominant, and so for this reason it is referred to as the method of will (*icchā-upāya*).

In the Method of Śiva, as already pointed out, it is will that plays such a dominant role as would lead to the abandonment of external forms of yogic discipline like *āsana* and *prāṇāyāma.*[23] Insofar as sensorial or intellectual activities of the individual are concerned, they are completely introverted not through such forms of concentration as would lead to the de-activation of the sense organs. Rather introversion occurs by itself and spontaneously. The thrust towards Śiva is so ardent and full of fervour that no form of doubt of any kind is entertained. Consequently, there surges up from the inner centre the intuitive illumination with regard to the self, which terminates in the realization of liberation in terms of the attainment of the transcendent state of ineffable God.[24]

One of the most significant concepts that the Trika has used in the Method of Śiva is that of "emptiness" (*śūnyatā*). Originally it were the Mahāyāna Buddhists who made use of this concept in relation to the Absolute as well as with regard to phenomenal existence. The Absolute is identified with emptiness because of it being so indeterminate as to be beyond all forms of conceptual determinations. The phenomenal existence is said to be identical with emptiness on account of it being devoid of intrinsic nature (*svabhāva*). The philosophical background of this concept lies in the perception that maintains that "all our experience is confined essentially to the realm of chance or becoming. The transitory and the momentary alone is available to us."[25] This idea of the Buddhists that believes in the existence of a single moment has greatly influenced the thinking of the Trika thinkers. The Trika thinkers arrived at the conclusion that the outer phenomena in terms of emanation, preservation, dissolution and ineffability are a continuous process[26] and the source of it is but the self. This process of emanation and dissolution of phenomena eventuates at such a rapid speed as would be impossible to observe it. While agreeing with the Buddhists concerning the existence of a single moment, the Trika, however, rejects the realistic understanding of time as being real, and thereby serving as the substrstum of instants in terms of connecting them to each other. The yogi, in the absence of time, through deep absorption so disconnects the frames of time as to be able to penetrate the void (*madhya*) that lies between two instants. In this manner the yogi so destroys time as to become the master of time by residing in instants. Thus the yogi immobilizes time and in terms of which he resides in an eternal present.[27]

The concept of emptiness is so used in the Trika system as would explain and establish the transcendental ineffability of the Absolute, who however is said to be nothing else than fulness itself. The void in relation to the Absolute denotes the pure act (*spanda*) of consciousness, which is linked to the undifferentiated Energy that is characterized by the absolute freedom (*svātantrya*). The identification of the self with the void explains the idea of the absence of the body, intelligence and life-force, which are the products of *prakṛti*, and so instantaneous. The indeterminate nature of the self as being free from such entities as the body, intelligence, etc., is linked also to "the expanse of ether,"[28] which is nothing but the void. It is this empty ether which, according to Abhinavagupta, is experienced as emptiness by consciousness. It is an experience that is characterized by such negations as, for example, "It is not, no, it is not," and for the yogi it embodies the supreme state of transcendence.[29]

The linking of the Absolute with emptiness explains basically the nature of non-dual reality, which means that the Absolute is completely devoid of all forms of determination. Thus by plunging into the non-dual void, there accordingly eventuates the illumination of the self. It would mean that the transcendence of the Absolute is such as to be comparable to the void of space. Thus the Absolute is beyond all forms of duality as well as discursive forms of thought. Thus the employment of the concept of emptiness frees the adept from the limitations and determination of thought.[30] It is because of this reason that the absoluteness of the Absolute is said to be even beyond emptiness (*śūnyātiśūnya*).[31]

The Method of Energy

The aspirants who are unable to cultivate the superior Path of Śiva are asked to take to the Method of Energy (*śākta-upāya*), which is one step below the *śāmbhava-upāya*. Since in this method much mental exertion is demanded, so it has accordingly been equated with the method of knowledge (*jñāna-upāya*). It is a method that terminates in the emergence of such knowledge as is characterized by the vision that is both simultaneously dualistic and non-dualistic (*bhedābheda-jñāna*).[32] It is a method in which the practice of meditation is so oriented as to be directed towards such concepts that are totally free from the taints of any kind. The cultivation of pure thoughts is considered to be necessary on account of the fact that the impure thoughts are seen as the source of bondage.[33] The impure thoughts are such thoughts that are either unintelligent or are based upon such beliefs that hold the view that the individual existent is identical with the bodily apparatus. It is such an intellectual viewpoint that does not view the pure consciousness as the substratum of what we are. While considering the world as being separate from the self, the upholders of this view look upon themselves as having knowledge that is limited, as having powers that are limited, and as being non-divine.

In contrast to impure knowledge (*aśuddha-jñāna*), we have pure knowledge (*śuddha-jñāna*), which thinks of the self as being of the nature of pure consciousness, as being identical with the perfect and ultimate Divine Principle as well as the source of the world out there. Thus the nature of pure knowledge is characterized by an orientation in terms of which the self is cognized as being non-different from the Absolute, which at the practical level of thought would mean that the so-called objectivity, too, is non-different from the self. It is so because it is the self from whom proceeds the world of objectivity.

The aspirant who, on account of the influence exerted by the impure thoughts, is unable to stay in the path of Śiva, is accordingly advised to take to the Method of Energy. There are no supports available in the Method of Śiva, not even the support of the mind. It is so because the mind is so dissolved as not to allow the emergence of any kind of prop. It is because of this fact that the spiritual practice that the Method of Śiva provides is devoid of supports (*nirālamba*). In the Method of Energy it is the pure concepts that are taken as supports or aids by the mind. Thus the mind of an aspirant engages itself in the practice of such conceptual knowledge that is pure and free from taints. Accordingly these pure ideas concerning the nature of the Absolute leave their desired impression upon the intellect of the aspirant.[34] This pure but factual knowledge leaves its impressions upon the screen of the mind in a variety of ways.

The main mode of this knowledge, however, is expressed by such terms as, for example, *yāga, homa, japa, vṛta,* and *yoga.*[35] All such-like concepts are firmly imprinted upon the screen of the mind through the various types of meditation.

These concepts represent the substances that are to be seen as having their existence in the Lord. As substances, they are offered, at the plane of the mind, to the Lord. It is the process of offering of the substances as oblations, at the mental level, that is known as *yāga*.[36] In contrast to *yāga*, we have *homa*, which is characterized by such thinking as would result in the realization of the substances as being nothing but the forms of divine light. In affirming firmly that the substances are nothing else than the pure forms of divine light, the aspirant accordingly so transforms them in the furnace of the fire of consciousness (*cidāgni*) as to be identical with consciousness itself.[37] Insofar as the repetition of the sacred name (*japa*) is concerned, it consists of in reflecting over and over again with regard to oneself as being non-diffetent from the intrinsic nature (*svarūpa*) of the Absolute, who is said to be perfect, pure, unrestricted and unconditioned freedom.[38] Likewise the aspirant must develop firm conviction (*vṛta*) with regard to the insentient substances (*jaḍa-padārtha*) as being nothing but the expression of pure consciousness. In other words, the aspirant has to see the substantive entities in the world as being the emission (*visarga*) of the Lord himself.[39] Lastly comes the practice of yoga. The Trika understanding of the Absolute is such as would make it impossible for the intellect to have any kind of grasp of it, which would mean that the nature of the Absolute is such as would be beyond the range of intellectual thinking. The Absolute, instead, always shines in itself and by itself—and it is the intrinsic nature of the Absolute to shine in and through its own light. It is this kind of reflection in which is affirmed the self-shining nature of the Absolute that is constitutive of what is known as *yoga*.[40]

There are certain other aspects of this method, such as, bathing (*snāna*), worship (*pūjana*), and meditation (*dhyāna*), which have to be explained briefly. The gaining of awareness concerning the factual state of existence in terms of neither being free nor bound is such a step that ultimately terminates in the very removal of thought-constructs. We think of freedom precisely because it has its opposite in bondage, which means that the empirical forms of thinking always rotate round the pair of opposites. Insofar as one subjects oneself to dialectical thinking in terms of pair of opposites, one has no possibility of knowing oneself as to who he essentially is. It is, therefore, asked of us to transcend such forms of thinking that is dialectical by engaging in such analysis as would give rise to the perception that views the individual existent as being neither bound nor free. It would mean that every form of thought-construct (*vikalpa*) has to be so tranquillized as would result in its cessation. The analytical process that terminates in the cessation of thought-constructs is in the Trika system called "bathing" (*snāna*). It is given this nomenclature on account of the fact that this internal bathing, like the external one, is responsible in removing impurity. The external bathing removes the dirt that may have amassed on the body, whereas the internal bathing removes the impurity of thought-constructs.[41] Similar is the case with worship, which is to say that reflection should be directed towards worship (*pūjana*) in terms of such thinking as would result in the sentiment of neither being appeased by the worship that is being performed nor nonappeased by its non-performance. It is "I" the worshipper (*pūjaka*) who really has to be present both in the act of worship (*pūjā*) as well as in the worshipped (*pūjya*). Thus the experiential sentiment should run like this: Since I am identical with the both worship and the worshipped, so it is I who really is being worshipped.[42] Likewise the aim of meditation, too, is nothing but to discover the presence of Śiva in everything that is being gazed upon by the senses. Whatever the senses may apprehend, it is to be viewed as but Śiva itself. It is such a kind of vigilant awareness that is called in the Trika system meditation (*dhyāna*).[43]

The fundamental aim or purpose of this method is to engage in such practices that are oriented towards the attainment of knowledge that is pure, supernal and free from the conceptual taints of the mind. It is the repeated practice of concepts that reveal the non-dual nature of reality which, at the conceptual level of thought, becomes firmly rooted in the mind. Once such thinking transforms itself into a firm conviction, then the aspirant succeeds in destroying the knots of difference that come about due to ignorance, which means that ignorance as doubt is totally eradicated. As a result of this firm conviction concerning the non-dual Absolute, there accordingly is attained the absorption (*samāveśa*) which results in the riddance (*nirmūlanam*) of impure thinking.

It is also the aim of this method to concern itself with the states of consciousness in such a manner as would facilitate the use of psychological practices for the purrpose obtaining immersion of individual consciousness in the cosmic consciousness, which is Paramaśiva. It is basically done through the process of correct reasoning (*bhāvana*) which ultimately leads to the removal of the veil of ignorance in terms of the disclosure or revelation of Paramaśiva. This method is so devised as would serve the point of transition between the inferior and superior methods. It accomplishes this task through the arousal of latent energy (*kuṇḍalinī*) within the individual, which occurs either on account of intense love for Śiva, or because of the intensity of such emotions as, example, fear, passion, love, terror, anger, etc. Also the method of elimination is made use of in such a manner as would lead to the absorption in a single thought. This deep absorption in a single thought results in the emergence of energy in its purest form.

The initial requirement that an aspirant is to fulfil is to abandon the method of concentration on concrete objects. Instead of concrete objects, he must cultivate his imagination in such a manner as would be rooted in the firm conviction of being non-different from Paramaśiva. It is within such a frame of mind that the intellect gets stabilized, and accordingly concentration gets focussed upon the primal Energy in its emergent and manifest form. As a result of such practice, the aspirant may undergo a variety of experiences, which could be in the form of bliss, knowledge, awakening of the *kuṇḍalinī,* or resonance in the interior of the spinal cord. The aspirant accordingly enters into deep contact with the undifferentiated Energy, and as a result obtains spontaneous repose that comes to be due to the emergence of such detachment that is natural and spontaneous.

This entrance into the undifferentiated Energy signifies such deep absorption as would lead to the destruction of limitations and structures of the individual's individuality. Upon transcending the complex of personality-driven structures, there flashes forth suddenly such intuition that completely frees the individual from the limitations of duality. However, mere mystical intuition cannot bring about repose that is lasting unless motivated by a powerful suggestion like—"I am Śiva, omnipresent and omniscient." It is such-like powerful suggestion that penetrates the source of Energy, and thereby causes the loosening of the complex knots of personality that has been allowed to emerge by the subconscious tendencies. In this manner is recast the personality of the adept, and so he gains peace and repose that is permanent. Through repeated contact with reality, the aspirant attains a state in terms of which is revealed to him the essence that is constitutive of a conscious subject—and this state is given the epithet of ineffability. This ineffable state is not an experience in terms of transcendence, but is characterized by immanence. It is an experience in which conceptualization is not transcended; rather it is existence that invites the yogi to its source—and it is at the source of life where conflicts are resolved forever.[44]

There is an another aspect of this method that is solely esoteric and *tāntrika* in orientation. And it concerns itself with the awakening of the latent Energy (*kuṇḍalinī*) within the body. The entire doctrine of *kuṇḍalinī* is based upon the notion that particular and the universal are identical, which in relation to the human body means that whatever exists out there in the cosmos exists potentially in the body. The aim, thus, is to cosmicize the body through mainly such absorptive techniques that Tantrism has devised. Also there is initiated, through the process of awakening the *kuṇḍalinī*, the experience of cosmic transcendence by bringing about the unification of the opposites. This cosmic transcendence is experienced at the point when the mystical union of Śiva and Śakti occurs in the *sahasrāra-cakra*, which is spoken of as being the Abode of Śiva. The yogi gains the experience of transcendence by focussing on such mystical centres in the body that are believed to be containing cosmic forces. The transcendence of cosmos is achieved by arresting time, viz., by eliminating it from consciousness. The practices that the yogi employs are of advanced nature. He so meditates on the mystical centres as to arouse the latent forces that are said to be residing therein. These centres (*cakra*-s), according to the *tāntrika* thinking, are located along the spinal cord—and the total number of them is believed to be either six or seven.

The initial circle or wheel is known as the Basic Support (*mūlādhāra*), and is said to be located at the base of the rectum. It is at this centre where the Coiled Energy (*kuṇḍalinī*) lies in the state of slumber, which is to say in the latent state. It rests at this centre in such a manner as to block the opening to the Gracious Vein (*suṣumṇā-nāḍī*).[45] The next circle is known as the Own Place (*svādhiṣṭhāna*), and is located at the base of the male genital organ. The third mystical centre, called the Jewelled City (*maṇipūra*), is located in the region of the navel, whereas the fourth centre, known as the Unstuck Sound (*anāhata*), is located opposite to the heart, which is considered to be the centre for the exhaled breath (*prāṇa*). Insofar as the fifth centre is concerned, it is called by the name of the Immaculate (*viśuddha*), and is said to be located at the base of the throat. The Command Wheel (*ājñā-cakra*) is the sixth circle and is located between the eyebrows. It is considered to be the seat of the cognitive faculty as well as of Śiva. The last centre is known as the one that has

Thousand Petals (*sahasrāra*). It is believed to be existing at the top of the head, which is considered as the Abode of Śiva. It is at this place where the Coiled Energy, upon ascending through the mystical centres along the spinal cord, ends her journey by merging in Śiva. This centre, however, is not related to the body on account of it being the plane of transcendence. It is because of this reason that most of the *tāntrikas* think that there are only six centres and not seven, which means that the *sahasrāra-cakra* does not pertain to the body, and so is not counted as one of the wheels.[46]

These mystical centres are provided with nourishment by the various channels that run through different parts of the body. Among them the most important are the three channels, of which two run to the right and to the left side of the Gracious Vein, respectively along the spinal cord. The right side of the spinal cord, which is considered as the region of Śiva, contains what is called the Yellow Vein (*piṅgalā-nāḍī*), which is the carrier of the descendent or inhaled breath (*apāna*) and it is through this breath that the various mystical centres are activated in the body. Insofar as the left side of the body is considered, it represents the region of Śakti, and the channel that carries the ascendant or exhaled breath (*prāṇa*) is known as the Vital Vein (*iḍā-nāḍī*). In order to awaken the Coiled Energy in the centre, called the Basic Support, the aspirant is asked, through the technique of breath-control (*prāṇāyāma*), to neutralize the incoming and outgoing breaths through the *piṅgalā* and *iḍā* channels, thereby forcing the vital air into the Gracious Vein.[47] Upon pushing the vital air into the Gracious Vein, there occurs the awakening of the Coiled Energy, and which, upon its awakening, moves upward by penetrating the mystical centres along the spinal cord. These centres, when activated, are heated up by the return passage of the Energy.[48] It is through this flaming heat that all forms of limitations are consumed, and thereby the realization of the supreme self is facilitated. While piercing one centre after another, the Coiled Energy, on her way, absorbs and devours the elements in the body. Accordingly the yogi experiences the purification of consciousness in proportion to the level each centre embodies until there takes place the mystical union of Śiva and Śakti in the higher centre of the brain, which results in the devouring of dual forms of thought.

Thus the ultimate goal of mystical realization is reached when perfect union of Śiva and Śakti occurs and in terms of which the yogi experiences the absorption (*samāveśa*) in Śiva. Once perfect absorption is realized, there remains nothing more to be accomplished, because the yogi

> arrives at a state of identity with Śiva (in terms) of the totality of categories. What sorrow, what delusion shall descend upon him who (has been so empowered as to have) the perception of all as (being identical with) the *brahman*.[49]

Accordingly the yogi offers as oblation

> All (forms) of mental duality in the effulgent flame of the Self (viz., of consciousness) and (accordingly) becomes one with the Light.[50]

The Individual Method

Lastly, we have the method which, according to the Trika thinking, is meant for such adepts who have not been successful in any of the above three methods. It is maintained that this method is appropriate for such aspirants whose mind is so congealed by impurities as would need lot of mental and physical effort for its removal. Since this method is at the lowest wrung of the spiritual ladder, so it is accordingly termed as the Individual Method (*āṇava-upāya*). It is also known as the method of action (*kriyā-upāya*), because in this method the aspirant has to exert himself energetically. This method is also known as the method of difference (*bheda-upāya*) on account of its functioning within the ambit of dualistic thought-structure.[51] As already pointed out above, the practitioner who follows the Method of Śiva does not need any such means as support upon which the mind would fix its attention, and thereby gain stability. For this reason this excellent method is said to be devoid of support (*nirālamba*). Insofar as the Method of Energy is concerned, it is such a method in which the mind is purified from the dross of conceptual thinking or impurities. While the mind is actively engaged in the task of actualizing the purity of conceptual knowledge, it, viz., the mind, however resorts to the self as its support. It is so because in this method reflection concerning the nature of one's essential nature (*svarūpa, svabhāva*) always plays a very dominant role. Rare are the aspirants who are qualified to cultivate the two superior methods of Non-Method and the Method of Śiva.

The Individual Method (*āṇava-upāya*), in contrast to the above methods, is so restricted in its operations that there is no any other way for the aspirant than to take the support, for the stabilization of the mind, of objects that are outside oneself. The support of external objects is taken in such a manner as would lead to thinking of them as being the appearance of the Lord. In this manner this method is ultimately transformed into the Method of Energy. However, there is a fundamental difference between the two methods, in that the purity of conceptual knowledge is given priority in the Method of Energy, whereas in the Individual Method the priority, however, is accorded to such objects that are external. In the Method of Energy the omnipresence of the self is so reflected as would allow the adept to have the vision of the entire universe as existing within one's own consciousness. However, in the Individual Method the knowable objects are so contemplated as to envisage their separate identity. It is because of this reason that this method has been equated either with action or with difference. Moreover, the effort has to be persistent and continuous. There is the danger of lapsing on the way or remain suspended in the mid-course. If such a situation arises, then the yogi will have to be born again so that he attains the state of Śivahood.[52] As the goal of realizing identity with Paramaśiva is difficult for them who follow this method, so the most they can achieve is the purification of dual forms of thought in terms of what may be called the state of pacification of thought.[53]

It is not the intrinsic nature of the self that is made as the contemplative support for the mind in this method. Instead the support is sought in such objects that are outside the self. The objects of meditation are mainly the aspirant's own intellect, life-force, body and the external world of objects.[54] Whenever an external object is taken as a support for the purpose of concentration by utilizing the services of the intellect, then we are in the zone of meditative concentration (*dhyāna-yoga*). The adept, while initiating this program of meditation, will have to bring together the subject (*pramātā*), object (*prameya*) and the means of knowledge (*pramāṇa*). In this way the divine effulgence of the self-shining consciousness is so ignited as to be of ineffable nature (*bhairava-bhāva*). Afterwards the aspirant is asked to apprehend the entire cluster of objects through the pathway of senses as well as through the mystical circle of energies (*śakti-cakra*). The devouring of objectivity has to be such as to let it stay within so that the entirety of externality is dissolved in the effulgent fire of consciousness. Through this practice the practitioner has the experience of emanation of objectivity (*sṛṣṭi*) as well as of its dissolution (*saṁhāra*). As a consequence of this experience the aspirant realizes his divine nature (*bhairava-bhāva*) and in terms of which he gains access to the limited absorption (*āṇava-samāveśa*) that is pervaded by the experience of Śivahood.[55]

Insofar as meditation on life-force is concerned, it is directed towards the category of self-monad (*puruṣa*) or towards the five operational functions of animation. When concentration is deepened, there ensues such repose (*viśrānti*) as would sequentially result in the experience of different planes of bliss. The bliss that results from concentration on subjectivity (*pramātā-tattva*), viz., on the self-monad (*puruṣa-tattva*), is termed as self-bliss (*nijānanda*).[56] There emerges the experience of bliss, called *nirānanda,* when meditation is objectless.[57] The next step that an aspirant has to take is that, upon the emergence of exhaling breath (*apāna*), he has to fix his attention upon its objectivity and upon the infinite objectivity that lies within through the process of inhaling breath (*apāna*). Upon the completion of this process, the aspirant has to repose his attention on both *prāṇa* and *apāna,* and as a result of this repose emerges the bliss that is known as *parānanda.*[58] Having become fully illumined, the aspirant accordingly unifies the multitudinous objectivity by reposing it on the equalizing breath (*samāna*), and the result that is obtained is in terms of the experience of bliss known as *brahmānanda.*[59] While ascending the planes of bliss, the aspirant now is in a position of dissolving all forms of conceptual objectivity as well as the means of knowledge into the intrinsic nature of the self by means of resting in the ascendent breath (*udāna*). In doing so, the aspirant has the bliss that is called the *mahānanda.*[60] The aspirant now reaches such a position whereby he, while reposing on the pervading breath (*vyāna*), so contemplates as to be free from all forms of adjuncts (*upādhi*-s), limitations and attributes. As a result of such contemplation he experiences accordingly the bliss called *cidānanda,* viz., bliss of consciousness. At this plane of bliss dependence (*ālambana*) on the so-called insentient objectivity completely falls off.[61] Upon having traversed the six planes of bliss (*ānanda-bhūmi*-s), the aspirant reaches a state whereby he is so empowered as to have the direct cognition of the power of animation (*prāṇa-śakti*). The bliss that he experiences at this final stage is limitless in the sense of it being of cosmic nature. The nature of this bliss is such that it shines as an uninterrupted presence in the entire objectivity that is constitutive of the world. The absorption is easeful, spontaneous and natural, which is to say non-exertive. It is at this stage of bliss that all forms of meditation are abandoned. This unlimited bliss that is experienced at the seventh plane is so universal as to be called cosmic bliss (*jagadānanda*).[62]

While lying buried in the universal repose of *jagadānanda*, the aspirant simultaneously takes note of the emergence of the life-force in the heart, and the process that is involved is technically called either *uccāra-yoga* or *prāṇa-yoga.* As to whether one has gained proficiency in this method depends upon the manifestation of six signs. If these six signs manifest themselves externally, then the aspirant has been successful in his task. The signs are (a) the experience of bliss,[63] (b) the experience of spilling over of bliss,[64] (c) the experience of trembling of the body, (d) the experience of sleep as well as (e) of inebriation.[65] All these experiences emerge when the life-force is made as the basis of contemplative practice. This yogic practice concerning the life-force is in no way identical with the practice of breath-control (*prāṇāyāma*) precisely because it is not considered as an internal practice that terminates in the realization of the state of absorption. The kind of bliss that is experienced is dependent on the nature of absorption. The level of bliss, thus, would be measured in terms of the degree of depth that absorption has gained. It is because of this reason that there eventuates variation insofar as the levels of bliss are concerned.

The adept has also the possibility of engaging in such yogic practice that is more concrete than the above one. The concrete form of spiritual practice is known as *karaṇa-yoga.* It is such a practice in terms of which the aspirant looks at his body as the divine temple of God, and accordingly so contemplates the various mystical circles/wheels in the body as to visualize the actuality of the entire universe. The visualization is such as would terminate in the realization of the universe as being but the display of the divine powers of the Lord. Thus the aspirant has the experience of his own body as well as of the universe as being nothing else than the manifestation of the glory of the Lord.[66] The so-called mystical awakening of *kuṇḍalinī* comes within the framework of contemplative practice. Although in some *tāntrika* schools the yoga of *kuṇḍalinī* is highly valued as a spiritual method, yet in the Trika system it is considered as one of the lowest spiritual methods, and accordingly is placed at the third plane on the spiritual ladder of *āṇava-upāya.* As the *karaṇa-yoga* is external in dimension, so the techniques that are used are also of external nature. It is because of this reason that the hand-gestures (*mudrā*-s) are extensively used in this method, as it is believed that their use results in the immediate attainment of absorption.

There is an another form of practice, which is one step below to that of *karaṇa-yoga*, and which is known by such names as the *varṇa-yoga* or the *dhvani-yoga.* It is believed that there occurs, due to the influence of the power of life-force, within the body a kind of sound (*nāda*) that is of wonderful and amazing nature.[67] This inward sound can be heard upon closing the opening of ears. The aspirant can attain the state of absorption by contemplating the inaudible sounds that are occurring constantly inside the body. All the letters of Sanskrit alphabet have their sound in this inward sound, and it so because it is within the crucible of this sound that the unity (*sāmarasya*) of all the letters can be discovered. It is through the reflective concentration on this inward sound that the seed syllables (*bīja-mantra*-s) concerning emanation and dissolution of the universe can be contemplated upon. This practice among the practitioners of *āṇava-upāya* is the easiest one, because the aspirant, without much effort, can fix his mind upon the mystical sound.

The adept who is unable to firmly fix his mind upon the intellect, life-force, body and the inward sound, is asked to engage in such external practices that would be easy to follow, and such a practice, according to the Trika, is known as that of *sthāna-prakalpana.* The places or centres (*sthāna*) of practice are said to be mainly three, namely, the breathing of air (*prāṇa-vāyu*), the gross body (*sthūla-śarīra*), and the external world of objects (*prameya*).[68] It is believed that the power of life-force is characterized by the pentad of exhalation (*prāṇa*), inhalation (*apāna*), equalizing breath (*samāna*), ascendant breath (*udāna*), and the pervasive breath (*vyāna*). However, the breath that is directly related to *sthāna prakalpana* is the breath that arises in the space of the heart from a distance of twelve fingers (*dvādaśānta*). It is this breath that is expelled through one of the nostrils. When expelled outside, the breath ends at a distance of twelve fingers outside in the space, and it is from this point from where the inhaled breath arises, which ends inside the body at a distance of twelve fingers from the heart. These two points are known as the outer and inner ends of the twelve fingers (*dvādaśānta*). It is within the space of these two points that concentration has to be fixed upon the outgoing breath (*prāṇa*) and the incoming breath (*apāna*). The concentration really has to be on the void (*śūnya*) that comes about between the moments when concentration on *prāṇa* and *apāna* occurs. The void emerges when the appearance and disappearance of two breaths eventuate at the point of twelve fingers.[69] Through this practice is achieved in steps the dissolution of thoughts in the mind. As a consequence of the disappearance of thoughts there occurs the absorption (*samāveśa*) that is appropriate to the *āṇava-upāya.*

Apart from the above spiritual methods of *āṇava-upāya,* there is an another technique of recognizing the state of Śiva, and the method is known as that of six paths (*ṣaḍadhva*). This method consists of two parts: word (*śabda*) and object (*artha*), which in the language of Vedānta is encapsulated by such terms as, for example, name (*nāma*) and form (*rūpa*). Insofar as the *śabda* is concerned, it consists of the triad of *varṇa, mantra,* and *pada,* whereas *artha* consists of the triad of *kalā, tattva,* and *bhuvana.* Both these triads in the Trika system are given respectively the nomenclature of the path of time (*kālādhva*) and the path of space (*deśādhva*). Since each path consists of a triad, so the total number of paths, thus, is six, and each path has to be so contemplated as would terminate in the required result.

Let us first take into consideration the path of time. The most subtle and the smallest unit of time is said to be moment (*kṣaṇa*). As to how a moment may be measured is quite uncertain. The Trika accepts the idea concerning time as being sequential (*kramātmaka*), which is to say that it is so oriented as to be cognized in terms of series. The subtlest moment of time is dependent on vibration in the mind, which amounts to saying that the moment lasts to the measure a thought lasts in the mind.[70] We know that the vibratory velocity of the mind in the states of waking (*jāgrat*), dreaming (*svapna*), and sleeping (*suṣupti*) is different. In the waking state it is dim, whereas in the dreaming state it is fast. In comparison to these two states, the vibration in the state of deep sleep is faster. The other two states, which are the Fourth (*turya*), and beyond the Fourth (*turyātīta*), the speed of pulsation is very fast. In the last two states the process of time, although eventuating sequentially, is not experienced at all. It is because of this reason that these two states are said to be of the nature of non-time-in-time.[71] It would mean that time is so subtle at the higher planes of consciousness that its enumeration is impossible to conduct.

The enumeration of time begins with the moment, and the duration of the moment is said to be that of thought. The perception of the moment falls within the ambience of knowledge, and knowledge is always actualized in terms of linguistic formulations, which means that it is always cognized in terms of words. There is no possibility of knowledge to occur apart from words. In the context of time it would mean that the understanding of time is dependent upon linguistic formulation, which is to say that the contemplation on time is in terms of words. It is the letter (*varṇa*) that explains the transcendent form of the word. It is through the association of the letter with the word that gives rise to the formation of seed *mantra* (*bīja-mantra*). And it is the power of *mantra* that terminates in the formation of a sentence (*pada*). It is through the reflective contemplation of the word, letter and sentence that the aspirant is able to pervade the entirety of time-sequence, viz., from the moment to an aeon. Accordingly does the aspirant absorb the vast expanse of time by focussing separately upon the pentad of animation till finally he is able to pervade over the time process of such categories (*tattva*-s) that are presided over by Brahmā, Viṣṇu, Rudra, Śrī-kaṇṭhanātha, Īśvara, and Sadāśiva.[72] Finally, he reaches such a state of accomplishment whereby he obtains complete freedom from the contraction (*saṁkoca*) that time initiates, which means that he is so empowered as to have the absorptive experience of the infinite lordship of the timeless Lord (*akāla*)

The subtle form (*sūkṣma-akāra*) of the thirty-six categories (*tattva*-s) consists of five planes, which extends from the *nivṛti-kalā* to the *śāntātīta-kalā*. In each plane are contained a number of worlds (*bhuvana*-s), and the total number of the worlds is said to be one hundred eighteen. An aspirant is asked to bring into contemplative focus the various worlds, categories as well as the *kalā*-s, viz., the container of the worlds and categories. Through contemplative absorption the aspirant has the experience of each world as being the form of the supreme Lord. While in deep contemplative absorption, the aspirant dissolves the pathway of space (*deśādhva*) into the body, body into the breath, breath into the intellect, intellect into the void, and void into consciousness (*saṁvid*). Through this process of dissolution the aspirant ultimately has such an experience of recognition in terms of which he realizes his essential nature as being nothing else but pure consciousness.[73] This realization of being essentially pure consciousness results in the experience of freedom from the contraction that the path of space implies. In this manner is removed the formation of contraction that these two pathways initiate and actualize.

Insofar as the categories are concerned, they are of two

types: subjective and objective, pure and impure. The thirty-six categories may, however, be termed as being the objective (*prameya-tattva*-s), whereas the seven experiential states are known as being subjective (*pramātṛ-tattva*-s). Thus the seven subjective planes, viz., from Sakala to Akala, and their corresponding powers (*śakti*-s) are recognized by the aspirant, while in contemplation, as being identical with his own essential nature. Technically it is known as the knowledge of fifteen (*pañcadaśī-vidyā*). The next step the aspirant is asked to take is to abandon the Sakala subject and contemplate only upon the six subjects and their powers, which is from Pralayākala to Akala. This process has to be repeated with regard to the remaining five planes until one reaches the plane of the Akala subject. In this way is thus contemplated the various categories, whether subjective or objective.

The Ancillaries

In order to achieve success in any one of the spiritual methods, it is necessary for the aspirant to take shelter under the wings of such a spiritual master (*guru*) who abides in the undifferentiated state of Paramaśiva. Although the Trika thinks of Paramaśiva as the real master, the liberator,[74] yet it is Paramaśiva who comes to the rescue of the disciple in human form. From a doctrinal point of view there is no essential difference between the spiritual master and the disciple, as both of them are essentially of identical nature. However, difference between the two remains to the measure the disciple has not attained the undifferentiated state of identity. The difference between the two fades away the moment both of them abide in the supreme state of non-difference. The disciple achieves such a state by identifying himself with the accomplished master, and through him with Paramaśiva.

The spiritual unfoldment of the disciple begins the moment he approaches an accomplished master. In doing so, he opens up to the possibility of receiving divine grace as the best antidote against the disease of bondage. The transmission of grace could either be intense, medium or dim, depending on the preparedness of the disciple. Upon whom grace is intense follow the superior spiritual paths of Non-Method and the Method of Śiva, whereas who follow the inferior paths of the Method of Energy and the Individual Method have the fall of grace either in moderate or dim form.

An accomplished master is said to be one who has the power of conferring full consecration (*abhiṣeka*) upon the disciple. It must be kept in mind that, according to the Trika, consecration must be distinguished from initiation (*dīkṣā*). The process of initiation is such as to be dependent upon the yogic practices and rituals. The spiritual master, while initiating the disciple, initially establishes certain identifications in the disciples, which means that the master identifies himself with the disciple, and thereby introduces the disciple to the spiritual path that the master considers being appropriate. Thus there is established such a kind of interpenetration between the master, the disciple and the universe as would terminate in the fusion with Paramaśiva. It is this fusion with Paramaśiva that delivers the disciple from the entanglement of bondage. Consecration, however, may be compared to the anointing of a king. It is in and through consecration that the master confers full illumination as well as the powers of omniscience and omnipotence upon the disciples, thereby making him liberated while alive (*jīvanmukta*). Thus the disciple attains himself the status of the master.

The next step that the aspirant has to take concerns itself with such meditative practices as would result in the quietude of thought in terms of its purification. And these practices are based upon a priori notion that the energy that activates the cosmos exists potentially in the human body. It is this idea that is confirmed by this aphorism of the *Śivasūtra*: "As in the yogi's body, so also elsewhere."[75] It is upon the arousal of this latent power in the body that the aspirant can obtain freedom from ignorance that is the cause of bondage, of transmigration. Whether the exercise concerns itself with the concentration on an object or image, or with the identification with the deity, or with the various bodily postures, or with the unification of the currents of thought, or with breath-control—all of them are directed at pacifying thought in terms of effecting the inward purification. Once the consciousness of duality is overcome, there ensues the undifferentiated state of absorption in Śiva. However, the repose of absorption that is attained through the Individual Method is that of tranquillity of thought.[76] It is such a state of mental calm in terms of which the mind is so purified as would not succumb any more to duality. Thus the mind rests in itself and thereby checks such motivation as would give rise to transmigration.

One of the redeeming features of the Trika practices is that that they are not so ascetical as are the yogic practices that have been prescribed by the *Yogasūtra* of Patañjali. It is because of this reason that Utpaladeva gave to the Trika spiritual practices the nomenclature of being such a path that is easy as well as new.[77] It is because of such an orientation that these practices come within the ambit of what is called the royal yoga (*rāja-yoga*). All these practices, from the Individual Method to the Non-Method, are so spoken because of them being free from such deprivation of the senses that are considered to be essential in the Yoga of Patañjali. In the Yoga of Patañjali the practices are so devised as would result in the suppression of the modifications of the mind.[78] Such is not the aim of the yoga that the Trika has prescribed. The Trika yoga, on the contrary, believes that the suppression in any form of the mind would make the mind more unstable and prone to delusion.[79] Instead of suppressing the mind or the senses, the Trika prescribes such contemplative methods as would engage the mind in such a manner that would lead to the emergence of what may be called the mood of Śiva, which, in other words, means that the mind, in a graduated manner, attains complete merger with Śiva. Once the introversive absorption becomes easeful and spontaneous, there accordingly is reached the state whereby the use of any kind of method automatically falls off. It is a state in which the fluctuations of the mind are dissolved, through deep absorption, into the indeterminate state of consciousness. It is not the dissolution of the modifications of the mind that in the Trika is referred to as yoga. It is, instead, the attainment of the state of recognition in terms of perfect indentity with Paramaśiva that it called Yoga.

References

1. *ĪPK*, 3.2.12: *mukhyatvam kartrāyās tu bodhasya ca cidātmanaḥ/ śūnyādau tadguṇejñānam tat samāveśa-lakṣaṇam//*
2. See *TAV*, 2.2: *upāyair na śivo bhāti*
   bhānti te tat prasādadaḥ/
   se eva ahaṃ svaprakāśo bhāse viśva-svarūpakaḥ//
3. *TĀV*, 2.2: *siddhānām yogininām ca darśanam cārubhojanam/*
   kathanam saṁkramaḥ śāstre sādhanaṃ guru-sevanam/
   ityādo nirūpāyasya saṁkṣepo'yam varānane/
4. *TS*, chap. 1: *upāya-jālam na śivam prakāśayed ghaṭena kiṁ*
   bhāti sahasra-dīdhitiḥ/ vivecayan-nittham-dvāra darśanaḥ
   svayaṃ prakāśam śivamāviśet kṣaṇāt//
5. *TĀ*, 1, 242: *tato'pi paramam jñānam-upāya-ādi-vivarjitam/*
   ānanda-śakti-viśrāntam-anuttaram-iha-uccayate//
6. K.C. Pandey, *Abhinavagupta: An Historical and Philosophical Study*, sec. rev. edn. Varanasi: Chowkhamba Sanskri Series Office, 1963, p. 315.
7. L.N. Sharma, *Kashmir Shaivism*. Varanasi: Bharatiya Vidya Prakashan, 1963, p. 315.
8. Pandey, op. cit., p. 303.
9. *TA*, 1.182:
   avikalpa-ātma-saṁvittau yā sphurattaiva vastunaḥ/
   sā siddhir na vikalpāttu vastu apekṣa-avivarjitāt//
10. *Pratyabhijñāhṛdayam, sūtra* 2.
11. *TA*, 1.182.

12. *PS*, v. 96: *paramārtha-mārgamenam jhātiti yadā gurumukhāt samābhyeti/ ati-tīvra-śakti-pātāt tadaiva nirvighnameva śivaḥ//*
13. *TĀ*, 8.173.
14. Pandey, op. cit., p. 80.
15. *ĪPV*, 4.2.2.
16. *TĀ*, 5.356; see also *VB*, vv. 15, 65–66, 72, 150, 152, 155.
17. *ĪPV*, 4.1.15.
18. Ibid., 1.230:
abheda-upāyam-atra-uktamśāmbhavam śāktam-uccayate/
bhedābheda ātmaka-upāyam bheda-upāyam tatha āṇavam//
19. *TS*, p. 10: *svātantrya-śaktim eva-adhikāṃ paśyan nirvikalpaṃ eva bhairava samāveśam anubhavati/* See also *Anuttarāṣṭaka*, v. 2:
mā kiṁcit tyaja ma gṛhaṇa virāma svastho yathāvasthitaḥ//
20. *TĀV*, 1.42: *sa (śāmbhava) eva parām kāṣṭhām prāptas ca an-upāya itya uccayate?*
21. *TS*, chap. 3.
22. *ŚD*, 1.24–25: *ghaṭa-ādi-gṛha-kāle 'pi ghaṭam jānāti sa kriyā/*
jānāti jñānam atraiva niricchor-vedarakṣatiḥ//
anumukhya ābhāvatas-tasya nirvṛttir nirvṛtti vinā/
dveṣye pravartate naiva na ca vetti vinā citam//
23. Sharma, op. cit., p. 253.
24. *VB*, vv. 140–44.
25. Sharma, op. cit., pp. 162, 164.
26. Pandey, op. cit., pp. 530–31.
27. *MM*, v. 54.
28. *VB*, v. 32.
29. *TA*, 6.10.
30. *VB*, v. 89.
31. *TĀV*, 6.10
32. Sharma, op. cit., pp. 54–55.
33. *TS*, chap. 4: *vikalpa-bhlād eva jantavo bāddham ātmānam abhimanyante/ so abhimānaḥ saṁsāra-prati-bandha hetuḥ/ ataḥ pratidvandva-virūpo vikalpa uditaḥ saṁsāra-hetum vikalpam dalayati itya abhya-udaya-hetuḥ//*
34. Ibid., chap. 4: *sa ca eva rūpaḥ-samastebhyaḥ parichinna-svabhāvebhyaḥ śivāntebhyaḥ tattvebhyo yat uttīrṇam aparicchinna samvin-mātra-rūpam tadeva ca paramārthaḥ . . . tadeva ca ahaṃ/ ato viśvottīrṇo viśātmā ca ahaṃ/*
35. Ibid., chap. 5: *sattarka eva sākṣāt tatra upāyaḥ/*

sa ca bahuprakāratayā saṁskṛto bhavati/tadyathā yāgo homo japo vṛtam yoga iti/

36. Ibid., chap. 4: *tatra bhāvānām sarveṣām parameśvara eva sithitiḥ/na anyat vytiriktam asti, iti vikalparūḍi prasiddhye parameśvara eva sarva bhāva arpanam yagaḥ/*
37. Ibid., chap. 4: *sarve bhāvaḥ parameśvara tejomayaḥ iti rūḍa-vikalpa-prāptyai parmeśa saṁvid-anata-tajasi samasta bhāva-grāsa-rasiktābhimate tattejo-mātra-āviśeṣatva saḥ samasta bhāva vilapanam bhomaḥ/*
38. Ibid., chap. 4: *evam vidham tat param tattvam sva-svabhāva-bhūtam ityantaḥ parāmarśanam japaḥ/*
39. Ibid., chap. 4: *parameśvara samatābhimānena dehasya 'pi ghaṭa āderāpi avalokanam vṛtam/*
40. Ibid., chap. 4: *tat svarūpa-anusaṁdhāna-ātmā vikalpa viśeṣo yogaḥ/*
41. *ŚD,* 7.87: *na me bando na me mokṣastau malatvena saṁsithitau/*
42. Ibid., 7/92: *pūjanannāsti me tuṣṭir nāsti khedo hi a pūjanāt/ pūjair-avibhedena sadā pūjeti pūjanam//*
43. Ibid., 7.79: *yena yena indriyena-artho gṛhyate tatra tatra sa/ śivatā lakṣitā styān dhāyanam iti vṛṇuyate//*
44. Mircea Eliade, *Yoga: Immortality and Freedom,* sec. rev. edn. Princeton: Princeton University Press, 1969, pp. 244–45.
45. Ibid., p. 241.
46. Ibid., pp. 241–43.
47. Ibid., pp. 236–41.
48. *VB,* vv. 26, 35, 52.
49. *PS,* v. 52: *ittham tattva-samūhe bhāvanayā śiva-mayatvamabhiyāte/ kaḥ śokaḥ ko mohaḥ sarvam brahmāvalokayataḥ//*
50. Ibid., v. 68: *ittham sakala-vikalpān pratibuddho bhāvanā samīraṇataḥ/ ātma-jyotiṣi dīpte juhvaj-jyotir-mayo bhavati//*
51. *TS,* chap. 5: *yadā tu upāyāntaram asau sva-saṁskāra artham vikalpo 'pekṣate, tadā buddhi-prāṇa-deha-ghaṭa-ādikan parimita rūpān upāyatvena gṛhanan aṇutvam prāpta āṇavam jñānam-āvirbhāvayati/*
52. *PS,* vv. 98–102
53. *TA,* 3.211.
54. *MVT,* 2.21: *uccāra-karaṇa-dhāyana-varṇa-sthāna-prakalpanaiḥ/yo bhavet sa samāveśaḥ samyag-āṇava uccayate//*
55. *TS,* chap. 5: *tatra pramātṛ pramāṇa-prameya-rūpasya vahni arka soma-tritayasya saṁghaṭṭam dhyāyet yāvat asau mahābhairava-agniḥ dhāyana-vāta-samiddākaraḥ sampaddayate/*

56. *TĀ*, 5.44: *nijānande pramātra-aṁśa-mātre hṛdi purā sthitaḥ/*
57. Ibid., 5.44: *śūnyatā mātra-virānter-nirānadam vibhāvayet/*
58. Ibid., 5.45–46: *prāṇodaye prameye tu purānandam vibhāvayet/ tatra ananta prameya aṁśa purāṇa-apāna nirvṛtaḥ// parānanadagatas tiṣṭhet apānaśa-śiśobhitaḥ/*
59. Ibid., 5.64: *tato ananta-sphuran-meya-saṁghaṭṭa-aikānta-nirvṛtaḥ/ samāna-bhūmim-āgamya brahmānanda-mayo bhavet//*
60. Ibid., 5.47–48: *tato 'pi māna-meya-augha-kalanā grāsa-tat-paraḥ/ udāna-vahanau viśrānto mahānandam vibāvayet//*
61. Ibid., 5.42: *nirupādir mahā vyāptir vyāna ākhya upādhi-varjita/ tadā khalu cidānando yo jaḍānupabṛmhitaḥ//*
62. Ibid., 5.50–52: *yatra ko'pi vyavacchedo nāsti yad viśvataḥ sphurat/ yad anāhata saṁvitti parama-amṛta-brahmhitam/ yatrāsti bhāvanādinam na mukhyā kāpi saṁsthitaḥ// tadeva jagadānandam-asmābhyam śambhurucivān/ tatra viśrāntirādheya hṛdaya-uccāra-yogataḥ//*
63. Ibid., 5.101: *atra bhāvanayā deha-gata upāyaih pare pathi/ vivikṣo pūrṇatā sparśāt prāṇa ānandaḥ prajayate//*
64. Ibid., 5.102: *tato'pi viddhutāpāta-sadṛśe deha-varjita/dhāmni kṣaṇam samāveśad udbhavaḥ prasphuṭam plutiḥ//*
65. Ibid., 5.103–5.
66. *TĀV*, 5.129.
67. *TS*, chap. 5: *asminna eva uccāre sphuran avyaktānukṛti-prāyo dhvanir varṇaḥ/... tad abhyāsāt para-saṁvitti-lābhaḥ/*
68. Ibid., chap. 6: *sa eva sthāna prakalpana-śabdena uktaḥ/ tatra tridhā sthānam-prāṇa-vāyuḥ śarīram bāhyam ca/*
69. *VB*, v. 51: *yathā tathā yatra tatra dvādaśānt manaḥ kṣepet/ prati-kṣaṇam kṣīṇa-vṛttera vailakṣaṇyam dinair bhavet//*
70. *TĀ*, 7.25.
71. *TS*, chap. 6: *yat tat sāmanasyam sāmyam tad-brahma/ asmāt sāmans yāt akālya kālān nimeṣa unmeṣa mātrataya proktā eṣa kāla prasara vilaya cakra-bramodayaḥ/ evaṃ asaṁkhyaḥ sṛṣṭi pralayaḥ ekāsmin mahā sṛṣṭi rūpe so'pi saṁvidi sa upādhau sa cimātre/cinmātrasya eva ayaṃ spando yad ayaṃ kālodayo nāma/*
72. Ibid., chap. 6: *evaṃ akhilaṃ kālādhvanam prāṇodaya eva paśyan sṛṣṭi saṁhārāṁs ca vicitrān niḥ saṁkhyāṁs tatraiva ākalayan, ātmanam eva parama-aiśvarayam pratyābhijñāna mukta eva bhavati/*
73. Ibid., chap. 7: *tam samastam adhvanam dehe vilāpya, dehe ca prāṇe, tam dhiyi, tam śūnye, tat saṁvedane nirbhara-paripāuṇa saṁvit samapadyate/*

74. *TĀ*, 13.159.
75. *Śivasūtra*, 3.17.
76. *TĀ*, 3.211.
77. *ĪPK*, 4.1.16: *iti prakaṭito mayā sughaṭa eṣa mārgo navo, mahā guru-bhir uccayate smaśiva dṛṣṭi śāstre yathā/ tad atra nidadhat padam buvana-kartṛtām-ātmano vibhāvaya śivatā mayīm nīṣam āviśaṁ sidhyati//*
78. *Yogasūtra*, 1.2: *yogaścittavṛttinirodhaḥ/*
79. *MVV*, 2.109.

7

The Śākta–Śaiva Perspective

IT HAS ALREADY BEEN POINTED OUT that the absolute powers of the Absolute are characterized by such aspects as would simultaneously express its transcendence (*viśvottīrṇatā*) as well as immanence (*viśvamayatā*). The transcendent aspect of Paramaśiva explains the immutable and indivisible aspect, whereas the immanent aspect is so characterized as would explain the glory of the lordly powers of the Lord. Thus the glory of the powers of the Lord continuously shine forth in terms of such movement or throb (*spanda*) that result in the emergence and dissolution of the phenomena. However, both these aspects the Absolute, viz., the transcendent and the immanent aspects, should not be seen as separate from each other; rather they are identical in the sense of pertaining to Paramaśiva alone. The identity of these two aspects constitutes the unity of the powers of the Absolute. The manifestation of these two aspects of the Absolute, at the theological level of thought, is represented respectively by Śiva and Śakti, or what popularly is called the Divine Couple. As Śiva is never devoid of Śakti, so Śakti accordingly is never separate from Śiva. Both these aspects exist continuously in identity with each other, and thereby express, both philosophically and theologically, the nature of the Absolute as being one-without-second.[1]

The transcendent aspect of the Absolute is as much embodied by Śiva–Śakti as is the immanent aspect as well as its various planes of existence. At no moment of time is transcendence or immanence devoid either of Śiva or of Śakti. Thus every manifest category or entity is found out, upon deep reflection, to be of the nature of Śiva as well as of Śakti. The three levels of difference (*bheda*), difference-cum-non-difference (*bhedābheda*) and non-difference (*abheda*) characterize this entire manifest order (*prapañca*). Śiva is continuously engaged, at these three levels, in the play of manifestation and withdrawal of the universe. Śiva through his own innate Energy, namely, Śakti, accomplishes this play of expansion (*prasāra*) and contraction (*saṁkoca*) of manifestation. The adept, at the level of spiritual practice, recognizes himself as being of the nature of Śiva only when he has the direct experience of the glorious powers of unimpeded will (*icchā*), knowledge (*jñāna*), and action (*kriyā*). It means that the adept obtains firm conviction concerning himself as being non-different from Śiva only when he has the knowledge of what he desires to know or is in a position of doing what he wants to do. Thus he comes to know himself as being identical with Śiva only through the medium of innate divine powers (*śakti*-s). Śakti accordingly is spoken of in the Trika system as being the mouth of Śiva.[2] It is Śakti through which the powers of Śiva are not only expressed, but equally are expressive of his being Śiva, which is to say that Śakti belongs to none other than Śiva himself. It is this Śakti that characterizes the absolute autonomy (*svātantrya*) of Śiva as Absolute.[3] Śiva and Śakti are identical with each other in the same manner as is fire and its burning capacity.[4]

The viewing of the Absolute in terms of its powers distinguishes Trika Śaivism from the absolutism of Śaṁkara. For Śaṁkara the Absolute is inactive and indeterminate, whereas such a conception of the Absolute is not acceptable to the Trika. The Trika thinks of the Absolute in terms of its powers, and so accordingly transforms itself into what may be called Śāktism. The philosophical thinking of Trika Śaivism, at the level of practice, is practically Śāktic in orientation. Whatever philosophical view any school of Śaivism may hold is, at the level of practice, so transformed as to be Śāktic. Likewise the philosophical views of Śāktism, at the level of reflection, are Śaivite in orientation. The scriptures that concern themselves with the practical aspects of spirituality are evidently disposed towards Śāktism, whereas the scriptures that have a philosophical bent are more prone towards Śaivism. However, both of them are so related to each other as to be inseparable, which is to say that they are essentially two sides of the same coin. Conceptually Śaivism and Śāktism may be distinguished from each other, but they are however one and identical when considered in terms of their essence.

The Perspective of Śāktism

Whatever be the nature of worship of Śiva, it is always performed in terms of one of its forms of Śakti. All such forms of Śiva that are being worshipped are nothing but the different forms of Śakti. All such incarnations of Śiva that are devotionally worshipped by the devotees are but the expressions of Śiva's own Śakti. The manifest order (*prapañca*) from the category of Śiva to that of earth is but the expansion (*vikāsa*) of Śiva's own Śakti. The five causal agencies like Brahmā, Viṣṇu, and others, are but the five forms of such *śakti*-s of Śiva are as emanation, preservation, dissolution, concealment, and revelation.[5] The entire universe appears to be shining (*sphurattā*) within Śiva's pure consciousness as reflection. For the appearance of this reflection Śiva is in no need of any support from such reflection that is different from, and external to him. The nature of Śiva is pure luminosity, which is to say that Śiva is of the nature of pure and luminous consciousness. Thus it is very consciousness that functions as the mirror for the reflection that is reflected within it. It is within this luminous mirror within which Śiva, through his unimpeded and free will, reflects his own infinite *śakti*-s or energies. It is this reflection within the mirror of consciousness of infinite *śakti*-s that is termed as emanation of the universe (*sṛṣṭi*). The maintenance of these reflections is called the act of preservation (*sthiti*). As and when Śiva re-absorbs these reflected energies within itself it is called the act of dissolution of objectivity (*saṁhāra*). With the dissolution of objectivity, there does not eventuate any more the appearance of reflection of energies. This entire play of emanation, preservation and dissolution of the universe is but the divine display of the lordly powers of the Lord, which is to say that it is nothing but the expression of Śiva's own Śakti. Thus the importance of Śāktism within the Trika framework is of great significance. Even if some aspects of Śāktism may be devoid of Śaivite perspective, yet the fact remains that it is Śāktism that is seen to be operating at the practical level of spirituality. Even if devotion and worship of a Śaivite is centered upon Śiva, yet it is Śakti that is found practically more useful than Śiva. Thus the Trika thinkers like Abhinavagupta have paid attention in equal measure towards both Śaivism and Śāktism. It all boils down to the fact that Śaivism and Śāktism are so interlinked with each other as to be inseparable. One cannot be Śaiva unless one is at the same time a Śākta, and similar is the case with those who are the adherents of Śāktism.

The Five Powers of the Lord

The absolute Lord, who in himself is full and perfect, is either referred to as the category of Paramaśiva (*Paramaśiva-tattva*) or as "the power of consciousness" (*cit-śakti*). Likewise the categories of Śiva (*Śiva-tattva*) and of Śakti (*Śakti-tattva*) have respectively been equated with "the power of bliss" (*ānanda-śakti*) and "the power of will" (*icchā-śakti*).[6] Śiva as the supreme category (*para-tattva*) is seen to be identical with "the power of consciousness" (*cit-śakti*) and accordingly his Energy is equated with bliss (*ānanda*).[7] Even in the *Śivadṛṣṭi* of Somānanda Śakti is said to be nothing else than the expression of Paramaśiva'a will (*icchā*). Insofar as the Trika path of spiritual practice is concerned, it accepts the category of Śakti as being equivalent with the power of bliss. In fact, Paramaśiva as pure consciousness is non-separable from his own power of bliss.

Insofar as "the power of knowledge" (*jñāna-śakti*) and "the power of action" (*kriyā-śakti*) of the Supreme Lord are concerned, they find their expression respectively in the categories of Sadāśiva and Īśvara.[8] Insofar as the category of knowledge (*vidyā-tattva*) is concerned, it is seen to be the embodiment of the Lord's power of knowledge. It would not be far-fetched to say that the power of knowledge and the power of action, when united inwardly, represent the power of will of the Lord. The external unification of these powers likewise embodies the power of knowledge of the Lord.

The Supreme Lord is said to be in possession of five supreme powers, and through the operation of which is conducted the emanation, preservation, and dissolution of the universe. The first two powers—consciousness (*cit*) and bliss (*ānanda*)—are not so much the powers of the Lord as much as they express his intrinsic nature. The other three powers of the Lord are will (*icchā*), knowledge (*jñāna*), and action (*kriyā*). Insofar as the power of will is concerned, it expresses the nature of the Lord, whereas the powers of knowledge and action are seen to be unfolding or expressing the expansion (*vikāsa*) of the Lord's innate nature. These five powers represent symbolically the five faces of the Lord. In order to give expression to these five divine powers as an act of grace, Paramaśiva incarnates himself as the five-faced Svacchandanātha, and through these faces discloses the esoteric teachings of the Śaiva scriptures. The five teachers of the scriptures of Southern Śaivism—Īśāna, Tātpuruṣa, Vāmadeva, Sadyojāṭa, and Aghora—are considered in the Trika as being the innate powers of Parameśvara.[9] These five powers are always throbbing within the Lord. It is because of the throbbing nature (*spanda-ātmaka*) of these energies within Paramaśiva that there eventuates the sequential emanation and dissolution of categories from Śiva to Mahāmāyā, of the lords of the categories from Śivanātha to Anantanātha as well as of such existents that hierarchically exist from Śāmbhava plane to Mantra (viz., Vidyeśvara) plane. Thus it is Paramaśiva himself who causes both the emanation as well as dissolution of categories that are pure, which is to say that they are free from the defect of difference that obtains among the categories that function under the influence of Māyā.

The Sixth Power of the Lord

The sixth power of the Supreme Lord is given the nomenclature of Vidyā. In the Vedānta of Śaṁkara the term *vidyā* is used to denote such supernal knowledge as would result in the realization of the self. In contrast to *vidyā,* we have *avidyā,* which signifies such contracted form of knowledge that would terminate in the actualization of bondage. In Śaivism, too, *vidyā* is considered from two perspectives, namely, from the perspective of pure knowledge (*śuddha-vidyā*) and impure knowledge (*aśuddha-vidyā*). The non-dual perspective of vision, in the midst of empirical difference of subject and object in terms of I-This (*ahaṃ-idaṃ*), is considered as being pure knowledge.[10] This type of pure knowledge belongs to such Akala subjects as, for example, Mantramaheśvara-s and Mantreśvara-s. Insofar as impure knowledge is concerned, it pertains to the limited individuals, viz., Sakala-s. It is a knowledge in terms of which the external objective world is cognized as consisting of difference. Thus the capacity (*śakti*) this kind of knowledge is limited both in scope and range. This Trika concept concerning pure and impure knowledge would mean that there does not exist, as does in Advaita Vedāna, such a thing as total ignorance (*avidyā*). If one were totally to be ignorant, then there would be no possibility for the ignorant individual to have any kind of knowledge. It is because of this reason that the Trika has equated ignorance with such forms of knowledge that are erroneous or imperfect (*apūrṇa-khyāti*). Thus the Vedāntic concept of ignorance would be considered by the Trika Śaivism as being nothing else but impure knowledge, which is characterized by error and imperfection. It is because of this reason that impure knowledge is said to be limited (*parimita*) and contracted (*saṁkucita*).

Insofar as pure knowledge is concerned, it is hierarchically so structured as to consist of various planes. The Mantramaheśvara subjects, though having knowledge of non-difference, are at the same time prone to the vision of difference in terms of I-Thou (*ahaṃ-idaṃ*). Likewise the knowledge of Mantreśvara subjects, though characterized by difference, terminates in non-dual knowledge in terms of This-I (*idaṃ-ahaṃ*). At the level of Vidyeśvara subjects pure knowledge is characterized by the vision of difference, which is to say that the subjects at this plane have perfect knowledge with regard to their essential nature, but consider entire objectivity as being of the nature of difference. Such pure vision is given in the Āgama-s the nomenclature of Mahāmāyā[11] which is one of the powers of the Lord, and whose functional operation will be explained below.

The Nature of Māyā

The notion of *māyā* within the Trika system has been accorded with many meanings. The perfect lordly powers of the Lord are also termed as being *māyā.* This transcendent power, called *māyā,* explains the unimpeded free will or power of the Lord. It would mean that the term *māyā* is so used in the Trika as would explain the intrinsic power of the Lord. In contrast to this Trika notion of *māyā,* the Advaita Vedānta considers *māyā* being an adjunct of *brahman* and not as his innate power. It is because of the glory of the powers of *māyā,* according to the Trika, that the Lord has his lordly powers. It is on the strength of the power of *māyā* that the Lord manifests himself in accordance with his will. The root cause for the entire objective universe to exist as reflection within

Paramaśiva is nothing but this transcendent power is called *māyā.* It is because of the pulsation of this creative power (*māyā-śakti*) that there eventuates the appearance (*avabhāsana*) of pure categories.

The other aspect of *māyā* is that it encapsulates the tendency within Paramaśiva towards externalization, which is to say that the natural tendncy of Paramaśaiva towards external manifestion is because of this transcendent power, called *parā-māyā.*[12] It is due to the influence of the power of *māyā (māyā-śakti)* that, at the lavel of Śadāśiva category, there partly begins the appearance of this (*idaṃ*), viz., of objectivity. With the incarnation of Paramaśiva as Anantanātha begins the process of emanation in terms of subjects and objects as being different from each other, which is to say that cach subject (*pramātā*) is different from other subjects, and likewise each object (*prameya*) is different from other objects. This vision of difference among the subjects is termed as being the *māyīya-mala,* viz., the impurity of *māyā.* This vision of difference among the subjects is termed as being the *māyīya-mala,* viz., the impurity of *māyā.* This impurity of *māyā* is also found among such subjects as Vidyeśvara-s. As and when this power of *māyā* envelops the subject, it thereby conceals his essential nature. Upon the concealment of the essential nature, the limited individual has the experience of himself as being a mere psychosomatic ego, which is simply a mental construct. Instead of thinking of himself of the nature of light of consciousness, the limited individual, as it were, is reduced to the status of inertness. This concealment of the essential nature as well as the reduction to the level of inertness is also called *māyā.* Thus it is this *māyā-tattva* that serves as the material cause for future emanation. It is so because it is this *māyā-tattva* that serves as the substratum for the inert manifestation. The cause of this *māyā-tattva* is the above-mentioned transcendental power (*māyā-śakti)* of Paramaśiva.[13]

There are some Śākta–Śaiva thinkers who adhere to the

notion that there exists one of the powers of Paramaśiva, called Mahāmāyā, between the categories of Śuddhavidyā and Māyā. Mahāmāyā is said to be the abode of such subjects as, for example, Vijñānākala-s. The field of Vijñānākala subjects is said to be somewhat of a lower status in comparison to that of Vidyeśvara subjects, although both of them have their abode in the Mahāmāyā category. This Mahāmāyā is believed to be nothing but the lower form of the expanded Vidyā.[14] The manifestation of appearance of the category of restriction (*niyati-tattva*) is eventuated by the power of restriction (*niyati-śakti)* itself. It is this power of the Lord that restricts the universe within the ambit of causal laws of restriction. Even Brahmā and other deities operate and function within the parameters of the law of restriction. The fruits of the deeds that have been performed are also reaped in accordance with this law of restriction. At every step of our activity the causal law of restriction makes itself so operational as to be unavoidable. Likewise there is the other power of the Lord through which are made operational time-bound activities in terms of their expansion and development—and this power is known as the power of time (*kāla-śakti)*.

The Concept of Twelve Kālī-s

It is through the infinite powers of the Lord that the affairs of this world (*prapañca*) are conducted as well as operationalized. The cause for initial proclivity of a human being towards any kind of action is nothing but the powers of the Lord, which is to say that initial push behind all forms of activity in the world are the infinite powers of the Lord. Likewise the activities of the senses too depend upon these powers of the Lord. The Lord, through his various powers, maintains and operates, at different levels or stages, this manifest world. The Lord, at the level of non-difference, operates this world through his transcendent power (*parā-śakti)*. At this level the world is recognized as being nondifferent from I-consciousness. At the level of the category of Vidyā, the world is operated in terms of difference-cum-non-difference (*bhedābheda*), which is to say in terms of I-This (*ahaṃ-idaṃ*). The power through which this operation is carried out is called *parāpara-śakti*. It is at the level of Māyā that the sense of difference (*bheda*) operates at its full speed and strength. The power through which the Lord carries out the operation of difference is called *apara-śakti*. In addition to this triad of powers the Lord has one more power, which is known as Kālasaṁkarṣiṇī-śakti. The Lord at the levels of emanation, preservation and dissolution of the universe operates through three powers, which totals to nine powers. And this entire activity is accomplished by adding one more power, and accordingly the entire number of powers that are made use of is said to be twelve, which is to say that when three is multiplied by four, we have the number twelve. These twelve powers have been spoken of in the Trika system as being twelve Mahākālī-s.[15] Abhinavagupta has beautifully explained in his *Kramastotra* the philosophical significance of the twelve Kālī-s. This multitude of powers is also known as the circle/wheel of powers (*śakti-cakra*).

Aghora, Ghora, and Ghoratara Energies

The Trika Śaivism is of the view that there are four Energies of the Lord that are responsible in conducting the play of emanation and resorption of the universe. The perdominant Energy among these four Energies of the Lord is said to be the transcendental Energy (*para-śakti*). This predominant Energy in the Śaiva scriptures is given the nomenclature of Ambā. It is such an intrinsic Energy of the Lord whereby he displays his transcendental powers. It is this Energy which manifests itself in three forms when engaged in the activity of emanation and resorptioin of the universe. Among these three Energies it is Jyeṣṭha that brings about the emanation of the universe, whereas Raudrī concerns herself with the preservation of what has been emanated. Insofar as Vāma is concerned, its preserve of activity is to bring about the dissolution of the manifest universe.[16] Jyeṣṭha as Goddess directs limited individuals towards such self-recognition as would result in the relization of non-dual state of Being. It is this Goddess whcih leads bound beings towards a competent teacher (*guru)* as well as towards the study of sacred scriptures. It is this Energy of Śiva that really is responsible in initiating such activities that would lead the bound beings to the realization of liberation from the bondage of transmigration. As the number of individual beings in the world is countless, so this Goddess manifests herself in numerous forms. The multitude of forms of Jyeṣṭha is termed as Aghora. These forms of energy of Jyeṣṭha are constantly engaged in leading bound beings to self-recognition in terms of their essential nuture as being non-different from Paramaśiva.[17]

If, on the one hand, the nonterrible energies (*aghora-śakti*-s) of Jyeṣṭha Goddess are engaged in such activities as would result in the liberation of bound beings, there are, on the other hand, the most terrible energies (*ghoratara-śakti*-s) of Vāma Goddess that push people towards bondage. This double-edged activity of the Lord's energies signifies that there are some individuals who attain the state of liberation, and at the same time there are some other individuals who remain tied to the peg of bondage. These energies of Vāma Goddess push people towards such activities that cause their spiritual downfall. The people who come under the influence of such energies take delight in sense pleasures or subject themselves to such dispositions that give rise to anger and lust.[18] Both these types of energies, viz., Jyeṣṭha and Vāma, function in accordance with the will of the Lord. The most terrible energies of Vāma Goddess function freely in the world where sinful activities take precedence over activities that are virtuous. In contrast to the energies of Vāma Goddess, the non-terrible energies of Jyeṣṭha Goddess function where righteousness is in ascendance.

Insofar as the Lord's Raudrī energy is concerned, it also manifests itself in infinite forms. The multitude of energies of Raudrī Goddess are given the appendage of being simply terrible (*ghora*). These energies are responsible in providing the necessary facilities to people that are pleasant, and accordingly people are made, though temporarily, to stay in the world. On account of the facilities provided by the energies people get more interested in such activities that are more religious than freedom-giving.[19] The multitude of these energies function under the three Goddesses, namely, Jyeṣṭha, Vāma, and Raudrī. These three Goddesses also operate in accordance with the will of the Lord's transcendent Energy, namely, Ambā Goddess. This Ambā Goddess as transcendent Energy is always one with Paramaśiva, viz., she cannot be separate from the Lord at all. In this manner are carried out, through these energies of Paramaśiva, both pure and impure activities in the world.

The Energies of the Senses

The sense organs of a living being become operational on account of the energies of Śiva, and these energies are known as the rulers of the circle/wheel of powers (*karaṇeśvarī-s*). The difference between a wise man and an ignorant person lies in this that the latter thinks that he enjoys the sense objects through the medium of sense organs, whereas the former thinks that it is the circle of energies who are responsible in offering the sense-objects to Śiva as oblations. A Śaiva adept thus looks at the sense objects as nothing more than the forms of Śiva, which is to say that, while obtaining the necessary knowledge of the objects through the senses, the adept at the same time has the disclosure or revelation of the objects as being the manifest forms of Śiva. Abhinavagupta has discussed this aspect of the sense objects as well as of the senses in his commentary on the

Bhagavadgītā, and the verses concerned are the following:

devān bhāvayatā'nena te deva bhāvayantu vaḥ/
parasparam bhāvayantaḥ śreyaḥ param avāpsyathā// (3.11)
iṣṭān bhogān hi vo deva dāsyante yajñabhāvitaḥ/
tair dattān apradayai 'bhyo yo bhuṅkte stena eva saḥ//(3.12)
tad viddhi praṇipātena paripraśnena sevayā/
upadekṣyanti te jñānam jñāninas tattvadarśinaḥ// (4.34)

Even Bhaṭṭa Kallaṭa has drawn attention, in his *Spanda-kārikā*, towards the energies as Goddesses that rule over the senses. Viewing the senses as being constituted by the energies as Goddesses, Bhaṭṭa Kallaṭa accordingly is of the view that the adept himself/herself should be seen as the lord of the energies of the circle of sense organs.[20] In this manner Śāktism received the necessary impetus for its development, both at the level of philosophy and theology, in the Trika Śaivism of Kashmir. Thus it proves that Śāktism is not different from the philosophical or theological persepective of Śaivism. It is so because the vision of the Absolute ultimately has to be in terms of Śakti.

References

1. *ŚD*, 3.2–3: *na śivaḥ śaktirahito na śaktir-vyatirekinī// śivaḥ śaktis-tathā bhāvanā icchayā kartum-īdṛśan/ śakti-śaktimator-bhede saive jātu na varṇyate//*
2. *VB*, vv. 20–21: *śaktyāvasthā-pragviṣṭasya nirvibhāgena bhāvanā/ tadāsau śivarūpī syācchaivī mukham-iha-uccayate// yathālokena dipasya kirnairbhāskarasya ca/ jñāyate digvibhāgādi tadvac-chaktiyā śivaḥ priye//*
3. *ŚD*, 3.6: *śakteḥ svatantra-kāryatvacchatvam na kvacid-bhavet/*
4. *VB*, v. 19: *na vahner-dāhikā śaktir-vyatiriktā vibhāvyate/ kevalaṃ jñānasattāyām prārambhoyam praveśane//*
5. *TĀ*, 6.177: *brāhmī nāma parasyaiva śaktistāṁ yatra pātayet/ sa brahmā viṣṇu-rudrādya vaiṣṇvavyāderataḥ kramāt//*
6. *ŚD*, 1.29, 30: *tadevaṃ prasṛto devaḥ kadacicchaktimātrake/ bibharti rūpam-icchātaḥ . . . //*

7. *TS*, chap. 1: *tasya ca svātantryaṃ ānandaśaktiḥ/ taccamatkāra icchāśaktiḥ/ prakāśa-rūpatā cichaktiḥ/āmarśa-ātmakta jñānaśaktiḥ/ sarvakara-yogitvam kriyā-śaktiḥ/*
8. *ŚD*, 2.11: *atha asmākam jñāna-śaktiryā sadāśivanīptā//*
9. *TĀV*, 1.18: *tatra hi parameśvara eva cidānanda-icchā-jñāna kriyātmaka-vaktra pañcakāsūtranena sadāśiva-īśvara-daśām adhiśyānas tad-vaktra-pañcaka melanayā pañca-śroto-mayam abheda-bhedābheda-bheda-daśoṭṭaṅkanena tat-tat-vaicitryātama nikhilaṃ śāstram-avatarayati/yad-bhir-vaikharī daśāyāṃ sphuṭam iyat/ tathā hi prathamam-īśāna-tatpuruṣa-sadyojātai . . . bhedapradhāna daśa śivabheda/ . . . eṣām eva vāmadeva-aghora-melanayā aṣṭā-daśa rudra-bheda bhavanti/*
10. *ĪPV*, 3.1.3: *atha tadadhiṣṭhātṛ dvya-gatam karaṇam vidhyā tattvam āha . . . ahaṃ-idaṃ iti samadhṛta-tulāpuṭa nyāyena yo vimarśaḥ sa sadāśivanāthe īśvara-bhaṭṭārake ca/*
11. *PTV*, p. 118: *mahāmāyā-abhāve māyāpad pralaya kevalānāmāvasthitaḥ vidyāpade ca videśvarādinam/iti kiṁ-iva tad vijñāna-kevalāspadam syāt//*
12. *ĪPV*, 4.1.4: *svarūpa-parāmarśatyāgenaiva tu yad bhinnatayāpi vimarśanaṃ svarūpa-parāmarśa eva viśrāntam, ahaṃ-idaṃ iti sadāśiva-īśvara-paramārtham sā bhagavato māyā-śaktiḥ/*
13. *ĪPK*, 3.1.6: *beheda dhīr eva bhāveṣu kartur-bodha-ātmano api yā/ māyā-śakty eva sā vidyety anye vidyeśvarā yathā//*
14. *PTV*, p. 199: *keṣucittu śāstreṣu sā mahāmāyā bheda-mala-abhāvopcārād vidyā-tattva aśeṣatyaiva nirṇīyate/ kvacit punar-ajñāna-mala-sadbhāvoparodhān-māyā-tattva-puccatayā/*
15. *TS* (KSTS edn.), pp. 29–30: *yayedaṃ śiva-ādi-dharanyantam avikalpya saṁvin-mātra-rūpatayā bibharti ca paśyati ca bhāsayati ca parameśvaraḥ, sāsya śrī parā śaktiḥ/ yaya darpaṇa hastya ādivad bhedābhedabhyām sāsya śrī-parāpara-śaktiḥ/yayā paraspara-vivikta-ātmanā bhedenaiva sāsya śrīmad-parā śaktiḥ/ etat trividham yayā bhāraṇam ātmanya eva krodhī kāreṇa anusaṁdhāna-ātmanā graste, sāsya bhagavatī śrīparaiva śrīman-mātṛsadbhāva-kālakarṣiṇyadi śabdāntara-niruktā/ etāṣṭau, sthitau, saṁhāre ca iti dvādaś bhavanti/. . . sṛṣṭau, sthitau, saṁhāre ca iti dvādaśa bhavanti/ . . . cakreśvarasya svātantryam puṣṇatyaḥ śrīkālī-śabda-vācyāḥ/ /*
16. *TĀ*, 6.57: *vāma saṁsāra-vamanā Jyeṣṭha śivamayī yataḥ/ dravaya-itri rūjāṁ raudrī ca akhilakarmaṇām//*
17. *MVT*, 3.33: *pūrvarvaj-jontu-jātasya śivadhāma-phala-pradaḥ/ parāḥ prakathitās taj-jñaira-ghorā śiva-śaktyaḥ//*
18. Ibid., 3.31: *viṣayeṣu eva saṁlīnān adho 'dhaḥ pātayatyaṇūn/ rudrāṇun yāḥ samāliṅgya ghorataryo 'parāḥ smṛtaḥ//*
19. Ibid., 3.32: *miśra-karma-phalāśakti pūrvaj-janayanti yāḥ/ mukti-mārga-nirodhinyasta syur ghora parāparāḥ//*
20. *SPK*, 1.6: *yataḥ karaṇa-vargo yaṃvimūḍho mūḍhavat svayam/ sahāntareṇa cakreṇa pravṛtti-sthiti-saṃhṛtiḥ//*

śabdarāśi-samutthasya śaktivargasya bhogyatām/
kalā-vilupta-vibhavo gataḥ san sa paśuḥ smṛtaḥ// (3.13)
seyaṃ kriyātmikā śaktiḥ śivasya paśuvartinī/
bandhayitrī svamārgasthā jñātā siddhya-upapādikā// (3.16)

Glossary

A: This first letter of Sanskrit alphabet stands for the Absolute (*anuttara*).

Ābhāsa: Divine manifestation as well as the phenomenal appearance devoid of illusion. This phenomenal manifestation, according to the Trika, is nothing but the appearance of what exists within the Supreme Lord, who is of the nature of consciousness.

Ābhāsa-vāda: It is such a philosophical viewpoint which considers that the essence of objectivity is characterized by its appearance, which means that an object or entity is nothing more than its appearance. Whatever exists objectively, exists in terms of its appearance. It is to this philosophical viewpoint to which Trika Śaivism adheres. The Buddhists, however, have interpreted the theory of appearance differently. For them it denotes the appearance of the world as consisting of impressions (*vāsanā*-s) that are stored in the store-house consciousness (*ālaya-vijñāna*). Insofar as Vedāntins are concerned, they are of the view that the appearance of Īśvara, of bound being and of the world is basically caused by the beginningless ignorance (*avidyā*). Upon the negation of ignorance, everything disappears, which is to say that the existence of objectivity is as real as are the dream-objects, which is to say that they are unreal.

Abhāva: It denotes absence, and thereby non-existence or non-being.

Abhinna: Non-different or identical.

Abhoga: It is an experience of spiritual expansion or delight, which is known as *camatkāra*.

Abuddha: An individual who is so unenlightened as to be unawake, which is to say that such an individual is in the grip of inherent and intellectual ignorance. As a result of this, the individual suffers from all the three impurities of *āṇava, māyīya,* and *kārma*.

Adhva: Such path as would denote the external spiritual practices of *āṇava-upāya*.

Adhva-aśuddha: The impure path that contains within itself all the categories from Māyā to earth as well as the various worlds, existents and the rulers of the worlds.

Adhva-śuddha: The pure path that contains within itself the categories from Śiva to Śuddhavidyā as well as the existents and the rulers of categories thereof.

Adhva-ṣaḍ: The sixfold pathway consisting of the course of time (*kālādhva*) as well as of the course of space (*deśādhva*). The former consists of *varṇa, mantra,* and *pada,* whereas the latter is made up of *kalā, tattva,* and *bhuvana*. Both these paths are used as supports of meditation in *āṇava-upāya*.

Advaita Vedānta: The non-dualistic school of philosophy as adumbrated by Gauḍapāda and Śaṁkara. It is mainly based upon such canonical Vedic texts as the Upaniṣads. The entire philosophical gamut is explained by Gauḍapāda in his commentary called *Kārikā* on the *Māṇḍūkyopaniṣad,* whereas Śaṁkara explained extensively each aspect of his philosophy in his commentaries on the *Brahmasūtra,* Upaniṣads, and the *Bhagavadgītā*.

Āgama: The sacred scriptures revealed by God, and as such are considered to be canonical with regard to matters that are theological. Insofar as the Trika scriptures are concerned, they are said to be sixty-four in number, and have been given the nomenclature of *Bhairava-āgama*-s. Some of the Trika scriptures are *Namakatantra, Siddhatantra,* and *Mālinītantra*. Apart from these scriptures, the other important texts are the *Svacchanda, Vijñāna-bhairava, Parātriśikā, Śivasūtra,* etc.

Aghora: Śiva is said to be having five forms, and *aghora,* which is his fifth form (*rūpa*), is such an aspect of his that is merciful.

Aghora-śakti-s: Such benevolent energies of the Lord as would lead people towards the path of liberation.

Aghoreśa: The incarnation of Īśvarabhaṭṭāraka at the plane that is below the Śuddhavidyā category. It is in the form of Lord Anantanātha that such categories as, for example, Māyā, etc. are given rise to.

Agni: It is the symbol of a knowing subject (*pramātā*).

Ahaṁ: It is a term that denotes the principle of self-identity, and so of self-awareness. When seen simply as a psychosomatic ego, then it gets itself differentiated from objectivity (*idaṃ*). In its fulness and plenitude it denotes I-consciousness as the Absolute.

Ahaṁkāra: The principle of psychosomatic ego.

Ahantā: In the Trika system the Absolute is said to be but I-consciousness.

Aiśvarya: The absolute glory and power of God, which is constitutive of his lordship.

Ajñāna: It generally denotes ignorance, which is characterized by erroneous or incorrect knowledge. This incorrect knowledge expresses itself particularly with regard to one's essential nature as being identical with such insentient elements as the body, life-force, intellect, etc. Accordingly, this erroneously conceived knowledge has a view of reality which is partial and incomplete, and the result is the non-recognition of one's essential nature as being non-different from Paramaśiva. This ignorance expresses itself in terms of primal limitation, which is to say that an individual being thinks of himself as having limited knowledge as well as having limited capacity for action. This kind of ignorance is called *pauruṣa-ajñāna.* The other type of ignorance is known as that of intellectual ignorance (*bauddha-ajñāna*)—

and it expresses itself in terms of such thinking as would be devoid of supernal knowledge.

Akala: Such existents that abide in the planes of Śiva and Śakti. They cognize themselves as being of the nature of pure I-consciousness. They are known as Śiva-s. It is as Śiva-s that they take the form Śāmbhava-s in the category of Śiva, and in the category of Śakti they are known as Śākta-s.

Akhyāti: Ignorance that is primal.

Akrama: The experience of the intrinsic nature in terms of timelessness, which eventuates either by following the yoga of knowledge (*jñāna-yoga*) or the yoga of energy (*śākta-yoga*) or the *uccāra-yoga* of *āṇava-upāya.*

Ālaya-vijñāna: It is a Buddhist concept that considers one of part of the mind functioning as a kind of store-house for impressions, and the instant appearance of these impressions occurs in the form of a continuous series, which is said to constitute the so-called individual.

Amayīya: Not pertaining to *māyā,* and thereby transcendent to *māyā.*

Ambā: The Transcendental Energy of the Absolute, which expresses itself in the form of such Goddesses as, for example, Jyeṣṭha, Raudrī, and Vāma.

Amūḍa: The principle of sentiency.

Anādaravirakti: The attainment of such spiritual state in which spontaneously emerges indifference towards the sensual delights.

Ānanda: It is one of the attributes of *brahman,* which along with being (*sat*) and consciousness (*cit*) explains the nature of the Absolute. It also constitutes one of the five outward signs of self-bliss that eventuates through the practice of *uccāra-yoga,* and the signs are *ānanda, udbhava, kampā, nidrā,* and *ghūrṇi.*

Ānanda-śakti: It is an innate, unlimited, unrestricted, pulsating and wonderful energy of bliss of Paramaśiva. This divine energy makes its appearance in the category of Śiva (*śiva-*

tanu).

Anantanātha: The object of worship, and thereby the presiding deity of Vidyeśvara or Mantra subjects. Also known as Aghoreśa. While descending to the level of Mahāmāyā, he, as the master of Māyā, gives rise to the limiting factors (*kañcuka*-s) as well as to *puruṣa* and *prakṛti*.

Anāśrita-śiva: It is such a state of Śiva that is completely free from the content of objectivity, which is to say that the objective universe exists potentially in him as does oil in the sesame seed.

Āṇava-mala: It is such an impurity in terms of which the limited individual being so identifies himself with insentient substances as to be reduced to doing only few limited things or knowing only few things. As a result of this identification with the inert, the individual accordingly begins to think of himself as being nothing more than his body or intellect. In the language of Trika it would mean of considering oneself as being destitute of the power of freedom (*svātantrya-śakti*), and so as inert as a luminous diamond. This innate impurity expresses itself in terms of inherent ignorance (*pauruṣa-ajñāna*) and intellectual ignorance (*bauddha-ajñāna*). Thus the ignorance of this impurity pervades the entire range of beings from heavenly gods to earthly creatures.

Āṇava-samāveśa: It denotes the state of absorption in the transcendent Self that is eventuated by following the method of *āṇava-upāya*.

Āṇava-upāya: Such Trika yogic practices that are dependent upon the external supports. These externalized spiritual practices are also known as *āṇava-yoga, kriyā-yoga, kriyopāya* and *bhedopāya*. The objects that are used as supports of meditation are either external (*bāhya*) or internal (*grāhya*). The internal objects could be the intellect (*buddhi*), life-force (*prāṇa*) or the breathing sound (*dhvani*). The external objects could be time and space, which have been classified each into three forms respectively, thereby totalling into six forms, which technically is known as the six paths of meditation (*ṣaḍadhvan*). If the intellect is made the object of meditation, then it is known as *dhyāna-yoga.* If the object is life-force, then it is called *uccāra-yoga.* If the object is body, then it is termed as *karaṇa-yoga,* and if the object is sound, then it is called *dhvani-*or *varṇa-yoga.* Likewise if the six paths of space and time are made as the objects of meditation, then it is referred to as the yoga of *sthānakalpana.*

Aṇḍa: A sphere that contains within itself a number of phenomenal elements, which conceal the essential nature of Paramaśiva.

Aṇḍa-catuṣṭaya: The four exterior coverings that conceal the essential nature of Paramaśiva—and they are the gross covering of earth, the subtle covering called *prakṛti,* the finer covering of *māyā,* and the purest covering of *śakti.*

Antaḥkaraṇa: The three interior organs, namely, intellect (*buddhi*), mind (*manas*), and ego (*ahaṁkāra*).

Antarmukhībhāva: It is such a state in which consciousness is so introverted as to have no link with the external world.

Aṇu[1]: Atom.

Aṇu[2]: Limited individual or subject under the influence of *māyā* (*māyā-pramātā*), and so signifying a conditioned being.

Anubhava: It denotes the highest spiritual experience.

Anugraha: The gratuitous grace of the Lord, and it is due to this grace that the bound being (*paśu*) is so empowered as would lead him to cultivate the divine path of salvation.

Anupāya: It is such a highly evolved spiritual path in which no external or internal exertion is involved. The adept has the spontaneous experience concerning his essential nature as being identical with Paramaśiva.

Anusandhāna: It is such a spiritual method in terms of which is conducted uninterruptedly intensive awareness concerning the essential nature of the Absolute. It also denotes such exercise as would terminate in joining the succeeding experience with the one that has preceded, and so, in the words of Kant, signifies the synthetic unity of apperception.

Anuttara: It is such a technical term among the Kaula-s as to signify the highest principle, which is but the Absolute. And the Sanskrit letter *a* is seen to be the symbol of this transcendent principle. The term has now become the part and parcel of overall lexicography of the Trika. Abhinavagupta has, in his *Parātriśikā-vivaraṇa*, discussed extensively the various aspects of the term.

Apāna: The outgoing breath, which is one of the five kinds of breath, and functions as a means of assimilating of what is taken into the body.

Aparokṣa: The realization of the Self without the support of thought-constructs.

Apavarga: The state of peace characterized by a feeling of emptiness towards the Self. In the philosophical systems of Nyāya and Vaiśeṣika *apavarga* is equated to the condition of liberation.

Apavedya-suṣupti: Such deep sleep in which even the subtlest object is not experienced. It is because of this reason that this state of sleep has been identified with emptiness, and has been equated by the Trika thinkers to the emptiness of Buddhist *nirvāṇa*.

Apohana: The process of differentiating, through the intellect, a specific object from other objects.

Apohana-śakti: The natural tendency within the Absolute of externalizing the innate nature, which in itself is full and without bounds. It is, thus, the power of differentiation and in terms of which one object is made to appear different from other objects. It is one of the three powers along with knowledge and memory through which the order of the world is maintained.

Ārambha-vāda: It is a theory concerning the origin of the world. According to this theory, the formation of non-existent world owes its existence to atoms. The followers of Nyāya-Vaiśeṣika mainly follow this philosophical view.

Aśuddha-vidyā: It denotes such form of knowledge of a bound being that is limited in range as well as in depth. It is also counted as one of the limiting factors (*kañcuka*), and so the source of bondage. It is to this kind of knowledge to which the *Śivasūtra* (1.2) refers as being the cause of bondage (*jñānaṃ bandaḥ*). For this reason this type of knowledge is spoken of as being impure, and so is equated with empirical knowledge.

Ātma-lābha: The realization of the Self.

Ātma-viśrānti: Reposing or resting in the Self.

Ātma-vyāpti: It is such realization of the Self that does not terminate in the realization of essential nature of Śiva.

Ātman: The Self as the ontological substratum of existence.

Avadhāna: An uninterrupted awareness that is sharp, attentive and quick.

Avāntara-pralaya: An aeon in which the dissolution of all mental and physical factors eventuates.

Āvaraṇa-traya: The three coverings that conceal the divine nature of consciousness, and thereby of the Absolute. The three impure coverings are the impurity of limitation (*āṇava-mala*), the impurity of differentiation (*māyīya-māla*), and the impurity of action (*kārma-mala*). The second impurity, viz., *māyīya-mala,* includes also the five limiting factors (*kañcuka*-s) as well as denotes such limitation as is imposed by the physical form.

Āveśa: The spiritual state in which absorption is of such kind as would result in the total submergence of the individual existent into Paramaśiva.

Avidyā: Ignorance as erroneous or incomplete knowledge, and not the absence of knowledge. If ignorance were to be considered equivalent to the absence of knowledge, then there would be no possibility for knowledge to arise on account of it, viz., of ignorance being innate to man. It is because of this consideration that the Trika has equated ignorance to incomplete knowledge (*apūrṇa-khyāti*).

Avikalpa-jñāna: Such a state of self-luminous experience in terms of which the mind is incapable of thinking about anything and the intellect accordingly loses the power of imagining objects in terms of name-and-form. It is, thus, said to be a state in which identity with the Absolute is experienced in its fulness. It is, thus, such indeterminate knowledge of the Absolute in which mental activity of any kind is not involved. It also represents the state of equilibrium between the power of knowledge (*jñāna-śakti*) and the power of action (*kriyā-śakti*).

Avikalpa-pratyakṣa: Such sensuous indeterminate awareness or knowledge that is devoid of perceptual judgement, which is to say that it is knowledge that is free from conceptual judgement.

Aviveka: It is ignorance in terms of which Being and Non-Being is not differentiated from each other. Due to this nondiscrimination between the real and the unreal an individual existent gets caught up in the cycle of transmigration from one existence to another. For the Sāṁkhya it signifies that the self-monad (*puruṣa*) would remain in bondage insofar as discrimination concerning the self-monad and *prakṛti* is not made.

Bahirmukhatā: Externalization of consciousness.

Bāhya: The external objects that are used as supports of meditation particularly in *āṇava-upāya*.

Bāhyārtha-vāda: It is such a realistic theory that maintains the existence of objects as being independent of consciousness and this theory is mainly maintained by the Buddhist realistic school known as the Sarvāstivāda school.

Baindavi-kalā: It expresses such absolute freedom of Paramaśiva whereby the knower always remains the knowing subject, and so is never reduced to the level of object that is to be known.

Bandha: Such bondage or limited knowledge that has its basis in ignorance that is primordial. It also means such yogic exercises through which certain organs of the body are both contracted and locked.

Bandhana: Such bound state in which knowledge is contracted. It also denotes the state in which the individual existent experiences himself as being limited with respect to knowledge and action as well as so dependent as to be non-free.

Bauddha-jñāna: Such determinate knowledge that is pure and in terms of which one considers oneself as being non-different from the highest Lord, namely, Paramaśiva.

Bauddha-ajñāna: Such determinate knowledge that is inherently erroneous, and as a consequence of this impure knowledge the limited subject identifies the essential Self with such inert elements as the subtle body, the gross body, the intellect, and the life-force.

Bhairava: Such perfect beings (*siddha*-s) who, while having divine bodies, have the vision concerning Reality as being non-dual. Also such sixty-four canonical texts that are non-dualistic in orientation insofar as philosophical as well as theological vision of Reality is concerned. Also such liberated Śiva-s who are engaged in preaching the non-dualistic sixty-four Bhairava Āgama-s. Finally, the term denotes the Absolute, viz., Paramaśiva. As an anachronistic term, it consists of *bha*, *ra,* and *va*, indicating thereby *bharana, ravana,* and *vamana* corresponding thereby to the maintenance, dissolution, and projection of the world. It would mean that Bhairava as the Absolute is the one who manifests, maintains and dissolves the objective world.

Bhairava/Bhairavīmudrā: It is a special kind of meditation in which attention is introverted, whereas at the same time gaze is directed outward. While engaged in this practice, there should occur no break in it.

Bhairava-samāpatti: The attainment of such spiritual state in which is realized perfect identity with Paramaśiva.

Bhava: Existence that is caught up in the net of transmigration.

Bhāva: The external and internal aspects of existence.

Bhāva-samādhi: Such mystical trance as would result from

the enhancement of emotions.

Bhāvanā: Such inward practice of meditation in which firm conviction is formed with regard to oneself as well as with regard to objectivity as being non-different from Paramaśiva. As a form of creative contemplation, it thereby envisages the apprehension of the inner and emergent divine consciousness.

Bhedābheda: A philosophical viewpoint that considers the relationship between God, man and the world to be of the nature of difference as well as of non-difference. It is the same kind of relationship that occurs between the body and its limbs.

Bhoga: The experience of sensual enjoyment.

Bhoktā: The experiencer of enjoyment.

Bhūcarī: While being presided over by Karṇeśvarī, the energies that pertain to *bhūcarī* are related to the external objects, which have colour, form, and so on. Insofar as the individual subjects, their sense organs of perception and of action as well as the inner organs are concerned, they are said to be the expression of the energies of *bhūcarī*.

Bhūta: The gross element.

Bhuvana: The Trika is of the view that there are 108 worlds, which are inhabited by different types of beings. At the level of meditation, it denotes the gross form of space, which is made use of in the meditative practice of *sthāna-kalpanā* of *āṇava-upāya*. Space, thus, constitutes one of the six paths of meditation (*ṣaḍadhvan*).

Bhuvana-adhva: The third meditative support with regard to the pathway of space.

Bīja: As an esoteric term it has many implied meanings, and one of them explains it to be such active light of the transcendent Energy as to be the cause of the manifest universe. In addition to it, it is seen to be denoting the vowels of Sanskrit alphabet, and thereby as mystical letters. The seed-letters form an essential part of a mantra of a deity.

Bindu: The *bindu*, which is a dot, is considered in the yoga of Śāktism as the embodiment of Śakti, which is said to be radiating between the two eyebrows. Thus an aspirant is asked to meditate on this dot that exists between the eyebrows. It is this *bindu* that is considered as the source of light. In the Trika, however, *bindu* parallels Īśvara Bhaṭṭāraka, whereas *nāda* parallels Sadāśiva. It is, thus, *bindu* and *nāda* that are seen as the primary results of the outward vibration (*spanda*) of *kalā*, which is the power of Paramaśiva. As the undifferentiated light of I-consciousness, it is at the same time viewed as a mass of indivisible energy that is found in the dot, which is ever ready to give rise to the manifestation of objectivity. It also denotes the nasal sound (*anusvāra*) as indicated by the dot on the letter *ha*. In the esoteric language of Tantrism, it simply means a drop of semen.

Bodha: Such awareness in terms of which consciousness is aware of itself as consciousness, which denotes that consciousness is always intentional. In the language of Pratyabhijñā consciousness, apart from being light, is at the same time of the nature of awareness.

Brahma-nāḍī: The mystical vein, called *suṣumṇā*, that runs along the spinal cord. It is through this vein that the latent Energy, called *kuṇḍalinī*, moves upwards by piercing the six mystical wheels (*cakra*-s) till it reaches its final abode, which is the *sahasrāra*.

Brahma-randhra: It is said to be such a centre of subtle energy that is located at the top of the head. When the Coiled Energy, which is located at the bottom of the rectum, reaches it by traversing the centres of energy along the spinal cord, the adept experiences, so it is maintained, complete freedom from bondage.

Brahman: The Advaita Vedānta considers *brahman* to be the Supreme Reality. However, it is such Reality as is devoid of powers, and accordingly is so lifeless as to have no capacity of performing any kind of action. Since *brahman* is destitute of the power of action, so it is said to be only of the nature of light of consciousness, which is to say that, though identical with knowledge, it is totally inactive. In contrast to this concept, the Trika thinks of *brahman* as being intrinsically unlimited and identical with absolute freedom. It is through the absolute free will that the Absolute performs such actions as those of emanation and dissolution of the universe. It is in the context of this thinking that the Absolute in the Trika system is said to be both *prakāśa* and *vimarśa,* which is to say that the Absolute is both consciousness and awareness.

Brahmānanda: The fourth plane of bliss that emerges by reposing consciousness on the equalizing breath (*samāna*), which results in the unification of entire objectivity. This meditative practice pertains to *uccāra-yoga* of *āṇava-upāya.*

Brahma-nirvāṇa: Such luminous state in which action is absent, and some schools of thought have identified it with liberation. In the Trika it is said to be equivalent to the plane of Vijñānākala existents.

Buddha: The one who has attained the state of supernal awakening.

Buddhi: Intellect, the faculty of understanding. As an aspect of intuitive consciousness, it is through it that the Self cognizes the truth. It is also known as *mahat.*

Buddhi-endriya-s: The five sense organs of perception, which are smelling, tasting, seeing, touch, and hearing. These organs of perception are also known as *jñānendriya*-s.

Caitanya: As absolute consciousness, it has the freedom of both knowing and doing.

Caitta: Intellectual ideas.

Cakra: The wheels of energy within the body. The number of such wheels is said to be six, and are located along the spinal cord. It is by penetrating these wheels that the awakened energy in the root-wheel ascends upward till it reaches the final destination, which is the thousand lotus-petelled wheel, the abode of Śiva.

Cakreśvara: The Lord of the circle or group of energies.

Camatkāra: The wonderful delight of the bliss of I-consciousness. It also denotes the sensuous delight that is aesthetic in nature.

Candra: In esoteric terms the moon is seen to be the symbol of the object of knowledge (*prameya*) as well as of breath that is exhaled (*apāna*).

Caramakalā: The supreme phase of manifestation that is known as *śāntyātīta* or *śāntātita-kalā.*

Caryā: Such esoteric *tāntrika* practices which only the heroes (*vīra*) are allowed to perform on account of the use of five prohibited items, which are meat, fish, wine, fried beans, and sexual intercourse

Cetanā: It signifies Paramaśiva, the Self as well as the conscious being.

Cetya: Such objects of consciousness that are knowable.

Cheda: It denotes the cessation of inhalation and exhalation, which is brought about through the practice of vowel-less (*añcaka*) sounds.

Cidānanda: The bliss of non-difference that is the intrinsic nature of the power of consciousness (*cit-śakti*). It constitutes the essential nature of Paramaśiva. It also denotes the bliss that emerges at the sixth spiritual plane. This form of bliss, which is free from the adjuncts, emerges by taking hold of the repose (*viśrānti*) of all-pervasive *vyāna* animation through the practice of *uccāra-yoga.*

Cit: As Absolute, it signifies such consciousness that is unchanging, and so is considered to be the foundation of the changing phenomena.

Citi: It is such power of consciousness of the Absolute through which is actualized the manifestation of phenomena.

Cit-śakti: The unlimited, full, pure and autonomous consciousness that shines forth as the essential nature of Paramaśiva.

Citta: In the Trika this term is used to denote the empirical understanding of the mind. In other words, it means that the Absolute as consciousness manifests itself as empirical consciousness.

Dakṣiṇācāra: Such type of Śaivī spiritual practice in which emphasis is laid upon the observance of injunctions and prohibitions, worship, austerity, etc.

Darśana: As seeing, it is equated with such supernal vision as would transcend the empirical. Thus philosophical reflection is considered to be of the nature of supernal vision, and so philosophy has a quite different role to play in India than what has been assigned to it in the West.

Deha-pramāṭā: Such Sakala existents who think of themselves as being identical with the intellect, the life-force and the body, which is to say that they are totally devoid of the knowledge concerning the essential nature of the Self.

Deśa-adhva: The path of space consists of *kalā, tattva,* and *bhuvana,* and they are used as external supports in the meditative practice of *āṇava-upāya.*

Dhāraṇā: Meditation in general. Esoterically speaking, it denotes the following Sanskrit letters: *ya, ra, la, va.*

Dhyāna: It forms the seventh limb in the eight-limbed yoga of Patañjali. It is such a meditative practice in which single idea is held uninterruptedly as the object of meditative concentration. In this continuous flow of meditation there must not occur any break or interruption due to dissimilar ideas.

Dhyāna-yoga: As the highest form of meditation in *āṇava-upāya* it must in no manner be identified with the *dhyāna-yoga* of Patañjali. It is a form of practice in which meditation is directed on the intellect. The practice of meditation is so conducted as would lead to the unification of the subject (*pramātā*), the means of knowledge (*pramāṇa*), and the object of knowledge (*prameya*) by offering them into the fire of consciousness (*cid-agni*) so that the fulness of I-consciousness is experienced in terms of realization of both subjectivity and objectivity as the aspects of *saṁvid.*

Dhvani-yoga: It is a special kind of meditation of *āṇava-upāya* in which concentration is focussed on the unstuck sound (*anāhata-nāda*) which arises in the body due to the pressure of life-force (*prāṇa-śakti*). It is also known as *varṇa-yoga*.

Dikcarī: It is presided over by Vāmeśvarī. The energies of space are related to the external senses (*bahiṣkaraṇa*-s) because the senses have the possibility of operating only in outer space.

Dīkṣā: The term is composed of *dā*, to give, and *kṣi*, to destroy. Thus as initiation it denotes such impartation of knowledge as would cause the destruction of ignorance and in terms of which the eradication of the latent traces of impressions of the past deeds in the mind is accomplished. Consequently there arises such supernal knowledge as would lead to the realization of the Self, which results in the attainment of liberation.

Divya-mudrā: The divine posture or seal as expressed by the *khecarī-mudrā*.

Gaganaṅgana: The power of consciousness (*cit-śakti*).

Garbha: As womb it denotes primordial ignorance (*akhyāti*), which is equated with Mahāmāyā, which lies between Śuddhavidyā and Māyā categories.

Ghora-śakti-s: These energies of the Lord, which are infinite in number, are responsible for providing the necessary wherewithal of enjoyment to the worldly beings. They are also responsible in giving rise to such obstructions in the path of spirituality as would hinder the attainment of ultimate goal of life, which is liberation from bondage.

Ghoratarī-śakti-s: These infinite but terrible energies of the Lord push the worldly beings further and further downward, so that they get fully trapped in the net of bondage.

Ghūrṇi: It is a kind of intoxicating experience in terms of which there occurs whirling movement in the head. This experience emerges upon practising *uccāra-yoga* of *āṇava-upāya*.

Gocarī: Presided over by Vāmeśvarī, it is directly related to the *antaḥkaraṇa*, which is the abode of the senses.

Grāhaka: The subject who is the knower and the experient of objects.

Grāhya: An object of experience or cognition. Also such internal objects like the intellect, life-force, breathing sound that are used as supports of meditation in *āṇava-upāya*.

Guṇa-tattva: It represents the state of agitation of the category called *prakṛti*. It is from this state from which proceed the five great elements (*mahat-tattva*).

Guṇa-traya: The three qualities or strands of *prakṛti*, namely, the peaceful (*sattva*), the passionate (*rajas*), and the inertial (*tamas*).

Ha: The symbol of divine power (*śakti*).

Haṭhapaka: Such an effort that is continuous with regard to the assimilation of experiences of the subject.

Hetu: Cause.

Hetumat: Effect.

Haṁsa: The individual soul.

Hrada: It denotes lake, and is the symbol of spiritual awareness. Inward spiritual awareness is compared to a lake because of it being pure, deep, and free from any kind of covering.

Hṛdaya: Heart as the symbol of supreme consciousness, which is considered to be the substratum of phenomena.

Icchā: It is the power of will of Paramaśiva, which is symbolically represented by the Sanskrit letter *i*.

Icchā-śakti: The power of will represents such tendency within Paramaśiva which terminates in the externalization of the infinite number of energies that exist within the Lord. It also manifests itself in the category of Śakti (*śakti-tattva*). It is considered to be such inward cosmic energy of Paramaśiva as to be inseparable from him. It is this energy that brings about unification among the other two powers of the Lord, namely, the power of knowledge (*jñāna-śakti*) and the power of action (*kriyā-śakti*).

Icchā-upāya: It is an another name of *śāmbhava-upāya*. It is also known as *icchā-yoga*.

Idaṃ: The objective world out there that is experienced through the senses, and so is considered to be opposed to the subjective awareness, which is *ahaṃ*.

Idantā: The consciousness or awareness that pertains to *This*, which is to say that the empirical consciousness is basically intentional by directing itself towards objectivity.

Indriya-s: The sense organs of perception and of action.

Indu: It means, among other things, the object (*prameya*), the breath that is inhaled (*apāna*) and the power of action (*kriyā-śakti*).

Īśāna: It is the first form of Śiva among his five mantra-forms.

Īśvara: As Lord, it represents such aspect of Paramaśiva that has manifested itself as the fourth category (*tattva*), and has also the power of knowing and doing according to one's will. It is in this category in which *this-ness* shines forth predominantly, although *I-ness* is still present.

Īśvara-bhaṭṭāraka: As a ruler over the category of Īśvara, he is thereby the object of worship for the existents of this category, namely, of Mantreśvara-s.

Īśvara-tattva: It represents that plane of qualified non-dualism among the pure categories within which the existents have the experience of non-difference within the ambit of difference. These existents have the experience in terms of *idaṃ-ahaṃ*, viz., in terms of the statement: "I am these objects."

Jagadānanda: It is such a kind of bliss that transcends the six planes of bliss, which occurs through the practice of *uccāra-yoga*. It is bliss that is full and unbounded. It is upon experiencing this form of bliss that one has the realization of being fully divine

Jāgrat: In the language of esotericism it denotes such knowledge as is free from delusion, which, in other words, signifies the knowledge that is pervaded by enlightenment.

Jāgrat-avasthā: It is in the waking state that the existents, through their gross bodies and sense organs, form contact with the external world. It is the first state among the four states of animation—the other three being dream state (*svapna-avasthā*), the state of deep sleep (*suṣupti*), and the fourth (*turya*). The state that transcends them all is called "the beyond the fourth" (*turyātīta*).

Jāgrat-jñāna: The empirical knowledge that is gathered during the waking state and is common among all people.

Jāgrat-sṛṣṭi: The external gross world, which, generally speaking, constitutes objectivity for the existents of the waking state.

Jīva: Such Sakala existents who think of themselves as being identical either with the life-force, or with the intellect, or with the body. As an empirical self it is so conditioned by the *saṁskāra* as would result in its identification with the gross or subtle forms of limitation.

Jīvan-mukta: Such an existent who considers the entire world as being the display of his own innate powers. He, thus, is never influenced in any manner by the activities that are carried out in the world. While living in the body, he remains totally free from the fetters of bondage. It also signifies such an existent who, while living in the body, has the partial experience of emanation, dissolution, etc., of the world. Thus it explains the state of a liberated person who, while leading an embodied form of existence, has at the same time the full taste of liberation. Thus such an individual is not conditioned by his gross or subtle constitution.

Jñāna: Complete and full knowledge concerning the actuality of objects. Also such knowledge that eliminates the consciousness of individuality, which emerges only upon receiving appropriate initiation from a competent teacher. It is knowledge in terms of which is realized one's Śivahood—and such knowledge is technically called *pauruṣa-jñāna*. There is also another form of knowledge, and it is known as intellectual knowledge (*bauddha-jñāna*). It is knowledge that is definite and conceptual, and occurs at the level of the intellect.

Jñāna-indriya-s: The five exterior sense organs of perception. These sense organs constitute, in an ascending order, the categories from sixteen to twenty. The five sense organs of perception have the power of smell, taste, sight, touch, and hearing.

Jñāna-śakti: An inward energy of the Lord through which, at the plane of Sadāśiva, occurs an unclear and incipient perception of objectivity. It also signifies such energy of the Lord through which is experienced incipiently the spiritual glory within the unity of luminous consciousness. This glory of consciousness expresses itself in terms of knowing and doing.

Jñāna-yoga: It is a form of yoga that pertains to the Method of Energy (*śākta-upāya*).

Jyeṣṭha: Such auspicious divine energy of the Lord through which people in general are so inspired as would lead them on to the path of spirituality. This energy of the Lord, at the popular level of religious practice, has been so anthropomorphized as would lead to the emergence of, in the form of worship of the Goddess, devotional spirituality.

Kaivalya: It is such a state of isolation of the self-monad (*puruṣa*) which, according to the Sāṁkhya-Yoga, is identical with liberation from bondage. The Trika, however, considers it to be equivalent to the vacuity that is experienced in deep sleep.

Kalā: One of the five limiting factors (*kañcuka*-s) caused by the operations of *māyā*. It is due to the veiling powers of *māyā* that an individual being experiences limitation both with regard to knowledge and action. In Śāktism the term is so used as would expresses the spiritual stir of the powers of Lordship, which, through the process of externalization, manifest in the form of *nāda* and *bindu*, denoting thereby sound and light respectively.

Kalā-adhva: The thirty-six categories have been classified into five basic subtle forms, which, when considered from top to bottom, are *śāntātīta, śānta, vidyā pratiṣṭhā,* and *nivṛtti.* It also consists of *kalā, tattva,* and *bhuvana* as supports of meditation.

Kāla-adhva: It is a method of meditation, called *sthāna-kalpanā* used in *āṇava-upāya.* This meditative practice takes hold of such supports as, for example, *varṇa, mantra,* and *pada.* Thus it constitutes the course of time.

Kāla-cakra: Such mystical wheels as the *mātṛkā-cakra, śakti-cakra,* and *devī-cakra;* also all the letters of Sanskrit alphabet from *a* to *kṣa.*

Kalanā: The process of outward manifestation of what exists within, and thereby affirms the Sāṁkhya causal doctrine of *satkārya-vāda,* which says that the effect exists potentially, prior to its actualization, in the cause.

Kāla-śakti: It is such a power of the Lord in terms of which the contracted aspect of time becomes manifest, and accordingly is expressed time in terms of sequence or succession.

Kāla-tattva: The capacity of doing only few things, which would mean the contraction of the power of action (*kriyā-śakti*). This limitation of action expresses itself in terms of succession of events or deeds, and accordingly is time so classified as would lead to its division in terms of present, past or future. Succumbing to this division of time, the finite being looks at himself as well as upon his deeds in terms of this time scale.

Kālī (twelve): The doctrine of twelve Energies of the Lord owes its existence to the Krama, or what is called the Mahārtha, school of Śāktism that originated in Kashmir. It is maintained that the Lord, through these Energies, engages at different planes in the process of emanation and dissolution of the universe. Insofar as the theology of twelve Kālī(-s) is concerned, it is as follows:

(a) *Sṛṣṭi-kālī*: As and when there emerges desire for manifesting the objective universe in Kālī, and at the same time the universe in outline shines within her, then she is known as *Sṛṣṭi-kālī*. In this way is explained the creative aspect of Energy in relation to objectivity.

(b) *Rakta-kālī*: This form of Energy explains the idea of preservation, through the five senses, of what has become manifest objectively.

(c) *Sthitināśa-kālī*: It explains such aspect of Energy as would result in the withdrawal of what has been manifested, which is to say it describes as to how extroversion of Energy reverts back to subjectivity.

(d) *Yama-kālī*: It is a form of Energy that transcends both the introvert and extrovert aspects of Energy, and so explains the indefinable (*anākhya*) aspect of reality, which is to say that the very nature of reality is such as to be beyond the objective description of words and concepts.

(e) *Saṁhāra-kālī*: This aspect of Kālī tells us that it is through the Transcendent Consciousness (*parā-saṁvid*) that the disappearance of objectivity in relation to the means of knowledge (*pramāṇa*-s) is effected. Upon the disappearance of objectivity is experienced perfect identity between the subject and the object, between the self and the Self, and because of this devouring of difference this aspect of Energy is spoken of as *Saṁhāra-kālī*.

(f) *Mṛtyu-kālī*: This aspect of Energy is so effective as to swallow even the traces of idea concerning objectivity. It accordingly goes beyond the operations of *Saṁhāra-kālī*.

(g) *Bhadra-kālī*: The term consists of *bha* and *dra*, denoting thereby the piercing (*bhedana*) as well as dissolving (*drāvana*) of objectivity in terms of getting them merged into the essential nature, which is embodied by the Goddess called *Bhadra-kālī*.

(h) *Mārtaṇḍa-kālī*: The term denotes the sun, which, in the language of esotericism, is seen to be the symbol of the group of twelve senses. As the senses illumine the object that is perceived, so the sun is considered to be the most appropriate symbol of the senses. The twelve senses are the five senses of perception, five of action, mind (*manas*) and intellect (*buddhi*). They become operational only when related to the ego (*ahaṁkāra*). This aspect of Energy, viz., the *Mārtaṇḍa-kālī*, is so referred to because she so dissolves the twelve senses in relation to the Ego as to become non-definable (*anākhya*).

(i) *Paramārka-kālī*: She embodies the power of emanation in relation to the limited subject (*pramātā*), and this is accomplished by dissolving the Ego into the creative power that is represented by the *Paramārka-kālī*. However, the limited subject here denotes the one in whom the limitation of objects and of senses has been dissolved, but who still suffers from the limitation of *āṇava-mala*.

(j) *Kālāgnirudra-kālī*: When the Transcendent Consciousness (*parā-saṁvid*) brings about identification between the individual self and the Self, then she is called *Kālāgnirudrakālī*. This aspect of Kālī represents the Energy of maintenance (*sthiti*) in the context of the limited subject, because it is she who makes the limited subject to repose in the cosmic Self.

(k) *Mahākāla-kālī*: This aspect of Kālī is responsible in bringing about the dissolution of the limited ego, and this limited ego always stands in opposition to the perfect I-consciousness.

(l) *Mahābhairava-ghora-caṇḍakālī*: This aspect of Kālī embodies the state of indefinability in the context of the limited subject. It represents such state of transcendence of the Transcendent Consciousness as would be beyond the description of words. Accordingly it is equated with Akula, which means that the subject, object and the means of knowledge are completely dissolved into I-consciousness. The first four Kālī-s, thus, represent emanation, preservation, dissolution and indefinability in the context of objectivity. The next four Kālī-s embody the powers that are related to the means of knowledge. The last four Kālī-s explain the state of indefinability in relation to the limited subject.

Kalpanā: Such mental construction or projection as is caused by imagination.

Kampa: It denotes such trembling that is experienced by practising the *uccāra-yoga* of *āṇava-upāya*.

Kañcuka-tattva: It is such a category that has the tendency of concealing the essential nature (*svarūpa*) of pure consciousness (*saṁvid*) by throwing, as it were, a cover over it. It also operates in terms of making manifest Paramaśiva in the form of a limited existent (*jīva*). It is this category through which contraction is brought about in the powers of knowledge and action. It has five aspects that are known as *kalā, aśuddha-vidyā, rāga, niyati,* and *kāla. Māyā* is considered to be its sixth aspect.

Kāraka-s: Such agents who are involved in performing an action.

Karaṇa: The means of knowledge and of action as well as the inner senses (*antaḥ-karaṇa*) and the external senses. It also denotes such concentration on the body as is made use of in the *āṇava-upāya*.

Kāraṇa-pañcaka: The five representatives, such as, Brahmā, Viṣṇu, Rudra, Īśvara, and Sadāśiva, who are seen to be responsible in operationalizing respectively the five acts of Paramaśiva, which are emanation of objectivity, its preservation and its dissolution. The other two acts are those of concealment and revelation.

Karaṇeśvarī-s: They are such energies as would rule over the senses, and are known as *khecarī, gocarī, dikcarī,* and *bhūcarī.*

Karma-indriya-s: The five sense organs of action, which are speaking (*vāk*), handling (*hasta*), locomotion (*pada*), excretion (*pāyu*), and sexual action (*upasthā*).

Kārma-mala: In fact, it is Paramaśiva himself who is the actual creator of the world, but the limited individual, owing to the influence of false egoism, thinks that it is he who is the actual doer. It is this false sense of egoism that transforms itself into what is called the impurity of action (*kārma-mala*), and so makes the limited individual responsible for the actions he performs. It is, thus, an impurity or limitation that give rise to *karma*.

Karma-saṁskāra-s: The impression of past actions left in the mind. These impressions exist there in potential or latent form.

Karma-sāmya: The simultaneous ripening of two mutually antagonistic past deeds. Since possessing equal measure of power, they thereby so restrict each other as would result in the negation of their fruit.

Kārya: An effect that emerges upon the cause becoming operational.

Kaula: A *tāntrika* denomination that is left-oriented in terms of its practice. It makes the use of five prohibited ingredients, or what is called the five *makāra*-s, for the purpose of hastening the spiritual experience of I-consciousness, and the items that are made use of are meat, fish, wine, fried beans, and sexual intercourse.

Kevala: A being who exists in the state of total isolation. In the Sāṁkhya system such a state is equated with liberation (*jīvanmukti*).

Khecarī: This Energy is presided over by Vāmeśvarī Śakti in such a manner as would be related to the empirical subject (*pramātā*). It also means the one that moves in the vast expanse of space (*kha*).

Khecarī-cakra: Such group of energies as move in the space/void of consciousness of the empirical subject.

Khecarī-mudrā: It denotes the unlimited pervasion of bliss of consciousness. It is also known by such terms as, for example, divine seal/posture (*divya-mudrā*) and the state of Śiva (*śivāvasthā*).

Kleśa: It is a term that embodies such forms of affliction which, according to the yoga system of Patañjali, express themselves as ignorance (*avidyā*), egoism (*asmitā*), attachment (*rāga*), envy (*dveṣa*), and love for life (*abhiniveśa*).

Krama: It is such a graduated yogic practice in terms of which is realized the Self, which is identical with *āṇava-samāveśa*, viz., self-absorption obtained through *āṇava-upāya*.

Krama-mokṣa/mukti: The attainment of liberation through the purification of ideas (*vikalpa*-s). The internal purification is effected by climbing the spiritual ladder in stages.

Krama-mudrā: Such absorption as would alternate between the internal Self and the external world as a form of Śiva.

Krama-naya: A Śākta denomination that has been very popular among the Śaiva-s of Kashmir. It is also known as Mhārtha-naya.

Krīḍā: It is such divine play of the Lord as would result in the emergence and dissolution of the universe.

Kṛtrima: Such knowledge of reality as is dependent upon determinate ideas, which is to say that this kind of knowledge of reality is a constructed one, and so artificial and non-actual.

Kriyā-śakti: The functional power of the Absolute as God. It is one of the innate powers of the Lord. It is through this power that the phenomenal manifestation is effected in such a manner as would be perceived to be characterized by difference, which, in fact, is non-different from Śiva. This power of the Lord basically so shines in the category of Īśvara as would lead to its extroversion in terms of the emanation of Vidyā-tattva and what follows thereafter. It is such a power as would have the capacity of assuming any and every form (*sarvākārayogitam kriyā-śaktiḥ*).

Kula: It is a term mainly used by the Śākta-s, which signifies the transcendent light of consciousness as well as tendency of Śakti of manifesting herself in all the thirty-six categories.

Kulāmnaya: Such tradition of the Śākta-s that makes use of the entire Sanskrit letters from *a* to *kṣa* as a means of realizing the Self.

Kulācāra: It embodies the religious discipline of those *tāntrikas* who follow Kaulism.

Kuṇḍalinī: The atomized form of Energy that is said to be located at the base of the rectum. It lies there in a dormant state. When awakened, it moves upwards till it reaches the crown of the head. It is at this place where she merges in Śiva, and as a result of this merger a yogi not only experiences the plenitude of bliss, but obtains final soteric liberation.

Madhya: The central mystical vein, namely, *suṣumṇā*. It is through this vein that the latent Energy, when awakened, moves upwards. It also is equated to the I-consciousness.

Madhya-dhāma: The *suṣumṇā-nāḍī* known also as *brahma-nāḍī*

Madhyamā: In the process of disclosure of the Word it is the middling stage in which the manifestation of mental reflection of awareness (*vimarśa*), in the form of ideas, eventuates. It is the second stage of manifestation of the Word, which exists within the subtle body (*puryāṣṭaka*), and lies between the seeing stage (*paśyanti*) and the stage of spoken speech (*vaikharī*).

Mādhyamika: The followers of the Buddhist School of Philosophy known as Madhyamaka. Nāgārjuna established this famous school of philosophy. It is this school that propounded the doctrine of emptiness (*śūnyatā*).

Mahāmāyā: It is a plane that exists below Śuddhavidyā and above Māyā, and it is in this plane in which the Vijñānākala existents abide. Also it is a plane in which the existents, though having the vision of themselves in terms of pure consciousness, are completely bereft of the autonomy of action. It also denotes the lower plane of Śuddhavidyā, which is the abode of Vidyeśvara-s. Vidyeśvara-s are such beings who, though having the knowledge of themselves as being of the nature of pure consciousness, are still under the influence of a vision that is dualistic.

Mahānanda: The fifth plane of bliss that emerges when concentration is reposed upon the ascendant fire, viz., on *udāna* life-force. This bliss is experienced by following the *uccāra-yoga* of *āṇava-upāya*.

Mahānaya: The Krama Śākta school.

Mahāpralaya: The total dissolution of the manifest order, which is to say of entire objectivity.

Mahārtha: Such Śākta school as the Krama. The term also means the supreme end or value, which is but I-consciousness.

Mahāsattā: The Absolute Existence or Being.

Mahat: It is considered to be such a cognitive faculty as would be unlimited. In the Sāṁkhya philosophy *mahat*, as the first evolute, is the result of the transformation of *prakṛti*. In the Trika system it is Śrīkaṇṭhanātha who causes disturbance in the equilibrium of *guṇa*-s of *prakṛti* by pushing up, through *rajas*, the strand of *sattva*. As a result of this disturbance, there occurs dominance of *sattva* strand over *prakṛti*, which, through the process of transfomration and change, results in the emergence of *mahat*. However, *mahat* itself is transformed into *ahaṁkāra*, or ego.

Mahāvyāpti: It is such a yogic experience in terms of which is experienced great pervasion. As a result of this experience, there occurs such whirling sensation in the head as would mark a kind of intoxication.

Maheśvara: The absolute lordship of the Absolute or Paramaśiva.

Māheśvarya: The glory of powers of the Absolute, namely, of Maheśvara.

Māheśvaryādayaḥ: Māheśvarī and other energies presiding over the group of letters.

Makāra: The five substances that begin with the letter *m*, which are used in a secret ritual by the left-hand *tāntrika*-s, and the substances are meat (*māṁsa*), fish (*matsya*), wine (*madirā*), sexual intercourse (*maithuna*), and fried beans (*mudrā*).

Mala: Inherited and adventitious impurities that conceal the divine nature of the Self by veiling it.

Mala-trayam: The three impurities known in the Trika as the impurity of limitation (*āṇava-mala*), the impurity of difference (*māyīya-mala*) and the impurity of action (*kārma-mala*).

Mālinī: Such energy of letters as would contain within itself the entire universe—a universe in which Sanskrit letters are arranged in an irregular manner from *na* to *pha*.

Mālinī-yoga: It is a yogic practice which is made use of in the *śāmbhava-upāya* in terms of visualizing the glow of innate powers in the form randomly arranged letters of Sanskrit alphabet beginning with *na* and ending with *pha*.

Manas: The psychosomatic organ called mind. In the Trika it is considered such a mental apparatus as would coordinate the functioning of the senses as well as the gathering of images and perceptions. It also is seen as the source of mental concepts.

Manthāna-bhairava: Such Bhairava who, through the process of churning, dissolves entire objectivity into I-consciousness.

Mantra: Such Sanskrit letters that are supposed to possess the power of supernal reflection as well as the power of protecting one from the danger of falling into the ocean of transmigratory existence. A *mantra* may be said to be a non-conceptual word-image, which is used as a means of gaining perfection through the process of meditation. Also the five *mantra*-s known as Īśāna, Tatpuruṣa, Sadyojāṭa, Vāmadeva, and Aghora constitute the five aspects of Śiva. A *mantra* is also such a being who, though having realized the category Śuddhavidyā, is not yet totally free from the yoke of *māyā*.

Mantramaheśvara-s: Such existents of Sadāśiva category in whom the vision of dualism, though of dim quality, has not completely vanished. Even then it is the vision of non-dualism that is pervasive among these existents. Thus the Self-awareness of the existents is characterized by the vision of "I am this" (*ahaṃ-idaṃ*).

Mantra-prāṇi: Such existents who, though devoid of erroneous concepts, still persists in looking at the world through the spectacles of dualism, because of being under the influence of *māyā*.

Mantra-vīrya: It denotes the energy of the *mantra* of I-consciousness, and so accordingly embodies the consciousness of Śiva and also of *parā-vāk*.

Mantreśvara-s: The existents that pertain to the category of Īśvara. It is such a category in which difference-cum-non-difference is predominant. The subjects of this category may have risen above the shadow of objectivity, yet their vision is as much focussed on non-dualism as it is on dualism. So their vision, thus, is characterized by the "this-ness" in terms of the statement: "This is myself."

Marici: Śakti.

Mātṛkā: Such words and letters that are seen as the source of knowledge, and so is equated with the power of Supreme Speech (*parā-vāk*) that causes the world to be.

Mātṛkā-cakra: Such group of energies that pertain to *mātṛkā*.

Mātṛkā-yoga: A yogic practice that pertains to *śāmbhava-upāya*. It is a meditative practice in terms of which one's divine powers are intuited through the medium of Sanskrit alphabet, which includes the sixteen vowels and consonants from *ka* to *kṣa*.

Māyā: In the Advaita Vedānta *māyā* is considered to be a beginningless cause of a world that is ontologically false. Although the cause of a world may be false, it itself however is considered to be false, because it can be negated through proper knowledge. As an adjunct of *brahman*, it is seen to be responsible in transforming *brahman* into Īśvara, who is seen to be a false product of a false cause. In the Trika system it is considered as the sixth *tattva* (category) in a descending order. Sometimes it is considered as constituting the sixth limiting factor (*kañcuka*). As a category, it is said to be impure, and so is the abode of all Sakala beings. Finally, it is seen such a deluding power through which an individual being forgets his essential nature, and as a result of which differentiates himself from other subjects as well as from objectivity.

Māyā-mala: A limited being who under the influence of *māyā* differentiates between the subject and the object, between one subject and the other subject, and between one object and the other.

Māyā-pramātā: The empirical individual who functions, and thereby carries out his activities, under the influence of *māyā*.

Māyā-śakti: Such vibratory energy of the highest Lord due to which is experienced difference within what essentially is non-different, and so also the source of *māyā-tattva*.

Māyā-tattva: It is on account of this category that the essential nature of consciousness is veiled—and due to this veiling of consciousness the limited individual identifies himself with such inert substances of the body, life-force, etc. The first category that is seen as the material cause of insentient objectivity, and so the source of five limiting factors (*kañcuka*-s).

Māyīya-aṇḍa: The sphere that contains within itself the five limiting factors (*kañcuka*-s), *puruṣa* and *prakṛti*. It is considered to be the exterior, but finer, covering of the Self.

Māyīya-mala: It is the impurity of *māyā*, and so operates in terms of differentiation.

Meya: Object.

Moha: Such delusion as would result in the identification of the Self with the body. It is because of this reason that it is seen to be a form of *māyā*.

Mokṣa: Liberation from bondage.

Mudrā: It is composed of *mud* (joy) and *ra* (to give). It means that *mudrā* is such a means as would bestow joy of the bliss of spiritual I-consciousness. It is so because it has the power of sealing up the universe in the being of *turya*-consciousness. It also denotes certain yogic postures of the body that are helpful in stabilizing concentration.

Mukta-śiva: The existents of the Akala planes, namely, Vidyeśvara/Mantra, Mantreśvara, and Mantramaheśvara.

Mukti: It is such liberation from the fetters of becoming in terms of which is recognized one's essential nature as being non-different from Paramaśiva. It is realized only upon abandoning the physical or divine body—and that is why it is called disembodied liberation (*videha-mukti*).

Mūla-prakṛti: It is considered as being such a root-substance that serves as the substratum of all instrumental and objective elements. It also serves as the basis for holding together the three *guṇa*-s in the state of equilibrium.

Nāda: It is the first flutter within the supreme consciousness (*parāsaṁvit*) towards the external manifestation, which takes the form of sound (*nāda*) and consequently evolves itself into the dot (*bindu*). Also sound as awareness is seen to be the source of names of sound. In the language of yoga, it denotes that primal unstruck sound (*anāhata*) that is experienced in the mystical vein called *suṣumṇā*.

Nibhālana: Perception as well as mental activity.

Nidrā: It is a mystical state that is experienced by the practitioners of *uccāra-yoga* of *āṇava-upāya*. It is such an experience in which a kind of drowsiness seizes the individual.

Nigraha-kṛtya: An act of concealment whereby the Lord hides his essential nature. It also denotes divine wrath.

Nijānanda: The first plane of bliss that is experienced when the adept, while making his existence as a support for meditation, focuses his attention on the principle of animation. This practice of meditation pertains to *uccāra-yoga* of *āṇava-upāya*.

Nimeṣa: It is such an inward movement of pulsation in terms of which is dissolved objectivity into subjectivity. It signifies the closing of the eyes of Śiva, which corresponds to the dissolution of the world, and thereby explains the act of involution of Śiva in matter.

Nimīlana-samādhi: It is such an inward form of meditation in which the individual consciousness gets totally dissolved into the universal consciousness.

Nirānanda: It is the second plane of bliss that emerges when the life-force is reposed in the void.

Nirbīja-samādhi: The highest yogic state that is attained by the followers of the yoga of Patañjali. It is such an indeterminate state in which is experienced complete absence of thought. However, the Trika considers it to be nothing more than the void that is experienced in *suṣupti*.

Nirvāṇa: The state of the void. For the Buddhists it is identical with liberation. The Trika considers it to be such state that is not different from deep sleep (*suṣupti*), and so equates it with such state that eventuates for the Pralayākala existents.

Nirvikalpa: Such indeterminate state of the mind in which supernal knowledge is obtained in the absence of thoughts. Thus a yogin is said to have the understanding of the perceptions that arise at the *paśyanti* level. It is, thus, such state as would be completely free from thought-constructs.

Nirvyutthāna-samādhi: Such state of inward absorption as would continue even when not engaged in any kind of meditation.

Nivṛtti: It is said to be one of the five *kalā*-s—and a *kalā* is considered to be the finest aspect of space as interpreted within the theory of six paths of meditation on external objects (*ṣaḍadhvan*). The *nivṛtti-kalā* contains within itself the solid earth, whereas the other *kalā*-s are the *pratiṣṭhā-kalā, vidyā-kalā, śānti-kalā,* and the *śāntyātīta-kalā.*

Niyama: It is a yogic discipline, which consists of five observances, namely, purity, tranquillity, austerity, study, and worship of God.

Niyati-śakti: Such divine power of the Lord in terms of which is experienced restriction with regard to cause-effect, knowledge and action. It is one of the veiling factors (*kañcuka*) among the five veiling factors. It is, thus, within the bounds of this law of limitation that the limited beings perform their deeds, which are either good or bad.

Niyati-tattva: Such restrictive power of Nature which is responsible in contracting or limiting the power of knowledge as well as of action of the subject. It basically serves as the source of phenomenal causation, and so accordingly brings into its own ambit of restriction the processes of knowing and doing of a phenomenal subject.

Nyāya-Vaiśeṣika: Both these schools of philosophy have developed a kind of realistic materialism in terms of which is upheld the existence of objectivity as being independent of consciousness.

Pada: A conceptual word-image. It is seen as being the embodiment of gross form of time, which is one of the six objects of meditation (*ṣaḍadhvan*) in the *sthāna-kalpanā* of *āṇava-upāya*.

Pañca-kāraṇe: Brahmā, Viṣṇu, Rudra, Īśvara, and Sadāśiva.

Pañca-kṛtya: The five acts of the Lord, which are creation (*sṛṣṭi*), preservation (*sthiti*), dissolution (*saṁhāra*), concealment (*pidhāna*), and revelation (*anugraha*).

Pañca-mantra: The five mantric forms of Śiva are Īśāna, Tatpuruṣa, Sadyojāṭa, Vāmadeva, and Aghora.

Pañca-śakti: The five energies or powers of Śiva, namely, consciousness (*cit*), bliss (*ānanda*), will (*icchā*), knowledge (*jñāna*), and action (*kriyā*).

Pañca-vaktra: The five symbolic faces of Paramaśiva, which are Īśāna, Tatpuruṣa, Sadyojāṭa, Vāmadeva, and Aghora.

Para: The Absolute.

Para-brahman: The philosophic absolute who as a theistic God has its basic nature as Godhead. The nature of the Absolute is said to be pure consciousness, and as God engages himself in the process of Becoming and in terms of which is emanated the objective universe. It is as God that the

Absolute tends to engage in the five divine activities of emanation, preservation, dissolution, etc.

Parama-advaita: It is a philosophical view that considers all the pair of opposites as being identical. Thus difference and non-difference, sentience and insentience, freedom and bondage, are seen to be synonymous.

Parāmarśa: It denotes as much mental apprehension as much as an experience.

Paramārtha: The supernal reality as actual truth and value, which is but God himself.

Paramārtha-satya: The absolute truth or value.

Paramaśiva: Such transcendent reality who, through its own innate energy, brings about both emanation and dissolution of all the thirty-five categories. This activity of emanation and dissolution of categories in no manner effect his essential nature, which consists of the fulness of pure consciousness.

Parameśvara: The highest Lord whose powers are so expansive and unbounded as would never suffer from depletion. It is because of his sweet will that Īśvara and Sadāśiva enjoy their lordly powers.

Parānanda: The third plane of bliss that is experienced by reposing consciousness in inhalation (*prāṇa*) and exhalation (*apāna*). This form of meditation pertains to *uccāra-yoga*.

Parāpara: It denotes an intermediate state in which are equally balanced both difference and non-difference, diversity and unity.

Para-pramātṛ: The supreme experient, which is but Paramaśiva himself.

Para-śakti: The supreme Energy of Paramaśiva, which is spoken of as *citi*.

Para-tattva: The Absolute or Paramaśiva.

Para-vāk: It explains such divine pulsation in the mind of the Absolute as would result in the external manifestation of objectivity. As pulsation, it is identical with the divine Logos.

Parasaṁvit: It signifies transcendental consciousness, and is made use of in equal measure both by the Trika Śaivites and the Śāktas. It also is known as *kālātīta* on account of it being identical with the spiritual stir of divine essence, which is nothing but Godhead, and so transcends *kāla*.

Pariṇāma: The transformation of the existing state of an object into another state, as, for example, milk transforming itself into curd. In this kind of transformation the transformed object cannot revert back to its original condition. The other kind of transformation is such in which the transformed object can revert back to its original condition, as, for example, in the case of gold and the ornaments that are made of gold.

Pāśa-s: The fetters of bondage.

Paśu: A bound being, viz., an existent enveloped by ignorance, and thereby by afflictions and in terms of which he is made to reap the fruit of his deeds done in the past lives. Such an individual, while under the influence of *māyā*, differentiates himself from other subjects as well as from the objective world out there.

Paśu-mātaraḥ: It signifies such divine energies as, for example, Māheśvarī. These energies are seen to be present in all the Sanskrit letters as well as are said to be controlling the life of an empirical subject.

Paśyanti: It is such Energy of Speech (*vāk-śakti*) as would go forth in terms of seeing, and so ready to give rise to manifestation, while in itself not having any kind of difference between the object (*vācya*) and the word (*vācaka*).

Pati: Such embodied beings who think of the world as being non-different from themselves. Such an experient or subject is said to belong to the category of Śuddhavidyā, and so is considered to be liberated. Pati also denotes the supreme Lord in relation to the bound being and his bondage.

Pauruṣa-ajñāna: The firm conviction of the individual existent concerning himself as being nothing else than a finite creature.

Pauruṣa-jñāna: When through the grace of guru the sense of limitation is eliminated, there emerges the cognition in terms of which is experienced identity with Paramaśiva.

Pidhāna-kṛtya: That display of the lordly power of the highest Lord due to which the limited individual forgets his essential nature.

Prajñā: It denotes the state of dreamless sleep (*suṣupti*).

Prakāśa: The Absolute as the light of consciousness is the basis for a sentient being to have the experience of his own glory as being a conscious subject. It is through the light of consciousness that all phenomenal entities become manifest. As light of consciousness, the Absolute also is cognitive awareness (*vimarśa*).

Prākṛta-aṇḍa: It is a sphere that consists of the root-element (*mūla-prakṛti*) as well as of its finer evolutes. It consists of elements from *mūla-prakṛti* to water.

Prakṛti: The basic nature of an object.

Prakṛti-tattva: The source of thirteen senses as well as of ten objective elements, viz., from *buddhi* down to earth. It also denote the state of equilibrium of three *guṇa*-s, viz., of *sattva, rajas,* and *tamas.*

Pralaya: Such state of dissolution (*saṁhāra*) in which the entire objectivity merges into what is called Māyā. It also denotes such state in which the manifest order up to Sadāśiva category is dissolved into Śakti, and Śakti itself merges into Śiva.

Pralayākala: The tranquil state of such existents who repose either in the void, or in the life-force, or in the pure intellect. They, as it were, are the creatures of deep sleep. While in *suṣupti,* they are affected only by *āṇava-mala,* and the other two impurities begin to effect them only when they come into the waking state. It is Śrīkaṇṭhanātha who awakens these beings from deep sleep at the time when he disturbs the equilibritun of *guṇa*-s of *prakṛti,* thereby initiating the process of evolution of the categories of existence.

Pramā: Knowledge that is exact and actual.

Pramāṇa: Such cognition that would authenticate the actual nature of an object.

Pramātā/Pramātṛ: The experiencing subject.

Prameya: The object that is known through appropriate means of knowledge.

Pramiti: Knowledge that is accurate.

Prāṇa: The life-force or the principle of animation, which is said to be of five kinds: *prāṇa, apāna, samāna, udāna,* and *vyāna.* It also denotes the breath that comes into the body from outside.

Prāṇa-bīja: In esoteric terms it signifies the letter *ha.*

Prāṇa-pramātā: The limited subject who thinks *prāṇa* to be identical with the Self.

Prāṇāyāma: A yogic exercise that consists in controlling the rhythm of incoming and outgoing breaths. It is the fourth limb in the eight-limbed yoga of Patañjali.

Prasāda: It signifies the *mantra sauḥ.*

Prasāra: It is such expansion of Śiva through his Energy that terminates in the manifestation of objective universe.

Pratha: To unfold, expand, shine or appear.

Pratibhā: It signifies the creative and spontaneous activity of I-consciousness. At the level of yogic praxis, it denotes such knowledge that is intuitive in character.

Pratibimba-nyāya: The point of view that establishes the manner of appearance of a reflection.

Pratibimba-vāda: It is a philosophical theory that establishes that the objective universe is nothing but the reflection of the powers of the Absolute as God, and this manifestation of the universe as reflection is the result of divine play.

Pratimīlana: It denotes both forms of indeterminate absorption, viz., the inward (*nimīlana-samādhi*) and the outward (*unmīlana-samādhi*) absorption.

Pratiṣṭha-kalā: One of the five *kalā*-s, and a *kalā* is but the finer aspect of a *tattva* as understood in the context of the theory of six paths of meditation (*ṣaḍadhvan*). This *kalā* contains the essence of all the categories from water to *prakṛti.*

Pratyabhijñā: Recognition of oneself in reverse order, which is to say of recognizing oneself as being identical with Paramaśiva. The essential principles of this school of philosophy were laid down by Somānanda in his *Śivadṛṣṭi*, which were further elaborated by his disciple, namely, Utpaladeva, in his seminal treatise called *Īśvarapratyabhijñā-kārikā*. It was, however, Abhinavagupta who, in his two commentaries, *vivṛtti-vimarśinī*, and *vimarśinī* on the treatise of Utpaladeva gave the final shape to this philosophy in such a manner as would attain the universal character.

Pratyāhāra: The fifth limb in the eight-limbed Yoga of Patañjali. The Trika does not consider it, along with *yama, niyama, āsana, prāṇāyāma,* as a direct means of Self-realization. It is a method that attempts to control the senses in such a manner as would not allow them to have any kind of contact with the external world.

Pratyavimarśa: Such reflection about oneself as would be opposite to the view one has of oneself and so denoting self-recognition.

Puṁs-tattva: The category of Puruṣa. The Sakala existent or the bound being.

Puruṣa: The self-monad of the Sāṁkhya, whereas in the Trika it is said to be the soul that is under the influence of *māyā*.

Puruṣa-tattva: The Trika Śaivism considers it to be the twelfth category of manifestation, whereas in the Sāṁkhya system it is the first category.

Puryāṣṭaka: It is the subtle body, called the city of the group of eight, which consists of the five subtle elements of external senses (*tanmātra*-s: smell, taste, colour, touch, and sound), the intellect (*buddhi*), the mind (*manas*), and the ego (*ahaṁkāra*).

Putraka-dīkṣā: It is such initiation in terms of which the initiated disciple becomes the son of his teacher (*guru*). It is through this initiation that the disciple is so empowered as to have the attainment of both the worldly enjoyment (*bhukti*) as well as liberation (*mukti*).

Rāga: Such form of attachment that accords great importance to one's body as well to the objects that are considered to be suitable. There always lurks the fear of loss of objects to which one is attached. Since much importance is accorded to the object of attachment, so this very object limits the range of action and knowledge of the subject.

Rajas: One of the three *guṇa*-s, which is a constituent of *prakṛti*. Being of the nature of passion, so it is considered to be the principle of activity, motion and disharmony.

Rāja-yoga: It is such a yogic practice in which austerities of any kind are not involved. The practice consists in focussing the mind on the Self in such a manner as would result in the natural cessation of inhalation and exhalation. This cessation of breathing results in the entrance of *udāna* into the mystical vein called *suṣumṇā*, and thereby allowing the Energy to go upwards till it reaches the centre called *brahma-randhra* at the top of the head. Consequently, there eventuates the experience of the Self as being unlimited and of the nature of pure consciousness.

Raudrī: Such divine energies of the highest Lord that provide the means of pleasure to the worldly beings. They are also responsible in keeping these beings in the state of bondage.

Ravi: In the language of esotericism the sun is the symbol both of life-force (*prāṇa*) and knowledge (*pramāṇa*).

Rudra: They are such Lords who bring about the dissolution of objective categories from earth up to the limiting factors (*kañcuka-tattva*-s). These Rudra-s also rule over these objective categories. The supernal being that resides at the base of the earth category, namely, *Nivṛtti-kalā*, is also called Rudra. He also causes the destruction of such realms as are known *bhū*, *bhuvaḥ*, and *svaḥ*.

Rudra-āgama: The eighteen Śaivite canonical texts that contain the viewpoint of difference-cum-non-difference.

Rudra-pramātā: The liberated Śiva-s or what is called *mukta-śiva*-s.

Śabda: Word or sound.

Śabda-brahman: God as sound. It also signifies the vibratory nature of self-cognizant consciousness. In the philosophical system of Bhartṛhari the Absolute is identified with the Word, and so is known as *śabda-brahman*. The Absolute as pulsating consciousness is such as would express perfect identity between the word and thought.

Śabda-rāśi: The multitude of Sanskrit letters from *a* to *kṣa*.

Ṣaḍadhva: The six paths of manifestation. The three paths consist of *varaṇa, mantra,* and *pada,* and embody the internal or temporal aspect of manifestation. The other three paths are those of *kalā, tattva,* and *bhuvana,* and represent the external or spatial aspect of manifestation.

Sadāśiva: The third category of the path of pure manifestation.

Sadāśiva-bhaṭṭāraka: The ruler over the Sadāśiva category as well as the object of worship therein.

Sadāśiva-tattva: The category in which the existents, who are of the nature of pure consciousness, have an unclear inclination towards objectivity. It means that in this category it is I-ness that is predominant while there is at the same time a faint awareness of this-ness also. It is the Mantra-maheśvara subject that has its abode in this category, while the ruler of the category is Sadāśiva.

Sādhanā: Spiritual practice.

Sadvidyā: The category of Śuddhavidyā. It is the fifth category of pure objective manifestation. While the experience of the subject of this category is characterized by "I am this," the "I" and "this" at the same time are held evenly, which is to say that the experience of subjectivity and of objectivity is of equal measure.

Sadyojāṭa: Śiva is said to be having five *mantric* forms, and Sadyojāṭa is his third form.

Sahaja: The essential nature.

Sahaja-vidyā: It is such knowledge of the essential nature as is characterized by the purity of consciousness, which means that there is complete cessation of mental constructs.

Sahasrāra: The seventh wheel of Energy located at the top of the head. It is often depicted as consisting of thousand lotus petals. As the abode of Śiva, it is characterized by transcendence, and so is not technically counted as being one of the wheels. When the awakened Energy reaches this transcendent abode, it merges in Śiva, which results in the experience of liberation for the yogi.

*Śaiva-āgama-*s: The canonical texts of Śaivism, which consists of ten dualistic, eighteen mono-dualistic, and sixty-four non-dualistic scriptures.

Sakala: Such a bound being in whom all the three impurities of *āṇava,* of *māyīyạ,* and of *kārma* operate, and due to which he remains in the grip of the cycle of births and deaths. And such bound beings are said to be from gods down to the tiniest of worms.

Sākṣād-upāya: The method of Śiva, viz., *śāmbhava-upāya.*

Sākṣātkāra: The initial indeterminate knowledge of the object that occurs through the senses. Also such direct knowledge concerning the Self that emerges by itself and without depending upon the senses or on the inner organs.

Śākta-pramātā: An Akala existent that abides in the category of Śakti.

Śākta-samāveśa: Mystical absorption attained through the practice of *śākta-yoga,* which consists in the contemplation of such ideas that are pure. It is through this absorption that one realizes one's divine essence.

Śākta-upāya: Such uninterrupted contemplation that is directed towards ideas that are pure and in terms of which one's own-being is seen as being essentially Śiva or I-consciousness.

Śakti: Capability or capacity of doing or knowing anything. The glorious or lordly powers of the supreme Lord and in terms of which both the emanation and dissolution of the universe is actualized. It also denotes the vibratory nature (*spandātmaktā*) of Paramaśiva, which is to say of I-consciousness. In this manner is, thus, explained immanent aspect of the Absolute.

Śakti-bhūmikā: The first two pure categories of Śiva and Śakti, which are completely free from the notion of dualism.

Śakti-cakra: The group of twelve Goddesses, namely, of twelve Kālī-s, which are said to be responsible in causing both emanation and dissolution of the objective manifest order. It also denotes such group of energies as those of the senses, of *mantra*-s, as well as energies known as *khecarī, bhūcarī, dikcarī,* etc.

Śakti-daśā: The state of the Absolute in term of which are held together the two pure categories of Śiva and Śakti.

Śaktimān: Maheśvara or Paramaśiva.

Śakti-pañcaka: The five innate energies of the Lord, namely, consciousness (*cit*), bliss (*ānanda*), will (*icchā*), knowledge (*jñāna*), and action (*kriyā*).

Śakti-tattva: The nature of Paramaśiva as being characterized by awareness, and so explains the mystery of the disclosure of his intentness towards objectivity. Thus it is the plane in terms of which is unfolded the blossoming of the power of will (*icchā-śakti*). It also denotes the second category among the thirty-six categories, which constitute both the pure and impure orders of manifestation.

Śaktipāta: Such descent of divine grace of the Lord in terms of which an individual turns towards the path of liberation. According to Abhinavagupta, the descent of grace is of three types, namely, immediate (*tīvra*), moderate (*madhya*), and slow (*manda*). These three types of grace have further been subdivided into nine types, which are *tīvra-tīvra, madhya-tīvra, manda-tīvra, tīvra-madhya, madhya-madhya, manda-tīvra, tīvṛa-manda, madhya-manda,* and *manda-manda.*

Sālokya: The attainment of the abode of one's *iṣṭadeva*, viz., of one's chosen deity.

Samādhi: It is such a state which is characterized by complete introversion of consciousness and in terms of which the whirls of the mind are stilled. It is at this plane of tranquil mind that there eventuates such experience in terms of which disappearance of distinction between the subject and the object is effected. There are many types of *samādhi,* and some of them are the *savikalpa-samādhi, nirvikalpa-samādhi,* and *nirbīja-samādhi.* In the Trika *samādhi* is seen as representing an excellent type of deep sleep (*suṣupti*).

Samanā: It is such power in terms of which mentation concerning phenomena are begun. It is so spoken of when the *unmanā-śakti* expresses herself in the form of the universe starting with Śiva and ending with earth.

Samāna: It is upon the unification of *prāṇa* and *apāna* that the equalizing breath (*samāna*) emerges. The function of this principle of animation is to assimilate what is taken in, namely, food, etc.

Samāpatti: It denotes the state of *samādhi,* which can be either determinate or indeterminate.

Samāveśa: Such a meditative practice of absorption in terms of which is experienced the shining nature of consciousness, and accordingly all objectivity, including one's body, is so dissolved as would result in the perfect experience of identity between objectivity and subjectivity.

Samaya-ācāra: Such religious discipline of the Vedāntins as would adhere strictly to the prohibitions and injunctions of the scriptures, and accordingly is effected appropriate differentiation between purity and impurity.

Śāmbhava-pramātā: An Akala existent that has its abode in the category of Śiva.

Śāmbhava-samāveśa: It is such immersion in Śiva or I-consciousness that is sudden and in terms of which is realized that one's being is non-distinct from Paramaśiva.

Śāmbhava-upāya: It is such a method of absorption in which occurs spontaneously the emergence of Śiva-consciousness without the support of thought-constructs. It is an emergence that occurs merely by indicating that oneself is not essentially different from Paramaśiva. This method of absorption is also known by such names as *śāmbhava-yoga, icchā-upāya,* or *icchā-yoga.*

Saṁghaṭṭa: It is union that is realized at the mental level through the process of concentration.

Saṁhāra-kṛtya: The dissolution of objectivity into its basic cause, which is but Śiva.

Samrasa: The state of identical feeling or consciousness.

Sāmrasya: Such unification of diverse objects as is found of the colourful plumage in the yolk of a peacock's egg.

Saṁsāra/Samsṛti: The world that is continuously in the process of becoming, and so implies an existence that undergoes unending births and deaths.

Saṁsārin: A being that is subject to cycle of births and deaths.

Saṁvedana: Such knowledge that has its origin in the senses and in the inner organs.

Saṁvedya-suṣupti: The state of deep sleep in which is experienced dimly both pain and pleasure, lightness and heaviness, etc.

Saṁvit/Saṁvid: The supreme consciousness as the embodiment of identity of *prakāśa* and *vimarśa,* thereby explaining the powers of knowledge (*jñāna-śakti*) and of autonomy (*svātantrya-śakti*) of the Absolute.

Saṁvit-devatā: The deities or energies which, when viewed from the macrocosmic point, are known as *khecarī, dikcarī, gocarī, bhūcarī,* and when viewed from a microcosmic point are referred to as being the internal and external senses.

Ṣāṇḍha-bīja: The four Sanskrit letters—*ṛ, ṝ, ḷ, ḹ*—are said to be so devoid of power as to be unable to give rise to any other letter.

Sandhi: Such union between the individual self and the Cosmic Self as is brought about by the practice of intense awareness. As such it denotes a process whereby is brought union between the two.

Śāntakalā: One of the five *kalā*-s in which are contained the four pure categories, viz., Śuddhavidyā, Īśvara, Sadāśiva, and Śakti.

Śāntyātīta: The fifth *kalā* which is considered to be the finest aspect of space particularly in the context of the doctrine of six paths of meditation (*ṣaḍadhvan*). In this *kalā* is contained the category of Śiva.

Sarvajñatva: Omniscience.

Ṣaṣṭha-vaktra: The sixth organ, namely, *medhra-kendra*, which is situated at the base of the rectum.

Sat: Being or Existence which, along with consciousness (*cit*) and bliss (*ānanda*), express the essential nature of the Absolute, viz., of *brahman*.

Satkārya-vāda: The Sāṁkhya causal doctrine that maintains identity between cause and effect, which is to say that the effect, prior to its actualization, exists potentially in the cause. The doctrine is so explained as would maintain that the entire objectivity exists potentially within what is called *mūla-prakṛti*. This potentiality manifests itself as the world in terms of transformation or change, as in the case of milk becoming curd or gold transformed into ornaments. In the case of curd, there is no possibility for it to revert to its primal condition, namely, to that of milk. In the case of ornaments, however, they can be brought back to their original condition. The Trika, while adhering broadly to this view of causality, maintains that this entire objectivity, called the universe, exists always within Paramaśiva as consciousness. The emanation of the universe occurs through the autonomous will of the Lord—and the process of emanation eventuates in the manner a reflection is reflected in the mirror. The theory of reflection is resorted to for the purpose of saving the integrity and indivisibility of Paramaśive as consciousness.

Sattarka: Such supernal logic as would explain the divine mystery—and Abhinavagupta has made use of this form of logic copiously. It is logic based on the supernal vision of the yogin concerning the nature of the Absolute. At its highest point it is called *bhāvanā*, and as *bhāvanā* it tears off the veils of ignorance, thereby allowing the light of Paramaśive to penetrate the heart and in terms of which is grasped that which appears to be objective is basically but one's own subjectivity.

Sattva: It denotes the principle of harmony, of being, and of purity, and also is one of the constituents of *prakṛti*.

Saugāta: The followers of Buddha.

Savikalpa-jñāna: Such conceptual knowledge of the object that is dependent upon name-and-form, and is obtained through *manas*.

Sārūpya: Such spiritual state of the aspirant in which he attains similar form as is of his chosen deity (*iṣṭadeva*).

Sāyuja: Such spiritual state in which the aspirant experiences partial identity with Paramaśiva. It is a state of difference-cum-non-difference.

Siddha: A perfect being.

Siddhi: Supernatural powers.

Śiva: It is a term that denotes that which is gocd and auspicious. In the Trika it signifies the ultimate reality as being of the nature of light (*prakāśa*).

Śiva-pramātā: Such an Akala existent in whom luminous aspect is predominant.

Śiva-tattva: That aspect of the nature of the supreme Lord in which light is dominant. It also represents the seed of the entire objectivity. Such transcendent category that has the capacity of unfolding objectivity. It is the first category among the thirty-six categories.

Soma: The moon. It is the symbol for the object (*prameya*) as well as for the breath that is exhaled (*apāna*).

Soma-nāḍī: It stands for the vein called *piṅgalā* and this vein carries the breath called *apāna*.

Spanda: It is such pulsation or vibration that is neither physical nor mental. It is, rather, spiritual activity of consciousness which pulsates simultaneously both inwardly and outwardly. It is within the framework of this view of consciousness that the Trika upholds the view that the Absolute, although tranquil and luminous, is not so inactive or indeterminate as is the *brahman* of Advaita Vedānta. It thinks that the Absolute always pulsates both inwardly and outwardly in terms of subjective and objective awareness as I-ness and This-ness. Thus the so-called outward manifestation of the world is but the blissful activity of *spanda,* which is the nature of the Lord. It would be erroneous to speak of *spanda* as being identical with Śakti. It is not so. Rather *spanda* is the manifestation of Śakti. Accordingly it is seen to be the stir of the power of bliss (*ānanda-śakti*) of the supreme Lord. In short, *spanda* is such throb in the motionless Śiva as would bring about the manifestation, maintenance and withdrawal of the universe. It is, thus, identified with the absolute and unimpeded freedom of the Absolute.

Sphurattā: Such intrinsic and shimmering freedom of the Lord through which is experienced the process of emanation, dissolution, etc., of objectivity.

Sṛṣṭi-kṛtya: Such an act of the Lord in terms of which the manifestation of diverse objectivity is emanated in the manner of reflection in a mirror.

Sthāna-kalpanā: The meditative practice of *āṇava-upāya* in which external objects are made supports of meditation, which at the same time is accompanied by meditation on the nature of Godhead. The objects of meditation that pertain to space and time are either fine, subtle or gross. The three objects of space and the three of time constitute what is known as the six pathways of meditation (*ṣaḍadhvan*). The three entities of space are *kalā, tattva,* and *bhuvana,* which are respectively fine, subtle, and gross. Insofar as the objects of time are concerned, they are *varṇa, mantra,* and *pada,* are respectively fine, subtle and gross.

Sthiti: It is such divine activity of God in terms of which the phenomenal world is sustained and preserved.

Sthūla-bhūta: Such gross elements as, for example, ether, air, fire, water, and earth.

Sthūla-śarīra: The gross physical body.

Śuddha-adhva: The pure path of supersensuous emanation from the category of Śiva to that of Śuddhavidyā.

Śuddha-tattva: Such pure categories that extend from Śuddhavidyā/Mahāmāyā to Śiva.

Śuddha-vidyā: The non-erroneous knowledge of Vidyeśvara-s, which also is known as Mahāmāyā. Also it denotes such vision of Mantreśvara-s and of Mantramaheśvara-s that is characterized both by difference and non-difference.

Śuddha-vikalpa: Such conceptual knowledge concerning oneself and the world that is definitive and determinate.

Sugata: The Buddha.

Sūkṣma-śarīra: The subtle body known as *puryāṣṭaka*, or a city with a group of eight.

Śūnya: The concept of emptiness was, for the first time, introduced by Nāgārjuna into the domain of Indian metaphysical thinking. Resorting to the middle path doctrine in terms of dependent origination of phenomena, Nāgārjuna arrived at the conclusion that things and objects arise dependently, and so they are accordingly devoid of intrinsic nature (*svabhāva*). It means that the phenomena, being devoid of nature, are simply empty. At the same time the Absolute, being indeterminate and devoid of attributes, cannot be spoken as this or that. It meant that the term that can best describe the Absolute is but emptiness. Since both the Absolute and phenomena are emptiness, so they are identical. It also denotes such state in which there is total absence of the knower, knowledge, and the object of knowledge, which, according to the Trika, signifies the state of absence.

Śūnya-pramātā: Such non-conscious state of deep sleep in which the sense of I-ness persists, and thereby denotes such an experient who considers it to be his nature. The Buddhists consider it to be a state of pure luminosity, and accordingly is said to be devoid of the subject, the means of knowledge, and the object. In the Trika it signifies the limited individual. It also denotes the category of Puruṣa. Moreover, it represents such state of the contracted "I" that is transcendent to the body.

Śūnya-suṣupti: The state of non-conscious sleep.

Suprabuddha: The fully awakened yogi, which is to say that the yogi is completely aware of the transcendental consciousness, and being aware, it is always present in him.

Sūrya: The sun that is considered as the symbol of life-force (*prāṇa*), knowledge (*pramāṇa*), and the power of knowledge (*jñāna-śakti*).

Suṣupti: Such state of deep sleep in which is experienced continuously the absence of objectivity, which is to say that the mind is so stilled as would allow the apparent cessation of the functioning of *prāṇa* and *apāna* to take place, and consequently there occurs the emergence of *samāna*, viz., of equalizing breath, which is a state of renewal. Also it denotes the incipient experience of objectivity at the subtlest level of consciousness. Finally, it signifies deep sleep devoid of dreams. According to the Trika, *suṣupti* is of two kinds, namely, the *savedya-suṣupti* and the *apavedya-suṣupti*. The former state is said to be of the same type as is the state of *apavarga* of Nyāya-Vaiśeṣika and the *kaivalya* of the Sāṁkhya–Yoga. Insofar as the latter type of *suṣupti* is concerned, it is said to be identical with the *nirvāṇa* of Vijñānavāda and of Śūnyavāda schools of Buddhism.

Svacchandanātha: One of the five-faced special forms of Lord Śiva. Svacchandanātha as the five-faced deity represents the five innate powers of the Lord, which are consciousness, bliss, will, knowledge, and action. These five faces of Svacchandanātha also represent the five deities that have *mantric* bodies, and they are Īśāna, Tatpuruṣa, Sadyojāṭa, Vāmadeva, and Aghora. Svacchandanātha is said to be the disciple of Śrīkaṇṭhanātha. Finally, Svacchanda denotes absolute freedom, which is of the nature of Śiva.

Svalakṣaṇa: The basic nature of an object, which is not related to anything, which is to say that an object is always limited by its particularity due to space and time.

Svapna-daśā: Such state of the individual existent in which the subtle body alone functions. The sense of identity with regard to the gross body remains absent.

Svapna-sṛṣṭi: Such state of the mind in which the dream-world and its objects are of subtle nature. Whatever activities eventuate in this state, they are of the nature of dream.

Svarūpa: Essential or intrinsic nature.

Svarūpapatti: The attainment or realization of one's essential nature.

Svasaṁvedana: The intuitive experience of the Self.

Svātantrya: It is such a philosophic concept in terms of which is established the absolute autonomy of the Absolute, and through the means of this self-autonomy as self-will are carried out the five divine activities of emanation, preservation, dissolution, concealment and revelation. This absolute autonomy of the Absolute is variously spoken of and some of the terms that are used are *caitanya, sphurattā, spanda, mahāsattā, parāvāk, parā, cit-śakti,* etc.

Taijasa: The dreaming state.

Tamas: It is one such constituent of the primordial materiality (*prakṛti*) that expresses itself in terms of inertia or delusion.

Tanmātra: The five sense-objects in their undifferentiated state—and the objects are sound (*śabda*), touch (*sparśa*), form (*rūpa*), taste (*rasa*), and smell (*gundha*).

Tarka-śāstra: The science that imparts the knowledge of logical reasoning.

Tatpuruṣa: One of the five *mantric* forms of Śiva.

Tattva: It is a term which basically denotes the general nature among the different classes of objects, and it is on the basis of a particular kind of nature that objects are classified. It also denotes the various groups of objects. Finally, the term signifies the thirty-six categories from the category of Śiva to that of earth, which are but the manifestation of Paramaśiva. The first five categories are said to be pure on account of them being free from the impurity of *māyā*, whereas the rest of the categories are said to be impure on account of them being under the influence of *māyā*. As thatness it denotes the essence or being of a thing.

Tattva-adhva: It is used as a support for meditation in *āṇava-upāya*, and in terms of which pervasion over all the categories, the seven subjects as well as their energies are accomplished.

Tattva-traya: The three principles of Man (*nara*), Energy (*śakti*), and God (*śiva*) corresponding to the Self (*ātman*), Knowledge (*jñāna*), and God (*Śiva*).

Tirodhana: Such an act of God in terms of which he conceals his essential nature, and accordingly pushes contingent beings further and further down into such conditions whereby their chains of bondage become stronger.

Trika-āgama: The three basic canonical texts of Trika Śaivism, and they are the *Siddhatantra, Namakatantra,* and *Mālinī-tantra.*

Trika-apara: The three ontological realities, namely, Śiva, Śakti, and Nara.

Trika-para: Light of consciousness (*prakāśa*) and consciousness as awareness (*vimarśa*), and the union of the two. Also the three energies of Paramaśiva, namely, will, knowledge, and action.

Trika-śāstra: Such theological texts that are based upon the Trika canon. The texts of this type would be, for example, *Tantrāloka, Tantrasāra, Śivadṛṣṭi, Īśvarapratyabhijñā-kārikā, Spanda-kārikā,* etc.

Triśūla: The trident that symbolizes the three powers of the Lord, and the powers are those of will, knowledge and action.

Turya: The fourth state of animation, which is equated with such state in which the revelation of the Self occurs. Transcending the three normal states of waking, of dreaming and of sleeping, it at the same time holds them together.

Turyātīta: It is that supreme spiritual state from which arise as well as into which merge the four states of consciousness, viz., waking (*jāgrat*), dreaming (*svapna*), dreamless (*suṣupti*), and the Fourth (*turya*). Annulling all the four states, it accordingly is full of bliss, and is free from the sense of difference.

Turya-daśā: It is that blissful and transcendent state in which the entire objectivity appears as the Self.

Turya-sṛṣṭi: The manifestation of the pure path (*śuddha-adhva*). The existents of the pure categories are always of the nature of pure consciousness (*śuddha-saṁvid-rūpa*).

Uccāra: It is one of the yogic practices that is mainly made use of in the *āṇava-upāya*. The practice consists of in taking hold of the point of emergence of the five forms of animation, which are *prāṇa, apāna, samāna, udāna,* and *vyāna*. It is through the practice of this technique that the different planes of bliss are experienced which are hierarchically situated. The first kind of bliss, called *nijānanda,* is experienced when attention is focussed on the I-consciousness. The second type of bliss—*nirānanda*—emerges when meditation is directed towards the void of I-consciousness. The bliss, called *parānanda,* emerges when attention is drawn towards the activity of *prāṇa,* which absorbs the objectivity that is contained in the *apāna*. The *brahmānanda* type of bliss arises when attention is focussed on the single point that constitutes the commonality of all forms of objectivity. The *mahānanda* bliss comes to be upon focussing attention on such fiery life-force, called *udānā,* due to which are reduced to ashes the differentiating notions of the subject (*pramātā*), the means of knowledge (*pramāṇa*), and the object of knowledge (*prameya*). The *cidānanda* form of bliss comes to the fore when the all-pervasive *vyāna* is meditated upon. It is such life-force that is totally free from the external adjuncts (*upādhi*-s), and so the bliss of this life-force, too, is not dependent for its illumination on anything that is external to it. Finally, we have the universal bliss, called *jagadānanda,* which comes to be so spontaneously as to be effulgent and is continuously augmented by the nectar of perfect I-consciousness. Also the aspirant undergoes five types of experience during the period of the practice of *uccāra* meditation, and the experiences are bliss (*ānanda*), temporary experience of a sudden upward jerk (*udbhava*), the experience of the trembling of the body (*kampa*), the experience of drowsiness (*nidrā*), and the experience of inebriation (*ghūrṇi*).

Ucchalattā: It is the upsurge of the bliss within Paramaśiva that is seen to be responsible in effecting both manifestation and withdrawal of objectivity.

Udāna: One of the five vital airs. In the Trika *udāna* is seen such a spiritual energy which goes upward through the spinal cord till its reaches its abode, namely, the *sahasrāra* at the crown of the head. While going upward, it not only burns all forms of conceptuality, but also produces such sensation which is very delightful.

Udaya: The emergence of the manifest order.

Udbhava: An upsurge of energy that the aspirant experiences when practising *uccāra-yoga*.

Udyama: Sudden and spontaneous emergence of I-consciousness.

Umāpatinātha: One of the incarnations of Īśvara-bhaṭṭāraka within the category of *prakṛti*. Also known as Svacchandanātha.

Unmeṣa: It is the externalizing pulsation of the power of will of the Lord. It is the initial movement towards manifestation of the power of action of the Lord. It also, however, signifies the emergence of I-consciousness in terms of its essential nature. In terms of yogic practice it denotes the emergence of such consciousness that is spiritual and accordingly serves as the basis for the arising of ideas.

Upādhi: It is such a limiting factor or condition that exists outside the Absolute. It is an element, though foreign, that gets itself somehow attached to the Lord, and is accordingly spoken as ignorance (*avidyā*).

Ūrdhva-mārga: As an upward path through which the *kuṇḍalinī*, upon its awakening, travels upwards till it reaches the abode of Śiva, which is known as the *sahasrāra* at the crown of the head. This upward path is identified with the mystical vein, namely, *suṣumṇā-nādī*.

Vācaka: Word as *varṇa, mantra,* and *pada* constitute the pathway of time (*kālādhva*), which is made use of as a meditative support in the *uccāra-yoga* of *āṇava-upāya*.

Vācaya: As object it is used, in the form of *kalā, tattva,* and *bhuvana,* as a meditative support in the *uccāra-yoga* of *āṇava-upāya*. It constitutes the pathway of space (*deśādhva*).

Vaha: It is the flow of the life-force in the channels of *iḍā* and *piṅgalā* situated to the left and right sides respectively of the *suṣumṇā-nāḍī*.

Vaikharī: It denotes such speech that is either spoken or exists in a written form. The four levels of speech in an ascending order are *vaikharī, madhyamā, paśyanti,* and *parāvāk*.

Vairāgya: Such renunciation as would result in total indifference towards the pleasure of sense-objects.

Vāma: The Divine Energy that vomits the universe. As the Energy of the Lord, she pushes the worldly beings further down towards the ocean of becoming, viz., towards the cycle of rebirths.

Vāmadeva: A supernatural being of the form of *mantra*. The fourth form of Śiva among his five forms.

Varga: A group of consonant letters like *kavarga, cavarga,* etc.

Varṇa: A letter that is non-conceptual, and thereby simply representing the image of a word. It also denotes the subtle sound of the nature of *anāhata,* viz., sound that is inaudible. The fifty Sanskrit alphabetical letters from *a* to *kṣa*. The sound-support used in the meditation is called *dhvani-yoga*.

Varṇa-yoga: A kind of yogic practice with regard to sound (*dhvani*) in which awareness concerning *mantra* is combined with that of breath. The object of meditation (*grāhya*) in this yoga is always internal. This form of yoga pertains to the *āṇava-upāya*.

Vāsanā: Mental impression. Such tendency towards the sense objects that terminates in experiencing or reaping the fruit of what one has done or is doing. According to the Vijñānavādin Buddhists, *vāsanā*-s are a series of past impressions left in the subconscious/unconscious part of the mind. They operate causally in such a manner as would become the innumerable sensations for the stream of momentary units of consciousness in terms of the thought processes that is constitutive of daily activity of an individual. Thus these sensations are seen to be responsible in giving rise to cognitions that determine the process of our daily activity.

Videha-mukti: Perfect merger in Paramaśiva upon the abandonment of the body, which is to say that such liberation is fully attained only upon the discarding of the body.

Vidyā: The category of Śuddhavidyā. The plane of Vidyā. The categories of Sadāśiva, Īśvara, and Vidyā. It also denotes *unmāna-śakti* or *sahaja-vidyā*. It also means such impure knowledge in terms of which an individual knows only few things, and so concretely expresses the limiting factors (*kañcuka*-s) of Māyā that veil one's essential nature.

Vidyākalā: One of the five *kalā*-s. As *kalā,* it represents the finer aspect of space in the context of the theory of six paths of meditation.

Vidyā-bhūmi: Such a plane in which the vision of unity-in-diversity is predominant. Also it represents the planes from the category of Śuddhavidyā to Sadāśiva category.

Vidyā-śakti: That Energy of the Lord through which is manifested the category of Vidyā.

Vidyā-tattva: The category of Vidyā, and so is accordingly dominated by the viewpoint of difference-cum-non-difference. It represents such a mood for an empirical being as to have attention focussed on Śiva. It also signifies such pure subjects in whom the vision of difference has not completely been eradicated.

Vidyeśvara-s: Beings residing in the plane of the category of Vidyā. They are also known as Mantra-s. The beings of this category generally take up such divine activities as are required to maintain the administration of the manifest order. Some such beings are Īśāna, Tatpuruṣa, Sadyojāṭa, Vāmadeva, and Aghora. These divine beings are said to be responsible in having revealed the canonical texts of Śaivism to some enlightened beings (*siddha*-s).

Vigraha: A particular or specific form or shape.

Vigrahi: The embodied being.

Vijñāna: To have a direct experience of the Self by making use of some principle or means. In Buddhism the term signifies the luminous nature of consciousness. Also it denotes the momentary appearances of consciousness.

Vijñānākala: Such an existent who considers himself as being of the nature of light of consciousness, while having no notion of himself as being also of the nature of action. The beings of this category are said to be on the borderline between impure and pure manifestation, and will remain tied to various types of limitation until they free themselves from the influence of *māyā*. Thus these beings are said to be residing above Māyā but below Śuddhavidyā.

Vijñānavāda: The Buddhist idealist school of philosophy established by Maitreya-Asaṅga, which through the philosophical contribution of Vasubandhu gained great prominence in Buddhism.

Vikalpa: The intellectual conceptualization of objects in terms of name-and-form. Also the erroneous conceptual knowledge concerning oneself as well as the world. It also denotes such definitive knowledge that is empirical. Finally, it signifies such supernal knowledge that is authentic precisely because it looks at oneself as being the product of divine play, whereas the world is seen as the outcome of the play of the Self.

Vikalpa-kṣaya: The dissolution of thought-constructs.

Vikalpanam: Such activity of the mind as would terminate in the emergence of differentiating thoughts-constructs.

Vikāra: Modification of a substance through the means of change or transformation, as, for example, milk changing into curd or gold transformed into various types of ornaments.

Vikāsa: The self-extension or expansion of Paramaśiva into the objective universe, which at the same time results in the contraction of divinity.

Vimarśa: The awareness of the Self as being of the nature of pure light. It also denotes the power (*śakti*) of consciousness. Consciousness in itself is light (*prakāśa*), whereas as light it is self-referential (*vimarśātmaka*).

Vindu/Bindu: While denoting surging of will, it so charges the divine will of the Absolute as would result in the objective manifestation of the universe.

Visarga: The emanation of the universe from Paramaśiva.

Visargabhūmi: The two dots one upon the other, representing thereby both Śiva and Śakti. Śiva is seen as the symbol of assimilation of what has been emanated, whereas Śakti represents the manifestation in terms of emanation of the universe.

Viśva: It denotes the waking state of contingent beings.

Vivarta: The appearance of the object in terms of its opposite nature. It is such a theory of appearance of Advaita Vedānta that is non-acceptable to the Trika Śaivism of Kashmir. The core of the theory lies in the assertion that whatever appears to the senses does not ontologically exist. The appearance is true to the extent it lasts, but upon its disappearance, it like an illusion becomes non-existent.

Vyāna: As the fifth principle of animation, it is seen to be so pervasive as to be shining in the Subject at the transcendental plane which is but *turyātīta*, viz., beyond the Fourth.

Yoga: This term in the system of Patañjali basically means such restraint of the fluctuations of the mind as would result in the attainment of *samādhi*. It also means union between the individual soul and the Supreme as well as the means that terminate in the attainment of this goal.

Yoginyaḥ: Such energies as *khecarī, gocarī, dikcarī, bhūcarī,* etc.

Yoni: Womb or source. It is also seen as representing the nine groups of consonants. As Śakti, it is considered to be the womb, whereas Śiva is said to be the seed (*bīja*). Finally, it is seen as the embodiment of four energies of Ambā, Jyeṣṭha, Raudrī, and Vāma.

Yonivarga: Māyā and its brood, which is objectivity. As the source of objective diversity, so it is equated with the *māyīya-mala*.

Bibliography

Primary Texts

Abhinavagupta, *Anubhava-nivedana,* in: K.C. Pandey, *Abhinavagupta: An Historical and Philosophical Study,* sec. edn. Varanasi, Chowkhamba Sanskrit Series, 1963.

—, *Anuttarāṣṭikā,* in: K.C. Pandey.

—, *Bhairavastotra,* in: K.C. Pandey.

—, *Kramastotra,* in: K.C. Pandey.

—, *Īśvarapratyabhijñā-vimarśinī,* 2 vols., ed. M.R. Shastri and M.S. Kaul, KSTS nos., 22, 33. Srinagar, 1918–21.

—, *Īśvarapratyabhijñā-vivṛti-vimarśinī,* 3 vols., ed. M.S. Kaul, KSTS nos. 60, 62, 65. Srinagar, 1938–43.

—, *Paramārthasāra* with the *Vivṛti* of Yogarāja, ed. J.C. Chatterji, KSTS no. 7. Srinagar, 1916.

—, *Parātriśikā* with the *Vivaraṇa,* ed. M.R. Shastri, KSTS no. 18. Srinagar, 1918.

—, *Tantrāloka* with the *Viveka* of Jayaratha, 12 vols., vol. 1 ed. M.R. Shastri and vols. 2–12, ed. M.S. Kaul, KSTS nos. 23, 28–30, 35, 36, 41, 47, 52, 57–59. Srinagar, 1918–38.

—, *Tantrasāra,* ed. M.R. Shastri, KSTS no. 17. Srinagar, 1918.

—, *Tantra-vaṭa-dhānika,* ed. M.R. Shastri, KSTS no. 24. Srinagar, 1924.

—, *Bodha-pañca-daśikā* with *Vivaraṇa* of Hara Bhaṭṭa Shastri, ed. J.D. Zadoo, KSTS no. 86. Srinagar, 1947.

—, *Dehastha-devatā-cakra-stotram,* in: K.C. Pandey.

—, *Mahopadeśa-viṃśatikaṃ,* in: K.C. Pandey.

—, *Paramārtha-carcā* with *Vivaraṇa* of Hara Bhatta Shastri, ed. J.D. Zadoo, KSTS no. 77. Srinagar, 1947.

—, *Mālinīvijaya-vārttikam,* ed. M.S. Kaul, KSTS no. 31. Srinagar, 1921.

—, *Parātriśikā-laghuvṛtti,* ed. J.D. Zadoo, KSTS no. 67. Srinagar, 1947.

Ādyanātha, *Anuttara-prakāśa-pañcaśikā,* ed. M.R. Shastri, KSTS no. 13. Srinagar, 1918.

Bhāskarakaṇṭha, *Bhāskarī,* ed. and trans. K.A. Iyer and K.C. Pandey, 3 pts.: pts. 1 and 2, Sanskrit text, pt. 3, English translation of *Vimarśinī* of Abhinavagupta. Delhi, Motilal Banarsidass, 1986.

Bhaṭṭa Nārāyaṇa, *Stavacintāmaṇi* with *Vivṛti* of Kṣemarāja, ed. M.R. Shastri, KSTS no. 10. Srinagar, 1918.

Cakrapāṇi, *Bhavopahāra* with *Vivaraṇa* of Ramyadeva, ed. M.R. Shastri, KSTS no. 14. Srinagar, 1918.

Dharmācārya, *Pañcastavī,* ed. and trans. J.N. Kaul. Srinagar: Ramakrishna Ashram, 1996.

Īśvarakṛṣṇa, *Sāṁkhya-kārikā,* ed. Sitarama Shastri. Varanasi, 1953.

Kalhaṇa, *Rājataraṅgiṇī,* ed. and trans. M.A. Stein, 3 vols., repr. Delhi: Motilal Banarsidass, 1979.

Kallaṭa Bhaṭṭa, *Spanda-kārikā* with his own *Vṛtti,* ed. J.C. Chatterji, KSTS no. 5. Srinagar, 1916.

—, *Spanda-kārikā* with the *Vivṛti* of Rājanaka Rāma, ed. J.C. Chatterji, KSTS no. 6. Srinagar, 1916.

—, *Spanda-kārikā* with the *Sandoha* of Kṣemarāja, ed. M.R. Shastri, KSTS no. 16. Srinagar, 1916.

—, *Spanda-kārikā* with the *Nirṇaya* of Kṣemarāja, ed. with English trans. M.S. Kaul, KSTS no. 43. Srinagar, 1925.

—, *Spanda-kārikā* with the *Pradīpikā* of Utpala Vaiṣṇava, ed. Gopīnātha Kavirāja, Yogatantra Granthamala 3. Varanasi, 1970.

Kṣemarāja, *Parāpraveśikā,* ed. M.R. Shastri, KSTS no. 15. Srinagar, 1918.

—, *Pratyabhijñā-hṛdayam,* ed. J.C. Chatterji, KSTS no. 3. Srinagar, 1911.

—, *Svacchandabhairava-uddyota,* ed. M.S. Kaul, 7 vols., KSTS

nos. 21, 38, 44–45, 51, 53, and 56. Srinagar, 1921–55.
—, *Netratantra-uddyota*, ed. M.S. Kaul, 2 vols., KSTS nos. 46, 61. Srinagar, 1926–29.
Madhurāja, *Guru-nātha-parāmarśa*, ed. P.N. Pushpa, KSTS no. 85. Srinagar, 1960.
Maheśvarānanda, *Mahārthamañjarī* with his *Parimala*, ed. V.V. Dvivedi, Yogatantra Granthamala. Varanasi.
Maitreya, *Madhyānta-vibhāga-sūtra* with the *Bhāṣya* of Vasubandhu, ed. and trans. Th. Stcherbatsky. Delhi: Sri Satguru Publications, 1992.
Puṇyānandanātha, *Kāmakalāvilāsa*, ed. M.R. Shastri, KSTS no. 12. Srinagar, 1918.
Sadyojyoti, *Nareśvaraparīkṣā* with *Prakāśa* of Rāmakaṇṭha, ed. M.S. Kaul, KSTS no. 45. Srinagar, 1926.
Somānanda, *Śivadṛṣṭi* with *Vṛtti* (incomplete) of Utpaladeva, ed. M.S. Kaul, KSTS no. 54. Srinagar, 1934.
Svatantrānandanātha, *Mātṛkā-cakra-viveka*. Datiya, Pitambara Saṁskṛt Pariṣad, 1977.
Utpaladeva, *Ajaḍa-pramātṛ-siddhi*, in: *Siddhitrayī*, ed. M.S. Kaul, KSTS no. 34. Srinagar, 1921.
—, *Īśvara-siddhi*, in: *Siddhitrayī*, ed. M.S. Kaul, KSTS no. 34. Srinagar, 1921.
—, *Saṁbandha-siddhi*, in: *Siddhitrayī*, ed. M.S. Kaul, KSTS no. 34. Srinagar, 1921.
—, *Īśvarapratyabhijñā-kārikā* with his own *Vṛtti*, ed. M.S. Kaul, KSTS no. 34. Srinagar, 1921.
—, *Śivastotrāvalī* with *Vivṛti* of Kṣemarāja, ed. with Hindi trans. Rājanaka Lakṣmaṇa. Varanasi: Chowkhamba, 1964.
Vasugupta, *Śivasūtra* with four commentaries, ed. and commented by Krishnanand Sagar, Shivoham Granthamala, 1984.
—, *Śivasūtra* with *Vārttika* of Bhāskara, ed. J.C. Chatterji, KSTS no. 4. Srinagar, 1916.
—, *Śivasūtra* with *Vimarśinī* of Kṣemarāja, ed. J.C. Chatterji, KSTS no. 1. Srinagar, 1911.
—, *Śivasūtra* with *Vārttika* of Varadarāja, ed. with Foreword by M.S. Kaul, KSTS no. 43. Srinagar, 1925.

Vatulanātha, *Vatulanātha-sūtra* with *Vṛtti* of Anantaśaktipāda, ed. with English trans. M.S. Kaul, KSTS no. 39. Srinagar, 1923.

Vijñānabhairava with commentaries by Kṣemarāja (incomplete) and Śivopādhyāya, ed. M.R. Shastri, KSTS no. 8. Srinagar, 1918.

SECONDARY SOURCES

Alper, Harvey P., ed., *Understanding Mantras*, repr. Delhi: Motilal Banarsidass, 1991.

Bamzai, P.N.K., *A History of Kashmir*, sec. edn. Delhi: Metropolitan Book Co., 1973.

Basu, Arbinda, "Kashmir Śaivism," in: *Cultural Heritage of India,* vol. 4. Calcutta: Ramakrishna Mission Institute of Culture, 1937–56.

Bhandarkar, R.G., *Vaiṣṇavism, Śaivism and Minor Religious Systems,* repr. New Delhi: Munshiram Manoharlal Publishers, 2000.

Bharati, Agehananda, *The Tantric Tradition.* New York: Samuel Weiser, 1975.

Bhattacharya, Narendra Nath, *History of the Śākta Religion,* sec. rev. edn. New Delhi: Munshiram Manoharlal Publishers, 1996.

Chakravarti, Chintaharan, *The Tantras: Studies on Their Religion and Literature.* Calcutta: Punthi Pustak, 1972.

Chatterjee, J.C., *Kashmir Śaivism.* Srinagar, 1916.

Dasgupta, S.N., *History of Indian Philosophy,* 5 vols., repr. Delhi: Motilal Banarsidass, 1975.

Dupuche, John R., *Abhinavagupta: The Kaula Ritual as Elaborated in Chapter 29 of the Tantrāloka.* Delhi: Motilal Banarsidass, 2003.

Dvivedi, Vrajavallabha, *Āgama aur Tantraśāstra.* Delhi: Parimal Publications, 1984.

Dyczkowski, Mark, *The Doctrine of Vibration: An Analysis of the Doctrines and Practices of Kashmir Śaivism.* Albany: Suny Press, 1987.

—, trans., *The Aphorism of Śiva with the Vṛtti of Bhāskarācārya.* Varanasi: Dilip Kumar Publishers, 1991.

—, trans., *Stanzas on Vibration: The Spandakārikā with Four Commentaries.* Varanasi: Dilip Kumar Publishers, 1994.

Eliade, Mircea, *Yoga: Immortality and Freedom.* Princeton: Princeton University Press, 1970.

Feuerstein, Georg, *The Essence of Yoga.* New York: Grove Press, 1974.

Ghosh, A.B., *Shiva and Shakti.* Rajshahi, 1935.

Gonda, Jan, *Vaiṣṇavism and Śaivism: A Comparison,* repr. New Delhi: Munshiram Manoharlal Publishers, 1970.

Grierson, A., and L.D. Barnett, eds. and trans., *Lalleśvarīvyākhyāyinī: The Wise Sayings of Lal Déd.* London: Royal Asiatic Society, 1929.

Gupta, Sanjukta, and Dirk Jan Hoens, *Hindu Tantrism.* Leiden: E.J. Brill, 1979.

Gurudatta, K., *Kashmir Śaivism.* Bangalore, 1952.

Hughes, John, ed., *Self Realization in Kashmir Śaivism.* Delhi: Satguru Publications, 1997.

Isayeva, Natalia, *From Early Vedanta to Kashmir Śaivism,* repr. Delhi: Satguru Publications, 1995.

Jash, Pranabananda, *History of Śaivism.* Calcutta: Roy and Chaudhury, 1974.

Jha, Yaduvamshi, *Śaivamata.* Patna: Bihar Rashtrabhasha Parishad, 1955.

Joshi, B.L., *Kashmir Śaivadarśana aur Kāmāyanī.* Varanasi: Chowkhamba Sanskrit Series, 1968.

Kachra, Durgaprasad, *Utpala: The Mystic Saint of Kashmir.* Poona, 1945.

Kavirāja, Gopīnātha, *Aspects of Indian Thought.* Burdwan: University of Burdwan, 1966.

—, *Bhāratīya Saṁskṛti aur Sādhanā,* 2 vols. Patna: Bihar Rashtrabhasha Parishad, 1963–64.

Kaw, R.K., *The Doctrine of Recognition.* Hoshiarpur: Visvesvarananda Vedic Research Institute, 1967.

Kotru, N.K., trans., *Śivastotrāvalī of Utpaladeva.* Delhi: Motilal Banarsidass, 1985.

Kramrisch, Stella, *The Presence of Shiva*. New Delhi: Oxford University Press, 1981.

Lakshman Joo, Swami, *Kashmir Śaivism: The Secret Supreme*. Delhi: Satguru Publications, 1991.

—, *Śiva Sūtras*: The Supreme Awakening with the commentary of Kshemaraja. New Delhi: Munshiram Manoharlal Publishers, 2010.

—, *Vijñāna Bhairava:* The Manual for Self-Realisation, ed. John Hughes. New Delhi: Munshiram Manoharlal Publishers, 2011.

—, ed. and trans., *Sāmbapañcaśikā*. Srinagar: Ishwar Ashram Trust, Samvat 2000.

Mishra, Kailashpati, *Kashmir Śaiva Darśana: Mūla Siddhānta*. Varanasi: Ardhanārīśvara Publication, 1982.

Mishra, Kamalakar, *Significance of the Tantric Tradition*. Varanasi: Ardhanārīśvara Publication, 1991.

—, *Kashmir Śaivism: The Central Philosophy of Śaivism*. Portland: Rudra Press, 1993.

Muller-Ortega, Paul, *The Triadic Heart of Śiva,* repr. Delhi: Satguru Publications,1997.

Murphy, Paul, *Triadic Mysticism: The Mystical Theology of Śaivism of Kashmir,* repr. Delhi: Motilal Banarsidass, 1986.

Pandey, K.C., *Abhinavagupta: An Historical and Philosophical Study*. Varanasi: Chowkhamba Sanskrit Series Office, 1963.

Pandit, B.N., *Aspects of Kashmir Śaivism*. Srinagar: Utpala Publication, 1977.

—, *Specific Principles of Kashmir Śaivism,* repr. New Delhi: Munshiram Manoharlal Publishers, 2009.

—, *History of Kashmir Śaivism*. Srinagar: Utpala Publications, 1989.

—, trans. and comm., *Īśvarapratyabhijñā-kārikā*. Delhi: Motilal Banarsidass, 2004.

—, *The Mirror of Self Supremacy or Svātantrya-Darpaṇa*. New Delhi: Munshiram Manoharlal Publishers, 1993.

Pandit, Moti Lal, *The Trika Śaivism of Kashmir*. New Delhi: Munshiram Manoharlal Publishers, 2003.

—, *Disclosure of Being: A Study of Yogic and Tantric Methods of Enstasy*. New Delhi: Munshiram Manoharlal Publishers, 2006.

—, *An Introduction to the Philosophy of Trika Śaivism*. New Delhi: Munshiram Manoharlal Publishers, 2007.

—, *From Dualism to Non-Dualism: A Study of the Evolution of Śaivite Thought*. New Delhi: Munshiram Manoharlal Publishers, 2009.

—, *The Philosophical and Practical Aspects of Kāśmīra Śaivism*. New Delhi: Munshiram Manoharlal Publishers, 2012.

Payne, Ernest, *The Śāktas*, repr. New Delhi: Munshiram Manoharlal Publishers, 1997.

Poddar, H.P., ed., *Kalyāṇa Śivāṅka*. Gorakhpur: Gita Press, 1990.

Radhakrishnan, Sarvepalli, *Indian Philosophy*, 2 vols. New York: Macmillan, 1958.

Raghavan, V., *Abhinavagupta and His Works*. Varanasi: Chowkhamba Orientalia, 1981.

Raju, P.T., *Idealistic Thought in India*. London: George Allen and Unwin, 1953.

Rastogi, Navjivan, *The Krama Tantricism of Kashmir*, vol. 1. Delhi: Motilal Banarsidass, 1979.

—, *Introduction to Tantrāloka*, vol. 1. Delhi: Motilal Banarsidass, 1987.

Kāśmīra Śivādvayavāda kī Mūla Avadhāraṇāyeṃ (in Hindi). New Delhi: Munshiram Manoharlal Publishers, 2002.

Rudrappa, J., *Kashmir Śaivism*. Mysore: Prasaranga, 1969.

Saksena, S.K., *The Nature of Consciousness in Hindu Philosophy*, Varanasi: Chowkhamba Sanskrit Series Ofiice, 1969.

Sharma, Debabrata Sen, trans., *Ṣaṭṭriṃṣaṭ-tattva* with the commentary of Rājanaka Ananda. Kurukshetra: Kurukshetra University Press, n.d.

Sharma, L.N., *Kashmir Śaivism*. Varanasi: Bharatiya Vidya Prakashan, 1972.

Siddhantashastree, R.K., *Śaivism Through the Ages*. New Delhi: Munshiram Manoharlal Publishers, 2010.

Sinha, Jadunath, *Schools of Śaivism*. Calcutta: Sinha Publishing House, 1970.

Śivaraman, K., *Śaivism in Philosophical Perspective*. Varanasi: Motilal Banarsidass, 1973.

Sundaram, S., *Śivapada, The Shaiva Schools of Hinduism*. London: George Allen and Unwin, 1934.

Tagare, G.V., *The Pratyabhijñā Philosophy*. Delhi: Motilal Banarsidass, 2002.

Temple, Richard Carnac, *The Word of Lalla the Prophetess*. Cambridge: Cambridge University Press, 1924.

Venkataramanayya, N., *Rudra Śiva*. Madras: University of Madras, 1941.

Woodroffe, John, *The Garland of Letters*, seventh edn. Madras: Ganesh and Co., 1973.

—, *Śakti and Śākta*, eighth edn. Madras: Ganesh and Co., 1975.

Zimmer, Heinrich, *Philosophies of India*, ed. Joseph Campbell. Princeton: Princeton University Press, 1968.

Index

ābhāsa 4, 8, 12, 19, 56, 61, 150; process of 20; theory of 19
Abhinavagupta 15–16, 20, 38–39, 47, 138, 149, 155, 183, 189, 191
Absolute 3–4, 6, 8–9, 11–12, 15–16, 19, 21–24, 27–28, 35, 40–41, 44, 49, 53, 59, 75, 96, 105–6, 114–15, 123, 132, 138, 147, 153–55, 191; absorption in 139; as consciousness 4, 10; aspects of 180; autonomy of 31, 55; bliss of 28; conception of 9, 11, 24, 36; devoid of 45; idea of 37; identity with 144, 147; nature of 6, 17, 38, 43, 45, 146, 157; of Advaita Vedānta 53, 133; of Śaṁkara 12; powers of 4, 180; view of 17; vision of 123
absorption 145, 154, 159, 163, 171; access to 146; methods of 145–46; point of 145; state of 167
Advaita (Vedānta) 3, 7, 11–12, 18–19, 22, 25, 36, 53, 64, 68, 87, 119, 132–33, 185; nature of 53; of Śaṁkara 3, 7, 50
Āgama 186
aghora 137; powers of God called 137
Aghora. *See* Jyeṣṭha
ahaṃ-bhāva. *See* I-ness
ajñāna 95, 119
Akala 63, 79, 102, 105, 108, 126, 134–35, 172, 185; state of 134
Ambā 191
an-upāya 145, 147–48, 151, 153, 164
ānanda-bhūmi 166
ānanda(*-upāya*) 11, 27–28, 41, 43–44, 53, 58, 60, 116, 147, 150, 153, 183; innate nature of 28
Anantanātha 65–69, 87, 105, 185, 187
āṇava-mala 99, 104, 107, 120, 123, 131–34
āṇava-samāveśa 89, 165
āṇava-upāya 89, 145, 164, 168–69
appearance 4, 8,12–13,18–21, 56, 80, 109, 114, 150–51, 187; doctrine of 87; forms of 114; process of 21; theory of 19–21
aśuddhādhva 67, 86
avidyā 12, 18, 26–27, 50, 53, 95, 98, 185

Barth, Karl 36
bauddha(*-ajñāna/jñāna*) 121–24
Becoming/becoming 9–12, 35–36, 43, 154; cycle of 133; nature of 132; process of 10; wheel of 49. *See also* Absolute
Being 8–12, 14, 30, 36, 63, 95,

112, 132; fulness of 14, 119; nature of 102; state of 190; unity of 13, 63, 124, 126, 134, 139, 147. *See also* Absolute
Bhāgavata 134
Bhairava 116, 126, 129; grace of 126
bliss/Bliss 3, 11, 17, 27, 41, 43–44, 47, 53, 58, 60, 63, 106–7, 114–16, 118, 127, 129, 135, 150, 153, 166–67; droplets of 45; experience of 125; form of 160; level of 167; nectar of 135; of Absolute 53; of Being 63; of *spanda* 47–48; pervasion of 149; planes of 166; plenitude of 134; power of 183–84; replete with 126; state of 128; method of 147
bondage 46, 48–50, 83, 112–14, 122–23, 134, 149, 158, 185, 190; bond of 96; cause of 174; disease of 173; entanglement of 173; fetters of 124, 147–48; grip of 122; play of 138; release from 118; source of 49, 84, 96–97, 156; state of 46, 118
Brahmā 30-31, 87, 89, 171, 182, 188
brahman 5,12,17, 41, 53, 64, 68, 132, 163; adjunct of 186; concept of 132; of Advaita Vedānta 36, 132; of Śaṁkara 5,17, 36, 40
brahmāṇḍa 166
Buddhist 70, 73, 109, 130–32, 153–54

cakra/-s, either six or seven, according to the *tāntrika* thinking 161: *ājñā* 161; *anāhata* 161; *mūlādhāra* 161; *maṇipūra* 161; *sahasrāra* 161–62; *svādhiṣṭhāna* 161; *viśuddha* 161
categories 10, 24, 53, 57, 59–60, 63, 67–68, 78, 88–89, 93, 101, 152, 185, 187–88; emanation of 25; number of 67; of manifestation 62; of existence 53, 106; path of 66
causal(-ity) 18, 24–25, 40, 99, 188
cause 18–19, 24, 54–55, 72, 98, 112, 121; emergence of 19
change 14, 39–41, 77
cidāgni 157
cidānanda 166
cit(-śakti) 5–6, 43–44, 58, 60, 96, 183–84
cognition 8, 22, 26, 103, 109, 151
Coiled Energy. See *kuṇḍalinī*
consciousness 4, 6, 9–10, 13, 19–21, 28, 37, 39, 44, 46, 48–49, 56–60, 66, 81, 95–96, 101, 103, 114, 118, 122, 146, 155–56, 172, 184; act of 154; aspect of 8; bliss of 166; descent of 59; essence of 38; fire of 157; intentionality of 97; light of 4, 6–10, 13, 23, 36, 115, 120, 132–33, 150, 187; mass of 26; mirror of 8, 20, 151–52; nature of 4, 11, 13–14, 25, 27, 40, 53, 74, 97, 110, 151; objectification of 96; ocean of 27; planes of 170; throb of 41, 48; womb of 17

Dakṣa 87
Devadatta 73
Dikpāla 31
Durvāsa 36, 127

effect 18–19, 24, 55, 99, 112; emergence of 24
Energy/energy 9, 10, 24–25, 149,

154, 159–62, 181, 189, 191; descent of 46; forms of 190; nature of 26; notion of 3; of Śiva 9, 88, 190; passage of 163; source of 160
essential nature, 2, 13, 23, 29–30, 49, 66, 69, 71, 83, 95–97, 122, 129, 135, 146, 164, 172, 186–87, 190
existence 1, 9, 44, 55, 79, 100, 105–6, 154, 157, 181; categories of 9, 44, 106; state of 158

freedom 2, 11, 15, 26–27, 37, 48, 59, 65, 72, 74–75, 97, 109, 114, 116, 128, 135–36, 147–48, 154, 158, 171–72, 174; abandonment of 46; curtailment of 73; devoid of 2; realization of 3; realm of 23; shining of 116; treasure of 135

God 6, 26, 41, 47, 54, 57, 105, 129, 136–38, 153; autonomy of 37; eyes of 47; gift of 129, 136, 138; powers of 137; surrender to 136; temple of 167; worship of 136
Goddess 10, 190–91; as Energy 10
grace 106, 118, 123, 127–29, 135–36, 140, 146, 148–49; classification of 138; concept of 135; context of 136; descent of 137; fall of 128, 137, 173; forms of 137; nature of 148; result of 136, 149; transmission of 123, 174; wonder of 138
Gracious Vein. See *nāḍī*/-s . . ., *suṣumṇā*
guṇa (-s) 74, 76, 78
guru 117, 122, 137, 146, 172, 190

Hegelian 12
homa 156

icchā 44, 181. See also *icchā-śakti*
icchā-śakti 58–59, 62, 145, 151, 183
I-consciousness 5–6, 9, 42, 60, 63, 75, 79, 83, 98, 119, 128, 140, 146; light of 5, 150; Absolute as 9
Ignorance 12, 28, 53, 66, 94, 96, 98, 120–24, 159, 185; cause of 98, 174; cessation of 124; freedom from 174; identical with 121; nature of 94–95; presence of 95; removal of 123; taint of 66; veil of 159
impure 58–59, 68, 86, 93–94, 101, 185
impurity 5, 21, 93, 95–96, 98–99, 101, 108, 117, 123, 158; concept of 95; devoid of 99; emergence of 101; forms of 121, 128; of action 101, 109; of difference 105, 109, 133; of *māyā* 100, 187; operation of 104; presence of 95, 101; source of 21; veil of 147
immanence 9, 23, 25, 36, 43, 117, 160, 180; principle of 9
immanent 9, 23, 36, 43, 180
I-ness 8, 11, 104, 121
Indian 1, 2
Individual Method 145, 163–64, 173–74
Īśāna 184
Īśvara(*-tattva*) 30–31, 59, 62–66, 68, 86, 103, 105, 134, 171, 184; of Vedānta 64
Īśvarapratyabhijñā-kārikā 29, 37–38
Īśvarapratyabhijñā-vimarśinī 38